THE TESTIMONY OF
JESUS

PAST, PRESENT, AND PROMISE

DENVER C. SNUFFER, JR.

First Edition
ISBN 978-1-951168-82-7

Cover art by David Christenson

Published in the United States by
Restoration Archive LLC

www.restorationarchives.com

TABLE OF CONTENTS

Preface

Repent, then, and turn to God,
so that your sins may be wiped out,
that times of refreshing may come from the Lord,
and that he may send the Messiah,
who has been appointed for you—even Jesus.
Acts 3:19-20 NIV

The beginning of the Protestant Reformation is dated from October 31, 1517 when Martin Luther published his 95 Theses. The 500th anniversary of that event arrived on October 31, 2017. The world has changed because of the Reformation, and this book is dedicated to commemorating the event and its legacy.

The word "Protestant" is based on the root word "protest." Luther protested Catholic practice, and as a result of widespread abuses by the Catholic Church, a chorus of others joined in to likewise protest against Rome.

Between the New Testament era and the 1500s, Roman Catholicism established a monopoly on Christianity in Western Europe. They abused their position, and many of the practices they used seem shocking today, even to Catholics. The celebration of Mass was performed in a language church members did not understand. The text of the Bible was unknown to parishioners. Governments were subject to the pope. Most of the land was owned by the Catholic Church. Bishops lived with aristocratic privileges, while peasants supported the church under a feudal system that exploited their labor. Critics were tortured and executed.

For many of the common Christians, it was the icons, statuary, tapestries, and paintings that defined Christianity instead of the words of Scripture. Today, both Catholics and Protestants would regard the

Catholic religion before the 1500s as completely alien to what now is regarded as "Christianity."

Catholicism brought reformation upon itself by its failure to provide a genuine Christian experience for the common man. When Luther, Calvin, Knox, Zwingli, Simons, and others started to oppose Catholic abuses, there was an eager audience wishing to be freed from Catholic domination. The protests unleashed against Catholicism quickly spread throughout Europe, and Protestantism succeeded because it was needed.

The Roman Catholic Church was changed by the Protestant Reformation. They responded, beginning in 1545, with the Counter-Reformation. The Council of Trent convened in twenty-five sessions from 1545 to 1563 to address needed church reform. In addition to condemning Protestantism, the council clarified Roman Catholic doctrine, reformed church administration, abolished some abuses affecting the sale of indulgences, established more rigorous clergy education and residential rules, affirmed that the Catholic Church was the ultimate arbiter of the meaning of Scripture, and explained the relationship of "faith and works" to counter Luther's doctrine of salvation by faith alone. It also reaffirmed many practices the reformers found offensive, including veneration of saints and relics, pilgrimages, indulgences, and veneration of the Virgin Mary. The Counter-Reformation lasted until the close of the Thirty Years' War in 1648 and addressed reconfiguring the church's structure, establishing religious orders, responding to spiritual movements, and political reforms.

Between the reformation outside of Catholicism and the counter-reformation within, the Protestant movement reshaped Christianity. In turn, Christianity was revitalized and held far greater relevance to the lives of the common man. Whereas before mere superstition informed most "Christian" beliefs, afterward Christians were expected to understand, even debate, the meaning of Christ's teachings. Once the Protestant leaders translated and published the Bible in the language of the common man, an aloof and educated clergy lost their monopoly over access to and the right to interpret Scripture. Every soul was entitled and expected to read the Bible for themselves.

In the wake of the Protestant Reformation, society in Europe transformed. This transformation spread to the New World, and North America was initially populated by fleeing Protestants. The government of the United States reflected Protestant values. The American political example, in turn, changed European rule. In time, the entire world has been influenced—directly or indirectly—by the changes which began with the Protestant Reformation.

The question remains, however, whether it is enough to protest and reform an apostate Christianity. Roger Williams concluded that *reformation* could never establish Christianity back to its original, but a *restoration* would be required for that. Once lost, only God could bring it again.

Many people agreed a restoration was needed, and several men have stepped forward in the past to restore the original primitive Christian church. Among them were Thomas and Alexander Campbell, father and son, and Joseph Smith, who likewise claimed to have restored the original, including twelve apostles, seventies, bishops, priests, deacons, and teachers. Smith's movement, which came to be known as "Mormonism," splintered into more than 80 different sects, all of which have dramatically changed from what he began.

Today, Christianity is a fragmented, quarreling, and inconsistent patchwork of denominational sects, many of which claim that they alone offer the truest form of Christianity. There have been many Christian thinkers who longed to see Christianity drop its internal disputes and find common ground. C.S. Lewis, Billy Graham, Charles Russell, and many others have made attempts to help Christianity find common agreement.

One of Christianity's greatest impediments to unity is the competing economic interests of the various denominations. To keep their congregations loyal and financially supporting their professional clergy, preachers, bishops, elders, and ministers pretend their version of Christianity will save, while others are false, or a cult, or inspired by the devil and teach false doctrine.

With the passing of the 500th year of Protestantism, the time has perhaps finally arrived when, once again, the common man can see through the conflicting claims and again protest against the denominational conflicts for what they actually are: competing economic structures. There is little difference between what motivated the Catholic abuses in the 1500s and the conflicts between denominations today. What Christianity needs is to practice what Christ taught and less of what the theological schools have overlaid in order to rebrand their version as "true." Ministers should not be paid. Tithes and offerings should help the poor. If there was no financial incentive to advance denominational conflicts, they would die out.

In marking the passing of the 500th anniversary of the Protestant Reformation, we likewise protest against the present state of Christianity and call again for reform. Beginning in 2017, I delivered eight talks that addressed Christianity's troubled history, present disarray, and potential future. These talks have been made available at learnofchrist.org and are included in their entirety in this book.

The time may yet come when Christians will achieve a unity of faith.

November 25, 2021
Denver C. Snuffer, Jr.
Sandy, Utah

INTRODUCTION

For He must remain in heaven until
the time for the final restoration of all things,
as God promised long ago through His holy prophets.

Acts 3:21 NLT

On October 31, 1517, Martin Luther published 95 criticisms of the Catholic Church's practice of selling indulgences. Although Luther intended to *reform* Catholicism (not break it apart), he accomplished both. On the 500th anniversary of his act of conscientious defiance, it is important to review how that moment changed the world religiously, economically, politically, socially, and intellectually. The upheaval stretched into every fabric of society, exceeding anything Luther could anticipate. The breadth of the resulting effect proclaims God's hand was involved. Although the reformation of Christianity began half a millennium ago, it has not completed its destiny.

The reformation movement was initially caused by the abuses of the Roman Catholic hierarchy. Reformers shared a common experience that included a conviction that Catholicism was different from New Testament Christianity and that it failed to either practice or preach Christ's gospel. These original reformers experienced first-hand abusive treatment by local Catholic leaders and sincerely wanted to practice a more pure form of Christianity. In their search to connect with God, they broke from Rome.

As the Reformation gathered strength, Protestant Christianity itself began to fracture. Once the Bible became available in the common languages of Europe, the widespread recognition that other institutions —in addition to Catholicism—failed to value different New Testament teachings led to multiplying denominations.

In the New World, Roger Williams reached the conclusion that the original could not be reformed back to its original state, and it would require a "restoration," which Christ alone could accomplish. He thought Christ would eventually send another apostle to restore the ancient, original church.

In 1820, Joseph Smith claimed Christ appeared to him and led him to establish a restored New Testament Church. However, following Smith's martyrdom, the course of Mormonism followed the course of Rome. Like the Catholics before, the institution became abusive, including a dark period while isolated in the Rocky Mountains when Mormon leaders intimidated, threatened, and eventually killed dissidents. The preaching of militant Mormonism led to the Mountain Meadows Massacre where over 120 people were killed. Fortunately, the American Army sent a force to the Utah Territory, displaced Brigham Young as Territorial Governor, and installed a secular government. Mormonism began as a revival of New Testament Christianity but devolved in less than 150 years to the same sad state of institutional abuse that Rome practiced in the 1500s.

The 500th year of the Christian Reformation has recently concluded, and Christianity has become a fractured, incomplete, and conflicted body of Christians. This half-millennial milestone marks an opportunity to consider where we are, how we have arrived here, and what can be done. Since its beginning with Martin Luther, John Calvin, and John Knox, and continuing to Roger Williams, John Wesley, and even Joseph Smith, devout men have sought in vain to recover the authentic Christianity once established by the Lord Jesus Christ. This book and its accompanying website learnofchrist.org serve as a commemoration of the efforts of these individuals to reform and restore Christianity and to better understand God's hand and role in these efforts.

A Brief History of Christianity

Christianity has a troublesome history. The Christian religion is not a single, monolithic entity but a cascade of divergent segments with great differences, even contradictions, between them. Christian history can be divided into the following periods:

The Apostolic Age (33 a.d. — 100 a.d.)

Christ originally sent twelve messengers to spread the news about Him. These messengers organized congregations of believers throughout the Mediterranean world, the Indian subcontinent, and beyond. These were diverse bodies of believer and (depending on which of the twelve organized them) reflected different priorities. They were all considered "Christian" and all followed Christ's teachings.

During this time, the body of Scripture used by the Christians consisted of the Hebrew Old Testament, primarily the Septuagint. The leading figures had known or met Christ, and they spread their testimony of Him. Paul was a towering figure, writing two-thirds of the letters which would later become "books" in a new addition to Scripture called the New Testament.

The Ante-Nicene Period (100 a.d. — 325 a.d.)

During this period, the testimonies of the Apostolic Fathers (the messengers sent by Christ) were collected and began to be regarded as Scripture. (By the 300s, these writings were well respected, but they would not acquire the official status as "New Testament" canon until the Council in Trullo in 692 A.D.)

Justin Martyr lived from 110-165 A.D. and wrote during this "sub-apostolic" period. His writings give a glimpse into how Christianity functioned in its earliest days. In his *First Apology*, he provides a description of Christian worship:

- They met in homes, having no church buildings.

- Before being considered a Christian, a candidate was baptized "in the name of God, the Father and Lord of the universe, and of our Savior Jesus Christ, and of the Holy Spirit."[1]

- Meetings began with a prayer and "saluting one another with a kiss."

- Then sacrament was prepared and administered using bread and a "cup of wine mixed with water," which was blessed by "giving praise and glory to the Father of the universe, through the name of the Son and of the Holy Ghost, and offers thanks at considerable length for our being counted worthy to receive these things at His hands."[2]

- The early Christians recognized there was an obligation for "the wealthy among us [to] help the needy." Therefore, after reading Scripture and "the memoirs of the apostles or the writings of the prophets," donations were collected. "And they who are well to do, and willing, give what each thinks fit; and what is collected is deposited with the president, who succors the orphans and widows, and those who, through sickness or any other cause, are in want."[3] The reference to the "president" is to the one who conducted the meeting that week.

These simple observances were resilient enough to preserve Christianity after the death of the apostles and before any great hierarchical magisterium arose. It was the power of baptism, the sacrament, Scripture study, and financial aid among believers that gave Christianity its power. But it was diffused and, therefore, incapable of destruction. When Justin Martyr was slain, the scattered Christians continued unaffected. It was just like when Peter and Paul were slain

[1] *First Apology*, Chapter LXI: Christian Baptism.
[2] Ibid., Chapter LXV: Administration of the Sacraments.
[3] Ibid., Chapter LXVII: Weekly Worship of the Christians.

and, before them, James was killed. The power of Christianity reckoned from the vitality of its original roots. These roots were in Christ and His message and teachings, which were employed to relieve one another by the alms shared from rich to poor.

HISTORIC/CATHOLIC CHRISTIANITY

Early Christianity included diverse and sometimes conflicting groups, all calling themselves "Christian." But conflicts grew in intensity over the centuries that followed. When the Roman Emperor Constantine saw the value in adopting Christianity, he did not realize Christianity was internally fighting over fundamental beliefs. Accordingly, in 325 A.D., Constantine forced an agreement among Christian leaders in Nicaea. The result was the Nicene Creed. This creed marked the beginning of a new era referred to as Historic Christianity. The consolidation of Christianity into a universal—or catholic—tradition followed Constantine's decision to make it the state religion of Rome. Though splinters remained, the state religion used coercion against the unorthodox groups and did its best to kill off other versions.

EAST-WEST SCHISM

In 1054 A.D., a split between Rome and Constantinople resulted in the division of the Roman Catholic Church and the Orthodox Christian Church, respectively. The division remains today, almost a millennium later. When they parted company, they also parted in beliefs, practices, and claims to authority. The Orthodox tradition prized the vision of God (mystic or gnostic knowledge) as superior, while Rome prized rational theology, reason, and philosophical knowledge, trusting it as the superior route to truth.

THE GREAT SCHISM

In 1517 A.D., Martin Luther posted a list of 95 abuses the Roman Catholic Church was practicing (known as "The 95 Theses"). This led to his excommunication in 1521 and, ultimately, to a rebellion in Germany against Roman Christian hegemony. Although he did not intend to found a church, the Lutheran Church claims Martin Luther as its founder. Among other things, the Roman Catholic monopoly on the possession and reading of Scripture was overthrown by Luther when he translated the New Testament into the common language. Additionally, the movable type press (invented by Johannes Gutenburg in 1440 A.D.) made widespread printing and distribution of the Scriptures possible. It was the alignment of Luther's religious rebellion, the availability of the printing press, and Germany's desire for independence from Rome that allowed the Protestant Reformation to begin.

Living at the same time as Luther, John Calvin aided in the Protestant fires against Rome. Luther and Calvin initially agreed with each other but fell into disagreement over the interpretation of the Eucharist.

John Knox also lived at the same time and led the reformation in Scotland. He is credited as the founder of the Presbyterian Church. He was troubled over the authority given to a female ruler by Catholic Bishops and questioned the "divine right" to rule in those circumstances. He wondered at the duty to serve and obey an idolatrous sovereign, asking John Calvin to counsel him on these topics.

Much of the Protestant Reformation grew out of the abuses inherent in combining church and state. When a state religion claims it is true and approved of God, then anything resisting the state religion is by definition both false and in rebellion against God. It was easy for "Christianity" to torture, kill, imprison, and abuse their victim-proselytes for more than a millennium. That was part of governing.

What began with Martin Luther has continued to divide and multiply into many Christian denominations, with different groups placing different emphases on different parts of the New Testament.

EVANGELICAL ERA

One of the most recent Christian developments is the innovation dubbed "Evangelical Christianity," which began in the 19th century. Those credited with laying the foundation for this innovation are John Wesley, George Whitefield, and Jonathan Edwards. Billy Graham caused it to spread internationally.

A BEWILDERING ARRAY OF "CHRISTIANITIES"

Christianity is anything but a smooth transition from a New Testament source to modern denominations. There were serious disconnects from the Apostolic age to the time of Constantine. If there was any legitimacy to the founding of the Roman Catholic Church, then the subsequent rebellion and excommunication of the reformation founders renders Protestant Christianity powerless to save. And if the Protestant Reformation was justified by the wickedness and apostasy of Rome, then the Roman Catholic Church forfeited their right to claim to be Christ's one-true-church. If Rome made herself a harlot by selling indulgences or forgiveness of sins, then the Protestant daughters are children of that harlot and hardly able to claim authority derived from Christ's ordination of apostles.[4]

Protestant, Orthodox, and Catholic Christians should be troubled about the legitimacy of their sects. Their denomination (whichever they accept) has taken a troubling route from the death of the apostles until today. The developing stages are so jarringly different from one another that the modern Evangelicals would be regarded as heretical and either forcibly converted or killed in the first fifteen-hundred years of "Christianity." Even after the Protestant Reformation, church and state remained intertwined, and heterodoxy was still dangerous for the non-Lutheran in Germany, the non-Anglican in England, and the non-Presbyterian in Scotland.

The English colonies and early states in the United States of America likewise had tax-supported state churches. The First Amendment prevented a "national" religion, but the states were free to adopt their own *state religion*. Virginia established the Anglican Church (or Church of England) as their state religion for 224 years (1606-1830). New York did likewise for 225 years (1614-1846). Massachusetts chose the

---

[4] "Ye have not chosen me, but I have chosen you, and ordained you, that ye should go and bring forth fruit, and that your fruit should remain: that whatsoever ye shall ask of the Father in my name, he may give it you" (John 15:16 KJV).

Congregationalist Church as their state religion for 204 years (1629-1833). Maryland adopted the Anglican or Church of England as the state creed for 235 years (1632-1867). Delaware, Rhode Island, and Pennsylvania did not have an official religion but supported clergy with tax dollars for 155 years, 199 years, and 109 years, respectively. Connecticut's state religion was Congregationalist for 179 years (1639-1818). New Hampshire was also Congregationalist for 238 years (1639-1877). Both North and South Carolina were Anglican or Church of England for 212 years (1663-1875) and 205 years (1663-1868), respectively.

Roman Catholicism was discouraged, even persecuted, in the American colonies and early states. The Puritans (who fled to the colonies to escape religious persecution) wanted freedom of religion for themselves, but they did not extend that freedom to other faiths—they were intolerant and opposed to religious freedoms for Catholics, in particular, and other religions, generally.

If the divergent Christian positions asserted by various Christian sects are taken at face value, then within the billions who have believed in some form of Historical Christianity, almost all will be damned because they have failed to believe in the "correct" version offered by competing groups.

DRIFT FROM ORIGINAL CHRISTIANITY

When a centralized hierarchy took control over Christianity, the money that was used for the poor, the widows, and the orphans was diverted to building churches, cathedrals, basilicas, and palaces. Ultimately, the wealth generated by the generosity of Christian believers became the tool used by the hierarchy to buy up armies, kings, lands, and treasures that were used to rule and reign as a cruel master over a subjugated population made miserable by the abuse heaped on them from Rome.

Even after the Protestant Reformation, Christianity continued to be ruled by hierarchies. Cathedrals and church buildings consumed—and still consume—resources which are to be used to help the poor. Christ built no building, although He accepted the temple in Jerusalem as His

Father's house. Peter built no church building—nor did Paul, nor James, nor John. Christianity in the hands of the Lord and His apostles needed no brick and mortar for its foundation. It was built on the hearts of believers and brought together by the charity and assistance shared between them.

Today, Christianity is not benefited but is weakened by hierarchies, cathedrals, edifices, and basilicas that house opulence, wealth, and art. Although the prophecies foretell of a temple to God in Zion and another in Jerusalem, there are no other structures foretold to be built by Christians or latter-day Israel. How much stronger would Christianity be today if wealth were reserved for the poor, and the hierarchies were stripped of their wealth?

Arriving at a "unity of the faith" (which Paul hoped could be achieved by Christians[5]) is a way off. Christianity has instead become the handmaiden of ambitious men who have diverted resources from the poor to serve themselves. The present state of Christianity is not markedly different from Jerusalem at the time of Christ. The Christian leaders today, like the Sadducees and Pharisees, shear the sheep and consume them and fail to serve them as Christ did.

Christianity began with personal worship and devotion in the homes of believers. Christ and His twelve built no cathedrals, chapels, or church structures but did give aid to the poor. Isaiah prophesied that only one kind of building would be built for God by His followers: a temple or House of God to be built on the mountaintop in Zion and another in Jerusalem.[6] Beyond those two structures, all other resources should help the poor, as was once done by early Christians.

In commemoration of the 500th anniversary of the Christian Reformation, a multi-part video series has been produced that briefly

---

[5] "And he gave some, apostles; and some, prophets; and some, evangelists; and some, pastors and teachers; For the perfecting of the saints, for the work of the ministry, for the edifying of the body of Christ: Till we all come in the unity of the faith, and of the knowledge of the Son of God, unto a perfect man, unto the measure of the stature of the fulness of Christ" (Ephesians 4:11-13 KJV).

[6] See Isaiah 2:2-3.

covers the Reformation (Christianity's past), the Restoration (Christianity's present), and the continuation of the Restoration today and tomorrow (the future of Christianity).[7] There are a total of 21 videos in the series, seven dedicated to each of these time periods.

The following three sections of this book are divided according to the same timeframes, and each begins with the content of the videos that cover the time period indicated.

---

[7] The complete series can be found at learnofchrist.org.

CHRISTIANITY'S PAST

Let no man deceive you by any means:
for that day shall not come,
except there come a falling away first.

2 Thessalonians 2:3 KJV

THE REFORMATION BEGINS
1300 A.D.

THE BACKSTORY

There is a backstory to the commencement of the Protestant Reformation. While it runs all the way back to the time of the post-Apostolic fathers and the events between the close of the New Testament and the Council of Nicaea, there were more immediate events that showed the obvious need to reform Catholicism.

Following the Council of Nicaea, the Catholic Church completely dominated Western Europe, and the extent of that domination was unlimited. Their authority reached into politics, government, education, religion, and economics. The Roman Catholic Church was the single largest landowner in the Western Europe of the Middle Ages.

In 1302, the pope issued an edict stating that salvation outside the Catholic Church was impossible and that all the authority in the Catholic Church was vested in the pope. Forty-five years later, in 1347, the Black Death fell upon Europe, and 25 million people died in a period of less than four years. Society under the complete control of the Catholic Church had been considered shaky previously, but following the Black Death, there were many whose faith had been shattered. Devout believers called upon God and received blessings from Catholic Bishops, and they did what they could to save the lives of the people. But they all failed—and because of that failure, there were many who began to rethink the order of things. They had called upon Catholic help, and Catholic help had been given—but it was ineffective.

Shortly thereafter, for a period of 31 years, there was an internal split within the Catholic Church. Two different popes each claimed to be the exclusive holder of the keys from Peter: one in Avignon, and the other in Rome. Then a third pope contended that *he* actually had the keys from St. Peter. What ensued was a three-way feud (from 1409 to 1415) between Gregory XII, Benedict XIII, and Alexander V over who held primacy and could claim to be the one exclusive holder of all authority in the Catholic Church.

Under these circumstances, doubts about the authority of Catholicism multiplied. People living at the time witnessed such a spectacle that many wondered if Catholicism could survive the crisis. The result was widespread questioning and doubting about the claims of the Catholic Church to be God's sole representative for salvation on Earth.

Johannes Huss (in Czechoslovakia) and Girolamo Savonarola (in Florence) spoke up. They were both regarded as rebellious doubters of Catholicism, and both of them were burned as martyrs because of their doubts. Catholicism was not going to share power willingly. These two martyrs were still part of recent memory when Martin Luther lived. Their deaths showed that strongly held convictions were necessary in order to muster the courage that Martin Luther summoned to question the Roman Church.

His questioning resulted in what we now refer to as the Protestant Reformation. When he protested against the church, recent history had proven that it was life-threatening to come out in opposition to Rome. There are few men who would have risked being burned at the stake to voice criticism against a powerful but corrupt religious hierarchy.

LUTHER'S COURAGE

Martin Luther's extraordinary courage was a strength shared by the other Protestant Reformation fathers. They opposed a monolithic political, economic, religious, and military power that was regarded by the European continent as *the* moral guide that God had provided. When they opposed it, they confronted the entire culture of their day.

In Martin Luther's case, his courage came from the conviction that his cause was godly and right. Although the Catholic hierarchy (both in Germany and in Rome) may have been cynical and hedonistic, Martin Luther was devoted, sincere, and self-disciplined as a committed believer in Christianity. He hungered and thirsted for his own salvation. He wanted his soul to be saved.

His sincere belief in absolute Christian virtue contrasted with what he witnessed in the behavior, policies, conduct, and politics of Roman Catholicism. He was *more devoted* to the religion than were his leaders.

But Martin Luther's success did not come from his conduct alone. Luther's success came because of others who had set the stage beforehand to make the Protestant Reformation possible. One such person was Johannes Gutenberg, whose invention of the printing press made publication and distribution of books widely available for the first time.

Luther's translation of the Bible from Latin (a language that most common people didn't speak or read) into the German familiar language was probably the most revolutionary and significant act that led directly to the Protestant success. The Bible translation, coupled with the Gutenberg printing press, allowed for widespread reading of the Bible by the common man; the four Gospels and the letters of Paul and the other apostles could be read and understood for the first time. The Catholic clergy had previously failed to communicate the New Testament to the common man in words the people could comprehend. All the Catholic Church wanted from them was money, obedience, and loyalty. Martin Luther, on the other hand, wanted people to understand Christ's Gospel.

Luther's translation of the Bible was revolutionary. Christians today take it for granted that they have access to the Bible in words they can read and understand. It is almost impossible for all Christians— Catholic and Protestant—to imagine the world before Luther.

PROTEST

The Protestant Reformation is dated from a specific event that happened 500 years ago. On Sunday, October 31, 1517, Martin Luther publicly published his list of 95 criticisms (referred to as the 95 Theses) of the corrupt and unscriptural Catholic practice of selling "indulgences."

"Indulgences" were marketed as a product the Catholic Church could provide that transferred virtue from an available reservoir of excess blessings acquired from the Saints that could then be allocated for the benefit of others. This could free a soul from Purgatory and the eternal punishment of sin. The right to allocate such indulgences was part of the "keys of St. Peter" that were held by the pope. This marketing of sale-able virtue was done as a blatant money-raising venture, authorized by the pope, and sold by Johann Tetzel (a monk), with the proceeds shared by a local nobleman and Pope Leo X.

In publishing the 95 Theses, Martin Luther faced a dilemma: If he was to criticize the church that claimed there was no salvation outside of itself, was he consigning his soul to damnation? Luther had to solve the dilemma about his personal salvation before he confronted and called the church to repent of its sins. He resolved the conflict through meditation on Paul's letter to the Romans: *For in it the righteousness of God is revealed from faith for faith, as it is written, 'The righteous shall live by faith'* (Romans 1:17 NKJV). From this statement, Luther concluded he could trust the Bible alone to obtain faith, and faith was the means for obtaining salvation. This meant he needed to (and safely could) reject the pope's claim that salvation outside the Catholic Church was impossible.

This was a bold step, especially for someone as sincere and devoted as Martin Luther was to his religion. When Luther took the leap of faith and published the 95 Theses, his original purpose was to reform Catholicism. But he instead set in motion changes that no one could control. The reaction of the Catholic Church to his criticism, the local political German environment, widespread discontent with Catholic domination of society, and the hope others saw for their own salvation independent of a hierarchy of men were forces waiting for the chance for change. Luther provided a rationalization for rebellion against Rome.

The fact that the Roman church owned so much of the land throughout Europe was a huge temptation to political leaders. They could reject Rome's control and seize the land, then diverting the resources to local nobility instead of exporting their value to the distant rulers of the church in Rome. Local leaders could get a new revenue stream taken directly from the Catholic Church. This all came together to produce a groundswell following Martin Luther's brave act that allowed the Protestant Reformation to succeed.

Martin Luther was chased, threatened, and hounded, and he went into exile. He was given protective custody by Frederick the Wise, a local political leader who favored Luther's view, and in time, there was a new church, the Lutheran Church—an accomplishment that was never the original objective of Martin Luther when he criticized the Catholic Church. He wanted a reform, but ultimately, he provoked outright protest because of the widespread acknowledgment that Catholicism was corrupt. Once the fire was lit, it could not be contained.

GOD'S TIMING

When God chooses to change the course of human history, His most effective means to accomplish that is to send the right people into the world at the right time to facilitate a revolutionary change in the course of human history.

This is what happened at the time of the American Revolution when there was a gathering of intellectual and moral giants in one generation living in the American colonies: George Washington, John Adams, Thomas Jefferson, James Madison, Alexander Hamilton, James Monroe, and many others were contemporaries in the British colonies of America. These men agreed it was necessary to both rebel against a distant and unsympathetic monarch and also to replace an unresponsive sovereignty with a form of government that guaranteed individual freedom. Every one of them were needed for the revolution to succeed.

Likewise, at the time of Martin Luther there were other courageous and moral men who believed Catholicism was corrupt to its core. Contemporaneous (that is, living at the same time as Martin Luther) were Protestant figures such as John Calvin and John Knox.

- Martin Luther lived from 1483-1546.
- John Calvin lived from 1509-1564.

- John Knox was born in 1513 and lived through 1572.

All of these men—as well as Bullinger, Zwingli, Simons, and others—shared the same view and had very similar experiences. They were all agreed that not only was Catholicism itself corrupted, but the local clergy with whom they had the most interaction proved to be not only corrupt but also abusive.

In the wisdom of God, the right personalities were present on the European stage at the same overlapping time. Luther, Calvin, and Knox not only lived at the same time, but their paths crossed, they had the same moral convictions, they were morally courageous, and each had witnessed local corruption in widely separated parts of Catholic Europe. God supplied the needed opposition for these men in the form of corrupt local clergy who had abused each of them.

If there is a common theme that produced the Protestant Reformation, it is the pattern of religious abuse, religious intolerance, corruption, and wickedness that was confronted by men of extraordinary moral character whose desire was to understand God and obtain salvation (each of whom feared they would not obtain salvation through the existing abusive political and religious establishment). Each of the Protestant leaders concluded Rome was misusing and corrupting the Christian tradition.

On the same European stage, at the same moment, God provided these different moral giants who were confronted by moral corruption, and all of whom longed to find a relationship with God that was authentic, real, and personal. When you add it all up together, the Protestant Reformation is not just the product of Martin Luther, although he's the one to whom is given the greatest initial credit. It was the timing and the confluence of many different people and circumstances aligning in the right moment that produced the success of the Protestant Reformation.

CALVINISM

John Calvin was a contemporary of Martin Luther. Calvin's teachings developed into the Five Points of Calvinism that summarize the core of Christian theology. These five principles and their meaning are as follows:

1. **The total depravity of man.** This circumstance exists as a consequence of the Fall of Adam, and the result is that every person is separated from God and a slave to a sinful nature. Therefore, men seek their own best interests and are prone to be not only in a state of rebellion against God, but also disinclined to love God. The extent of this human failure is "total" or as widespread as humanity itself; hence, the "total depravity" of mankind. Without some outside source redeeming mankind, they have nothing but depravity—because men are fallen and require a Savior.

2. **God's unconditional election.** God will decide who will be saved, and that decision is unconditional. His choice is independent of the faith of those saved, and the decision is made from eternity to either extend or withhold saving mercy, thereby producing salvation or damnation according to God's choice. If God intends to save, He has the power to save despite the shortcomings of any person. Salvation comes from God, and God's wrath is justified toward the damned because of their sins against God. When God elects someone, they are saved without any condition apart from God's grace.

3. **A limited atonement.** This does not mean that Christ's atonement was not fulsome enough to save everyone but, instead, that the atonement Christ provided is limited in its application. Christ's atonement is applied fully to those that are elect and not applied fully to those who are not elect. Therefore, the limitation was based upon the election of the individual or limited in application but not in its potential effect. Christ suffered and died for an intended group of the saved, and the rest are left to be punished for sins. This has been described by Calvinists: "The atonement is sufficient for all and efficient for the elect." While all could be saved (because

Christ's suffering was sufficient for all), God intends only to save some.

4. **Irresistible grace.** Saving grace is effectually directed on behalf of those whom God intends to save who are His elect. For those, this grace of God overcomes any resistance caused by the Fall of Adam and secures for the elect saving faith. When God intends to save an individual, that person will be saved. The mechanism for infusing this irresistible grace is the Holy Spirit, which cannot be refused by the elect. While preaching the Gospel may be resisted by sinners, the elect cannot resist it.

5. **The perseverance of the Saints.** If a person is actually elect, they will persevere to the end. Correspondingly, if a person fails to persevere to the end, then they were never elect in the first place— which implies that they resisted God's grace, managed to reject God's election, and failed to secure part of Christ's atonement, remaining depraved despite all God might have done to save them had they been willing. This final principle restores some measure of balance to the foregoing four principles.

This bundle of principles was based on Calvin's understanding of the writings of Paul, and Paul's exposition concerning grace.

John Calvin's recognition of his own failures, his realistic assessment of his limitations, and his sincere desire to be saved all led him to conclude that men were totally depraved, God's election was irresistible, and Christ's atonement was unconditionally applied to the elect—because if it were otherwise, Calvin could not be saved. His own sin and failure, like every other believer, was enough to forever separate him from the grace of God. Therefore, these core principles gave Calvin (and every other earnest seeker) the pathway for God's grace to save them.

John Calvin and Martin Luther met and agreed on many things, but they ultimately split on these principles because Martin Luther had a more benign view of how God's grace worked. Despite their disagreement on how God saved His sheep, both men were certain that salvation could be obtained independent of the corrupt and abusive

Catholic Church. Therefore, they both contributed to the Protestant Reformation, even while disagreeing on how salvation was provided to mankind by Christ.

RECONSIDERING EVERYTHING

Ten years after Luther's 95 Theses, Ulrich Zwingli published his 67 Articles or criticisms of Catholicism. Unlike Luther's specific topic of the sale of indulgences, Zwingli attacked Catholicism generally. His first statement directly rejected the 1302 Catholic claim that there was no salvation outside the Roman Catholic Church. Zwingli declared: "All who say that the Gospel is invalid without the confirmation of the Church err and slander God." It should be apparent to all that salvation outside the Roman Catholic Church needed to be possible for the Protestant Reformation to survive. Therefore, that was the first issue Zwingli addressed.

Today, many of Zwingli's expansive criticisms of Catholicism are taken as common sense by the Protestant world. But he made these points first and defended them in January 1523. The echoes of his defense are still with us.

Zwingli declared, "Christ is the only way to salvation for all who ever were, are, and shall be" saved by God.[8] He redefined the "body of Christ" as "believers" rather than the institution headquartered in Rome.[9] He defined Christ, not the pope, as the head of the church.[10] He condemned any Catholic practice that failed to acknowledge Christ as the head and any ordinance that did not originate with Christ.[11] Accordingly, he condemned, "clerical (so-called) ordinances, concerning their splendor, riches, classes, titles, laws, a cause of all foolishness, for they do not also agree with the head."[12] It should seem self-evident that the life Christ led contrasted and contradicted the lives

---

[8]   "The Sixty-seven Articles of Zwingli," Article 3.
[9]   Ibid., Article 7.
[10] Ibid., Article 9.
[11] Ibid., Article 10.
[12] Ibid., Article 11.

of Catholic clergy occupying the basilicas and cathedrals clothed with silk-robed splendor.

He proclaimed, "In the Gospel one learns that human doctrines and decrees do not aid in salvation."[13] He also proclaimed, "That Christ is the only mediator between us and God."[14] No pope, bishop, nor priest can interfere with or prevent the salvation of believers. He claimed that institutional leaders could not excommunicate a believer, but only the congregation itself possessed that right.[15] His criticism of pretentious Catholic set-prayers mirrors the instructions given by Christ in the Sermon on the Mount: "Real petitioners call to God in spirit and truly, without great ado before men. Hypocrites do their work so that they may be seen by men, also receive their reward in this life."[16]

Once Catholicism was openly criticized about the sale of indulgences by Luther, the scope of open criticism was bound to expand to include other subjects. Zwingli was the harbinger of much more that would follow. Today's Protestant sects take for granted these important themes, but they originated in the painful and dangerous world in which the Protestant Fathers began their protest.

Conclusion

The Protestant Reformation dramatically impacted the world. Even the target of the protest, Roman Catholicism, was improved by the rebellion. Unchallenged Catholic hegemony over political, economic, and religious life in Europe led naturally and inevitably to abuse. When Protestants gave people a choice, it forced Catholicism to compete.

An early result was the Catholic Counter Reformation. Although the Counter Reformation also had abuses—including the Spanish Inquisition—it also provoked needed reforms. Catholicism attempted a much-needed return to its spiritual foundation. The Counter Reformation began with the Council of Trent in 1545 and lasted more

---

[13] Ibid., Article 16.
[14] Ibid., Article 19.
[15] Ibid., Article 31.
[16] Ibid., Articles 44-45.

than a century. Pope Paul III wanted the corruption of clergy, the sale of indulgences, and financial corruption in the church addressed. While much of Catholicism remained unreformed, the church addressed the long overdue and needed education and moral training of its clergy. Political appointments of bishops ended, and ecclesiastical discipline was improved. New religious orders were founded that were dedicated to higher morality and better clerical service for local parishes.

One of the most important new religious orders was the Jesuits, founded in September of 1540. The founder of this order, Ignatius of Loyola, set out its laudable purposes, including:

> ...after a solemn vow of perpetual chastity, poverty, and obedience, to strive especially for the defense and propagation of the faith and for the progress of souls in Christian life and doctrine, by means of public preaching, lectures, and any other ministration whatsoever of the Word of God, and further by means of retreats, the education of children and unlettered persons in Christianity, and the spiritual consolation of Christ's faithful through hearing confessions and administering the other sacraments, ready to reconcile the estranged, compassionately assist and serve those who are in prisons or hospitals, and indeed, to perform any other works of charity, according to what will seem expedient for the glory of God and the common good.[17]

Once the Protestant movement began, its momentum carried beyond religion and into politics and economics. Rome lost control of Europe's nation-states, as they independently considered their interests above the dictates of a pope.

The Protestant Reformation came only two decades after the Americas were discovered. Early colonialists in North America were largely Protestants. These Protestant refugees knew the terrible history of Roman hegemony. Those lessons inspired a political viewpoint that was incorporated into principles of the Constitution of the United States.

---

[17] Puca, Pasquale (30 January 2008). *St. Ignatius of Loyola and the Development of the Society of Jesus*, L'Osservatore Romano Weekly Edition in English.

The American government was directly influenced—indeed, made possible—by the Protestant Reformation.

When the full measure of the Protestant Reformation is considered, the entire world was changed by what began with Martin Luther posting the 95 Theses. Like the stone cut out of a mountain without hands (as explained by Daniel interpreting King Nebuchadnezzar's dream), it has grown to fill and change the whole world.

The year 2017 marked the 500th anniversary of the Protestant Reformation. Mankind should look back in gratitude and recover its energy by applying the virtue of God's word in their own lives.

KEY FIGURES IN THE PROTESTANT REFORMATION

The following is a series of short biographies of the "Protestant" Christian Reformation Fathers who lived from 1330 A.D. to Present as well as some background on the main tenets of modern Protestant and Evangelical Christianity.

JOHN WYCLIFFE (1330-1384)

Nearly two hundred years before the Protestant Reformation, John Wycliffe was a reformer who foreshadowed what was coming. Although the world's circumstances were then not developed to permit the Reformation, many of Wycliffe's criticisms of Catholicism and his translation of the Bible would prefigure the coming Reformation.

Wycliffe lived through the Black Death, when 25 million people died in Europe. That catastrophe delayed his completion of a doctorate at Oxford until 1372. He became a dissident, and although sanctioned and opposed by the pope (five edicts from Pope Gregory XI condemned him for 18 errors and called him "the master of errors"), he believed and taught that the pope and the church were second in authority to Scripture. He conceived of an invisible church of the elect who were recognized by Heaven, rather than an organization on Earth that controlled salvation. Many of his ideas would later be advanced by the Reformation Fathers.

His arguments with Rome were first political (1366-1378) and later theological (1378-1384). During his last six years of life, he provided a continuing written campaign against the pope and the entire church hierarchy of the time. By the end, he came to equate the pope to the Antichrist.

Among his issues, he disputed transubstantiation: "The bread while becoming by virtue of Christ's words the body of Christ does not cease to be bread." He condemned indulgences: "It is plain to me that our prelates in granting indulgences do commonly blaspheme the wisdom of God." He repudiated confession to the priests: "Private confession… was not ordered by Christ and was not used by the apostles." He viewed faith as saving: "Trust wholly in Christ; rely altogether on his sufferings; beware of seeking to be justified in any other way than by his righteousness."

He believed every Christian ought to be able to read Scripture. At a time when only Latin Bibles existed in England, he began translating it into the common English language. He was assisted in this by John Purvey, and when Wycliffe died before it was completed, Purvey finished the translation. Rome condemned this as an act of rebellion:

> By this translation, the Scriptures have become vulgar, and they are more available to lay, and even to women who can read, than they were to learned scholars, who have a high intelligence. So the pearl of the gospel is scattered and trodden underfoot by swine

Wycliffe responded with this explanation: "Englishmen learn Christ's law best in English. Moses heard God's law in his own tongue; so did Christ's apostles."

Wycliffe believed church officials ought not to live in wealth but should instead sacrifice to serve. Church wealth should be directed to help the poor. He encouraged English leaders of both church and state to stop sending wealth to Rome and instead use it to help those locally in need.

Wycliffe died before authorities convicted him of heresy. After his death, the Council of Constance declared him a heretic, ordered his remains to be removed from consecrated ground and burned, and his ashes thrown into the River Swift. Pope Martin V confirmed the edict, and it was carried out. However, Wycliffe's influence could not be suppressed, and as one writer observed, "Thus the brook hath conveyed his ashes into Avon; Avon into Severn; Severn into the narrow seas; and they into the main ocean. And thus the ashes of Wycliffe are the emblem of his doctrine which now is dispersed the world over."

MARTIN LUTHER (1483-1546)

Martin Luther was a Roman Catholic priest who devoutly believed in and practiced his religion. That devotion led to dismay because of the disconnect between the righteous ideals of Christianity and the institutional corruption of his church. When he publicly proclaimed his criticisms, the Catholic clergy's reaction ranged from thinking him demonic to thinking him the only correct teacher in the church. 500 years later, he is less controversial, and even Catholics respect his contribution to the course of Christian history.

Luther's devotion included prolonged prayer, fasting, depriving himself of sleep, inflicting physical discomfort to subject the body to the spirit, and even abusing himself with a whip to attain mastery over the flesh. His personal zeal resulted in a growing chasm between his self-discipline and the institutional indulgence of sin. It is fitting that the great breach between him and the Roman Catholic hierarchy came over the issue of selling indulgences to profit the church.

Indulgences were believed to come from an available storehouse of merited blessings earned by the Saints, over which the Roman Catholic Church held discretionary authority because of the keys given to St. Peter. The original practice of conferring an indulgence required acts of devotion or penitence to merit the grant from the pope. It was later changed to allow for purchase, independent of any penitence or devoted service. By the time Luther confronted the practice, it had grown into a wealth-producing market of selling these rights for the living and their dead ancestors, allowing the wealthy to escape accountability for sinful misconduct by purchasing relief. Luther's revulsion at the sale of indulgences provoked his written list of 95 charges against the practice. The 95 Theses were made public on Sunday, October 31, 1517. This event, in hindsight, became the milestone from which the Protestant Reformation is dated. His 95 Theses are presented in their entirety in the next chapter.

Despite the attention given to the 95 Theses, Martin Luther's greatest contribution to the Protestant Reformation was another project: the translation of the Bible into the common German language, making it possible for laymen to learn the content of Scripture. The New

Testament was published in 1522 and the complete Bible (including the Apocrypha) in 1534. This was the event that made permanent the fracture between Protestants and Roman Catholicism. Once the language of the Bible could be read by the common man, the false traditions, hypocrisy, and violation of Jesus' teachings were exposed to view. Those who were most religious were unable to reconcile Catholic conduct with the biblical canon, and soon the Bible was being translated into the commonly spoken languages of Dutch (1526), French (1530), Polish (1563), Spanish (1569), Czech (1549), and English (1526). Like a stone cut out of the mountain without hands, gathering energy and strength as it rolled forward, Martin Luther set events in motion that forever changed the history of western civilization.

Religious societies multiplied as different bodies placed greater emphasis on different facets of the Bible. Unfortunately, the example of persecution (learned over a millennium and a half of Roman Catholic intolerance) was not abandoned by the different Christian societies. Most of these daughters of Rome opposed, sanctioned, and even violently persecuted those holding different religious views from the locally organized majority faith—thus, the Protestants followed the unfortunate example of the church in Rome.

The early American colonialists fled to a new continent to escape persecution but likewise proved to be intolerant of minority religious practices in their new land. By the time of the American Revolution, the revolutionary political leaders had centuries of history to draw upon to deal with the question of how to address freedom of religion. The American Constitution, including the First Amendment, is the product of events set in motion by Martin Luther many years prior.

The influence of Luther's life on the world cannot be overstated. He began a revolution that a half-millennium later still affects the world culturally, politically, religiously, and educationally. He was far more than merely a religious figure. He is one of the few people who has literally changed the world.

ULRICH ZWINGLI (1484-1531)

Ulrich Zwingli was the city chaplain of Zurich in 1523. Luther's reform movement in Germany had influenced the Swiss Confederation, and reform was in the air. Like Luther, he made a list of charges—his consisting of 67 Articles. His began with, "All who say that the gospel is invalid without the confirmation of the church err and slander God." His 67 Articles are presented in their entirety in the next chapter.

Also a contemporary of Luther, the two men met and discussed Christian practice. They disagreed on The Real Presence of Christ in the Eucharist. Zwingli led an alliance that attempted—unsuccessfully —to blockade Catholic cantons, and the Catholics attacked. He was among those killed in the battle in 1531. He left a legacy that still influences Christian thought beyond the Reform Churches.

MENNO SIMONS (1492-1561)

Menno Simons was another contemporary of Luther that moved the Reformation forward in the Swiss Confederate states. He influenced the Dutch Anabaptists, and the Mennonites are named after him.

He became a priest at the age of twenty-four but thought himself, and the other clergy, careless and self-indulgent. He had doubts about transubstantiation, and his research led him to some of Luther's writings. Because of this, he studied the New Testament, which he had previously been afraid to read.

There was a dispute about the correct age for baptism following the 1531 execution of Sicke Freerks Snijder for his re-baptism as an adult. Menno's search left him discontent with inconsistent answers he found comparing Luther, Bucer, and Bullinger. He resolved to rely on Scripture alone. Upon this decision, he became an evangelical preacher.

His preaching provoked opposition, then persecution. "The error of the cursed sect of the Anabaptists…would doubtless be and remain extirpated, were it not that a former priest Menno Symons…has misled many simple and innocent people," complained a letter to the regent of the Netherlands in 1541. "To seize and apprehend this man we have offered a large sum of money, but until now with no success. Therefore we have entertained the thought of offering and promising pardon and mercy to a few who have been misled…if they would bring about the imprisonment of the said Menno Symons."

Holy Roman Emperor Charles V joined in and offered 100 gold guilders for Menno's arrest. But Menno successfully avoided arrest. He reacted to his opposition by adopting pacifism, believing that ideas were more powerful than armies. He said, "The regenerated do not go to war, nor engage in strife. They are children of peace who have beat their swords into plowshares and their spears into pruning forks, and know no war." His preaching changed those who followed them to become likewise pacifist and moderate.

Even before leaving Catholicism, he rejected the Catholic teaching of transubstantiation because he detected nothing in the bread and wine he dispensed at Mass to suggest it transformed into Christ's body and blood. This was a position he did not adopt lightly, and his decision came only after careful examination of the question. "Finally, I got the idea to examine the New Testament diligently. I had not gone very far when I discovered that we were deceived, and my conscience, troubled on account of the aforementioned bread, was quickly relieved."

His view on Christian duty can be summarized in his statement: "True evangelical faith, cannot lie dormant, it clothes the naked, it feeds the hungry, it comforts the sorrowful, it shelters the destitute, it serves those that harm it, it binds up that which is wounded, it has become all things to all creatures."

After leaving Catholicism, he became an Anabaptist leader. Though many of their preachers were enthusiastic, even fanatical, he exemplified sober, thoughtful Christian life and tried to be a meek follower of Christ. His followers were thought to be dangerous and were persecuted and mistreated. When they endured it well, the authorities came to regard them as both different and non-threatening.

He was not the founder but was the regenerator of the Anabaptist movement. He was their most significant spokesman in the Netherlands during the sixteenth century. Menno provided moderate leadership and prolific writings to unify the nonviolent Dutch Anabaptists. Their peaceful beliefs have made their survival in surrounding violent societies a cause for admiration.

Menno took 1 Corinthians 3:11 as his motto: "For no one can lay any foundation other than the one already laid, which is Jesus Christ." He made this a theme for his ministry, and his teachings are therefore defined as Christ-centered. After leaving Catholicism, he married and fathered three children.

Menno's followers were referred to as Mennonites, a name used to deride them. Later, however, the Swiss Anabaptists who emigrated to America adopted that name. Today there are almost 1.5 million Mennonites in 75 countries.

WILLIAM TYNDALE (1494-1536)

William Tyndale was educated at Oxford. He earned a Master of Arts degree before he was allowed to begin to study theology. He complained about his education that, "They have ordained that no man shall look on the Scripture, until he be noselled in heathen learning eight or nine years and armed with false principles, with which he is clean shut out of the understanding of the Scripture." He was fluent in seven languages, including Greek and Hebrew.

He was inspired by the work of Martin Luther and translated the Bible into English. He concluded, "Christ desires his mysteries to be published abroad as widely as possible. I would that [the Gospels and the epistles of Paul] were translated into all languages, of all Christian people, and that they might be read and known." Because of opposition to translating the Bible in England, he traveled to the Lutheran city of Worms where he safely completed the work. He used both Hebrew and Greek sources, rather than the popular Latin Bible used by the Catholic Church, which had been translated by Jerome. He described his effort, "I call God to record against the day we shall appear before our Lord Jesus, that I never altered one syllable of God's Word against my conscience, nor would do this day, if all that is in earth, whether it be honor, pleasure, or riches, might be given me."

In his translation, he used the word "congregation" rather than "church" for the Greek "ecclesia." Tyndale's translation of this word was not only correct, it was revolutionary. Although this small correction may seem insignificant to readers today, at the time it undermined the Roman Catholic claims to be the only true church and, therefore, the exclusive body meant by the word "church." Likewise, by rendering the Greek word "metanoeo" as "repent" and not as "do penance," the translation challenged the financial interests of the church in the sale of pardons and indulgences. He translated "agape" as "love" instead of "charity," which also had an economic impact on church donations. In each case, Tyndale's translation conveyed the better meaning, but it came with an economic impact on the church and, therefore, offended the church.

The Bible translation was considered an act of defiance of both English law and the Roman Catholic Church. He was said to have predicted that not many years following his work on the Bible, "I will cause the boy that drives the plow to know more of the Scriptures than" the Catholic clergy. When the New Testament translation made its way to England in 1525, it was condemned by King Henry VIII, Cardinal Wolsey, Sir Thomas More, and others. Thomas More called it the work of the "Antichrist."

Tyndale was opposed to King Henry VIII's planned annulment to Catherine of Aragon in order for him to marry Anne Boleyn and published a work condemning it as unscriptural. This made him the King's enemy. In 1536, Tyndale was convicted of heresy, stripped of the priesthood, strangled to death, and his body burned at the stake.

During his lifetime in England, possession of a copy of his translation of the Bible resulted in a death sentence for unlicensed possession of Scripture in English. He consoled himself and others while he was in prison awaiting trial on heresy by writing: "...if God be on our side, what matter maketh it who be against us, be they bishops, cardinals, popes." Within three years following his execution, however, King

Henry VIII decreed that an English translation of the Bible should be available in every Parish for the public to read. It was Tyndale's Bible translation that was used to produce The Great Bible for the Church of England, as well as the King James Bible in 1611. The King James Version copies Tyndale in 83% of the language of the New Testament and 76% of the Old Testament.

Tyndale summarized how to find happiness in everyday life: "There is no work better than to please God; to pour water, to wash dishes, to be a cobbler, or an apostle, all are one; to wash dishes and to preach are all one, as touching the deed, to please God."

JOHN CALVIN (1509-1564)

John Calvin was an early convert to the Reformation movement. Like others, he began as a Roman Catholic but broke with them because of his conviction that they erred in doctrine and practice. He was influenced by Luther but broke from the Lutherans, also.

He consolidated a number of beliefs that originated from others but gave a clarity and defense of a body of beliefs that resulted in "Calvinism" as a religious system of belief. His influence on John Knox took many of his theological ideas into Presbyterianism. He split from Catholicism and then from Luther, forging his own body of stern beliefs. However certain his teachings may seem, he had an underlying humility about his certitude. He said, "A perfect faith is nowhere to be found, so it follows that all of us are partly unbelievers."

Calvin is given credit for five principle points or doctrines, known as the Five Points of Calvinism, which were described in the previous chapter. These center on the proposition that God has the ability to save every individual upon whom He chooses to show mercy, despite the failure or inability of the object of God's grace.

Calvin declared, "We should ask God to increase our hope when it is small, awaken it when it is dormant, confirm it when it is wavering, strengthen it when it is weak, and raise it up when it is overthrown."

Calvin's statement in opposition to abortion seems as timely now as when he first framed it: "If it seems more horrible to kill a man in his own house, then in a field…it ought surely to be deemed more atrocious to destroy a fetus in the womb before it has come to light."

JOHN KNOX (1513-1572)

John Knox is credited as the founder of the Presbyterian Church of Scotland. Educated at St. Andrews, he was influenced by the local corruption of the Catholic Church and literature imported from Martin Luther's movement in Germany. He lived in violent times, and he developed a violent response to the corrupt Christianity he believed needed to be overthrown.

The Catholic Church owned a majority of the land in Scotland and drew nearly eighteen times the income of the Scottish Crown. Catholic clergy were more political than religious, the local archbishop, Cardinal Beaton, having fathered 10 children with various women. It took little more than the import of smuggled Lutheran literature to open Knox's mind to protesting against the horrid state of Christianity.

Knox joined in a rebellion that resulted in the murder of Cardinal Beaton, which led to his arrest and exile. While exiled he worked for the Church of England, becoming a chaplain to King Edward VI. The death of Edward put a Catholic on the throne (Mary Tudor), and Knox was forced to resign and leave the country. He moved to Geneva and met John Calvin, then to Frankfurt to head an Anglican refugee congregation. But his teachings were controversial, ending any further participation in the Church of England.

He returned to Scotland and led the Protestant Reformation there, which overthrew the reign of Mary of Guise, putting Mary Queen of Scots on the throne. She allowed him the freedom to lead the Protestants, and he in turn criticized her Catholicism. He chafed under the rule of women and believed a woman had no right to rule over men. He declared,

To promote a woman to bear rule, superiority, dominion, or empire above any realm, nation, or city, is repugnant to nature; contumely to God, a thing most contrary to his revealed will and approved ordinance; and finally, it is the subversion of good order, of all equity and justice.

Queen Mary confronted him, and he explained he was as content to live peaceably under her rule as the Apostle Paul had been to live under Nero's. Queen Mary defended her allegiance to Rome, and Knox responded,

Wonder not, Madam, that I call Rome an harlot; for that Church is altogether polluted with all kind of spiritual fornication, as well in doctrine as in manners. Yea, Madam, I offer myself to prove, that the Church of the Jews which crucified Christ Jesus, was not so far degenerate from the ordinances which God gave by Moses and Aaron unto His people, when they manifestly denied the Son of God, as the Church of Rome is declined, and more than five hundred years hath declined, from the purity of that religion which the Apostles taught and planted.

Because church and state were involved throughout his life, Knox addressed these subjects with pen and sermon. He said, "Resistance to tyranny is obedience to God," and "A man with God is always in the majority." He also stated, "Let a thing here be noted, that the prophet of God sometimes may teach treason against kings, and yet neither he nor such as obey the word, spoken in the Lord's name by him, offend God."

Knox was fearless, and he devoutly believed the Bible should be followed, not merely read. He believed it required him to stand up to corrupt church clergy, kings, queens, and society. The force of his personal convictions still echo in Protestant thought beyond the Presbyterian Church he is credited with founding.

Roger Williams (1603-1683)

Born and educated in London, Roger Williams went from Anglican to Puritan when he concluded the church was corrupt and false. It was dangerous to hold unorthodox views in England: Alexander Leighton published a book that was critical of the Anglican church and was punished with prison for life, fined ten thousand pounds, degraded from his ministry, whipped, pilloried, his ears cut off, his nose slit, and his face branded with a hot iron. This intolerance of religious beliefs and cruel punishment for expressing them influenced Williams throughout his life.

Roger Williams moved to the English Colonies in America in 1631 where he became a Reform Baptist, then later a Free Will Baptist, and ultimately founded the First Baptist Church of Providence.

Williams was an abolitionist and organized the first attempt to prohibit slavery in the British American Colonies. He was also an advocate for separation of church from state. His ideas percolated among colonists and led to the First Amendment to the U.S. Constitution. He wrote,

> When they have opened a gap in the hedge or wall of separation between the garden of the church and the wilderness of the world, God hath ever broke down the wall itself, removed the candlestick, and made His garden a wilderness, as at this day.

His words were echoed by Thomas Jefferson in the letter to the Danbury Baptist Church, which repeated the words "wall of separation" between church and state. Jefferson's Danbury letter has been cited in several U.S. Supreme Court decisions as if it were part of the First Amendment.

Williams founded the first place in modern history where citizenship and religion were separate. His society also adopted majoritarian democracy. These ideals took root and directly influenced the American Revolution a century later.

His search for pure religion led him to eventually separate from any organized church, and from 1639 onward, he waited for Christ to send a new apostle to reestablish an original, pure, and authoritative church. He carefully studied religious societies and history and came to the conclusion that every denomination was flawed and each church was corrupt, though they differed in their flaws and virtues. He was persuaded that Christianity had departed from the truth early in history and had been corrupt ever since. He wrote, "Christianity fell asleep in the bosom of Constantine and the laps and bosoms of those Emperors who professed the name of Christ." This sober reflection led to his conviction that freedom of conscience was necessary to allow every soul to search for and accept all truth they could find. He declared, "There is no regularly constituted church of Christ on earth, nor any person qualified to administer any church ordinances; nor can there be until new apostles are sent by the Great Head of the Church for whose coming I am seeking."

Williams thought the British treatment of American Indians was inequitable and urged the land be purchased from the Indians rather than taken from them. This view caused conflict between him and the colonial authorities. He was convicted in 1635 of sedition and heresy and banished from Salem.

Despite his conflict with colonial leaders, he became a trusted friend by several native tribes in New England, even negotiating the end of conflicts between Indians and Rhode Island for nearly forty years. Twice he allowed himself to be taken hostage (1645 and again in 1671) to guarantee the return of an Indian leader summoned to court.

Williams has grown in influence over time, with many of his revolutionary ideas becoming commonplace generations later. He helped to create an American society that welcomes diverse religious views and protects freedom of conscience.

Although he did not believe the Christian churches preserved the original, he nevertheless practiced Christianity. He summarized what should be done briefly:

> ...the two first principles and foundations of true religion, or worship of the true God in Christ, are repentance from dead works, and faith towards God, before the doctrine of baptism or washing, and the laying on of hands, which contain the ordinances and practices of worship.

JOHN WESLEY (1703-1791)

One of the towering Protestant figures following Martin Luther was John Wesley, credited with founding the Methodist Church. He was educated at Oxford and became a minister in the Anglican Church. By the time of his death, there were 71,668 followers in Great Britain.

Wesley's ministry began before experiencing a direct connection with God. On May 24, 1738, he wrote in his journal about a life-changing connection:

> In the evening, I went very unwillingly to a society in Aldersgate Street, where one was reading Luther's preface to the Epistle to the Romans. About a quarter before nine, while he was describing the change which God works in the heart through faith in Christ, I felt my heart strangely warmed. I felt I did trust in Christ, Christ alone for salvation, and an assurance was given me that he had taken away my sins, even mine, and saved me from the law of sin and death.

This experience created within him the conviction that he had experienced God's love and would be saved. Persecution of his views began the next year, 1739, and never abated the remainder of his life.

Wesley did not accept the predestination teachings of John Calvin and was criticized and barred from preaching in his mother Anglican Church. He launched a new direction, with people meeting in private homes, praying, reading Scripture, discussing spiritual concerns, and collecting money for the needy. As fellow-believers grew in numbers, they were dismissively labeled "Methodists," but the term was accepted by them and in time became the accepted name of a new Christian denomination. During his lifetime, Wesley thought Methodists could in good faith remain members of the Anglican Church. Following his death, the two separated.

Wesley believed in pursuing and attempting Christian perfection in which men and women could live in this world in a state where God's love "reigned supreme in their hearts," which would reflect godly holiness—not as an imaginary concept, but as a living reality.

Like Luther before him, Wesley recognized the corruption of the professional clergy and the failure to preach repentance to sinners. He thought himself called to revive dying Christianity with a new voice crying repentance and promising God's forgiveness to the earnest seeker. He was loyal to both the Bible and prior orthodox Christian traditions. He believed every soul could be saved by faith in Christ and rejected the idea some were elected by God to salvation while others were doomed to damnation, as Calvin had taught. Salvation by grace could be experienced and known, as he explained: "...an inward impression on the soul of believers, whereby the Spirit of God directly testifies to their spirit that they are the children of God." This made salvation personal to each individual. He explained his fear:

> My fear is not that our great movement, known as the Methodists, will eventually cease to exist or one day die from the earth. My fear is that our people will become content to live without the fire, the power, the excitement, the supernatural element that makes us great.

He acknowledged the decline of the gifts of the Spirit recorded in the New Testament and noted they disappeared early in Christian history, once Constantine issued the Edict of Milan decriminalizing Christianity (313 A.D.). This led in turn to Christianity becoming the state religion of Rome in 380 A.D. In Wesley's sermon "The More Excellent Way," he explained,

> The cause of this [decline of spiritual gifts following Constantine] was not, (as has been vulgarly supposed,) "because there was no more occasion for them," because all the world was become Christians. This is a miserable mistake; not a twentieth part of it was then nominally Christian. The real cause was, "the love of many," almost of all Christians, so called, was "waxed cold." The Christians had no more of the Spirit of Christ than the other Heathens. The Son of Man, when he came to examine his Church, could hardly "find faith upon earth." This was the real cause why the extraordinary gifts of the Holy Ghost were no longer to be

found in the Christian Church; because the Christians were turned Heathens again, and had only a dead form left.

Wesley's teachings have influenced Christian thinking far beyond the bounds of the Methodist Church. He is a widely respected and studied Christian thinker. He is credited with posing the question, "Though we cannot think alike, may we not love alike?"

His dying words were, "The best of all is, God is with us," which he repeated twice.

MARY BAKER EDDY (1821-1910)

Mary Baker Eddy was a teacher, author, and religious leader whose ideas about spirituality and health were set out in a book published in 1875, titled *Science and Health with Key to the Scriptures*. Her approach was called Christian Science. Four years after its publication, she founded the "Church of Christ, Scientist," a new denomination which has grown worldwide. She began (and the denomination continues to publish) *The Christian Science Monitor*, now a leading and highly respected international newspaper. She described its purpose was "to injure no man, but to bless all mankind."

Mary was born in New Hampshire and raised in a religious Congregational family. While still young, she rejected the Calvinist principle of predestination and sought guidance through prayer and Bible study. She married in 1843 and was widowed the following June, while six months pregnant. She returned to her parents' home and was married a second time in 1853, but it was an unhappy relationship; he abandoned her in 1866, and they divorced in 1873 on the grounds of desertion.

She had health problems all her life. Chronic illness and personal losses made her preoccupied with health issues. The physicians of her day administered remedies which caused additional suffering with limited, if any, meaningful relief. She studied homeopathy and investigated a variety of new approaches to medical care. She subjected herself to new "cures" to see if things ranging from hydropathy to placebos—even mental suggestions (hypnosis)—would help. While doing so, she continued to study the Bible.

She sustained a serious injury in 1866 from a fall, and while convalescing and studying her Bible, she read about a miraculous healing and found it suddenly, likewise, healed her. This was when she discovered Christian Science. After nine years of study, she published her *Science and Health with Keys to the Scripture* to attempt to set out the principle of Christian healing. She believed Jesus performed healing using a natural and repeatable system. She explained,

> During twenty years prior to my discovery I had been trying to trace all physical effects to a mental cause; and in the latter part of 1866 I gained the scientific certainty that all causation was Mind, and every effect a mental phenomenon.

With time, her system came to be widely taught, and hundreds of men and women established successful healing practices based on her work.

When other denominations refused to welcome her system, she obtained a charter for the "Church of Christ, Scientist" in 1879 "to commemorate the word and works of our Master, which should reinstate primitive Christianity and its lost element of healing." While she did not want to start a church, rejection of the things she believed to be true led her to this inevitability. Her organization is local—that is, congregationally organized and democratically run by the participants.

She advocated practical steps to improve mankind: "Sin makes its own hell, and goodness its own heaven." "True prayer is not asking God for love; it is learning to love, and to include all mankind in one affection." She is regarded as one of the 100 Most Influential Americans of All Time.

WILLIAM BOOTH (1829-1912) & CATHERINE BOOTH (1829-1890)

William Booth was the founder of the Salvation Army. He was born in Nottingham, England and married Catherine Mumford in 1855. They worked together in their joint desire to help fight the poverty that surrounded them.

William Booth was no stranger to poverty, even in his childhood. His father died when he was only 14, and his family was nearly destitute as a result. He served as a pawnbroker's apprentice, which exposed him to the direful plight of the poor that resulted in his hatred of the effects of poverty.

William became a Christian at 15, and his potential as a preacher became noticed while he was yet a teenager. His passion to help the down-and-out brought him into the streets where the people who needed most to find hope in Christ were to be found. He later became a traveling Methodist evangelist but returned to the streets as his primary ministry. His exposure to poverty and his experience on the streets of the London slums led him to found The Salvation Army.

Catherine was born in Ashbourne, Derbyshire. She was a thoughtful child from a strong Christian family. She is said to have read the Bible cover-to-cover eight times by the time she was 12 years old. When 14 years old, she became seriously ill and spent a lengthy time convalescing and reflecting on her beliefs, including the problems alcohol caused in society. This would foreshadow her later work to address the problem.

William and Catherine met when he came to preach at her Methodist church. She began to help him in his ministry, and following a three year engagement, they were married in a simple ceremony. Even on their honeymoon, William continued to preach, because they both believed it was important to be used by God. They had eight children and adopted a ninth. Seven of their children became well-known preachers, all of whom also published hymns.

William led the fight against prostitution in London, which involved 13- to 16-year-old girls who became trapped in the trade while seeking relief from poverty and hunger. His campaign resulted in legislation against "white slavery." The Salvation Army led to the formation of the USO, which operates 3000 service units for people serving in the armed forces. Catherine's concern about the ill effects of alcohol led to the development of The Salvation Army's alcohol rehabilitation program, which has now helped people for 100 years.

The focus of The Salvation Army from the very beginning has been to help the poor, the homeless, the hungry, and the destitute. William and Catherine took their mission to the streets and met the needs where the needs existed, rather than remaining at a pulpit to minister to a traditional congregation. He once asked her (referring to the streets of London), "Where can you go and find such heathen as these, and where is there so great a need for your labours?"

William Booth took the fight for Christian belief to those who most needed hope. He said,

> While women weep, as they do now, I'll fight; while little children go hungry, as they do now, I'll fight; while men go to prison, in and out, in and out, as they do now, I'll fight; while there is a drunkard left, while there is a poor lost girl upon the streets, while there remains one dark soul without the light of God, I'll fight—I'll fight to the very end!

William Booth cautioned us about the trends he saw in both society and religion:

> I consider that the chief dangers which confront the coming century will be religion without the Holy Ghost; Christianity without Christ; forgiveness without repentance; salvation without regeneration; politics without God; and Heaven without Hell.

In 1860, Catherine began to also preach publicly, and by her success, she changed her husband's view about the potential of female ministers. The Salvation Army would become an advocate of sexual equality in the ministry, leaving a legacy of an expanded role for women in churches far beyond The Salvation Army. She was an agent for social reform and advocated better conditions and pay for women. She is remembered by the Salvationists as "The Army Mother."

DWIGHT LYMAN MOODY (1837-1899)

Dwight L. Moody was one of the great evangelists of the 19th century. Born to a poor Northfield, Massachusetts family of nine children, his father died when he was four. He only received a fifth-grade education and left home at age 17. He became a Christian at 18 and moved to Chicago. Rather than seek a personal fortune, he focused on helping the poor, establishing a Sunday school in a Chicago slum in 1858. He refused to fight in the U.S. Civil War, claiming that, with respect to war, he "was a Quaker"—meaning a pacifist. Nevertheless, he worked to evangelize Union troops.

By 1861, his missionary activities were so successful that he withdrew from business to devote himself full time to missionary work. In 1870, he partnered with Ira Sankey, and the two spent years touring in evangelistic campaigns in the United States and Great Britain. He believed that music would be an effective tool as part of preaching and recruited Sankey to join him and sing hymns to the crowds. Their selection of hymns became popular and widely used and generated over a million dollars in royalties. It is estimated that more than 100 million people attended the Moody-Sankey revival meetings.

He became convinced there was a need to train other evangelists, both men and women. He established the Northfield Seminary for girls in 1879 and the Mount Hermon School for boys in 1881. In 1886, he founded the Bible-Work Institute of the Chicago Evangelization Society, later renamed the Moody Bible Institute. The royalties from his successful hymnal were used to fund these projects.

He believed in being Christian above every other thing in life. He taught, "Christians should live in the world, but not be filled with it. A ship lives in the water; but if the water gets into the ship, she goes to the bottom. So Christians may live in the world; but if the world gets into them, they sink." He could give a profound sermon in a single quip: "Moses spent forty years thinking he was somebody; forty years learning he was nobody; and forty years discovering what God can do with a nobody."

He lived his life trying to be an example of Christian faith and taught those who heard him to do likewise. He admonished Christians, "Out of 100 men, one will read the Bible, the other 99 will read the Christian." Also, "The world does not understand theology or dogma, but it understands love and sympathy."

He believed in the Calvinist tradition. His sermons were filled with insightful quips, personal allusions, and penetrating insights. His limited education did not control his destiny, and he had a formidable command of the English Bible text. He could be blunt and had little pretense in his demeanor. Although he was praised and respected, he never seemed to fall under its control. He stressed God's love and mercy rather than God's anger and the risk of hellfire.

CHARLES TAZE RUSSELL (1852-1916)

Charles Taze Russell founded the Bible Student Movement. He made a systematic study of the Bible the focus of his ministerial effort. His study resulted in publishing a journal—now called *The Watchtower*—in which he made a contrast between what the Bible said compared with what various churches taught. After his death, the Jehovah's Witnesses developed from his followers.

He published a six-volume study of the Bible between 1886 and 1904, titled *Studies in the Scriptures,* that sold over 19,900,000 copies while he was still living. Always a prolific writer, in 1912 he was responsible for distribution of 35,520,475 free pamphlets, magazines, and tracts. His sermons were published in newspapers across America. His last major project was a motion picture project titled "Photo Drama of Creation" that was released in 1914. It was in four parts, two hours per part, and dealt with the earth's history.

Although a gifted preacher, Russell claimed no special revelation or vision, nor did he claim any special authority to justify his calling. He did not intend to create a new denomination but rather to gather Christian believers together. Reason alone was sufficient to figure out what the Bible taught.

His early religious exposure made him fearful of eternal punishment while still a teen. He was unable to reconcile this with the love of God, and for a time, he became a skeptic. By 1870 he concluded that the Bible may be correct, but the competing denominations of Christianity were the culprit in causing believers to err. He wrote, "The various creeds continually conflict and clash; and as each claims a Bible basis, the confusion of thought, and evident discord, are charged to God's word."

After concluding that the Bible was reliable and the various denominations were misrepresenting its content, he decided there was no religious organization that could be identified as the "true church." He believed there had been an early apostasy from the truth, writing that "the predicted 'falling away' had begun to work even in the Apostolic times." He taught that the Dark Ages were caused by the neglect of truth and the strife of sectarianism. Despite this, he did not attempt to reorganize the "true church."

Despite his dislike of denominational Christianity, he thought Martin Luther, John Wycliff, John Knox, and other Protestant fathers were bold defenders of God's words. Apart from this, he regarded clergy generally as weak, ineffective, and errant.

Using his reason as a guide to interpret the Bible, Russell searched the Bible for types and determined that the period from 1813 B.C. until 70 A.D. was parallel to the period from 33 A.D. until 1915 A.D. He believed the World's Parliament of Religions held in 1893 in Chicago was an example of Christians compromising the purity of their beliefs. He believed simplicity was the primary basis for early Christian worship in the Apostolic age.

Jehovah's Witnesses have described his ministry in these words:

> Among that group of sincere Bible students was a man named Charles Taze Russell. While Russell took the lead in the Bible education work at that time and was the first editor of The Watchtower, he was not the founder of a new religion. The goal of Russell and the other Bible Students, as the group was then known, was to promote the teachings of Jesus Christ and to follow the

practices of the first-century Christian congregation. Since Jesus is the Founder of Christianity, we view him as the founder of our organization.

Russell explained, "If it is not proper to unite with any of the present nominal churches, would it not be well to form a visible association of our own? Yes, that is what we have—a society modeled after that of the early church. We think we have come back to primitive simplicity."

In many respects, Russell was responding to widespread recognition (shared by many of the leaders of the Protestant movement) that Christianity was deeply flawed and needed to be reconsidered. Christianity once held great power to save souls and descended into squabbling factions. He sought to return to an original simplicity to avoid conflict.

C. S. Lewis (1898-1968)

Clive Staples Lewis is known to his readers as C.S. Lewis. While originally an atheist, he became known as a prolific Christian apologist. He progressed from atheism to theism and then to Christianity. His conversion to Christianity came in 1931.

He was born in Belfast, Ireland. Lewis entered the University of Oxford in 1917 and remained close by thereafter. He taught at Oxford beginning in 1925 and later at Cambridge from 1954 to 1963, where he married an American English teacher, Joy Gresham, in 1956. She died of cancer in 1960.

He wrote *The Pilgrim's Regress: An Allegorical Apology for Christianity, Reason, and Romanticism* in 1933 as his first Christian apology, and he went on to write 25 Christian books that sold millions of copies. Many people associate him with *The Chronicles of Narnia*, an allegorical Christian series of seven books which has sold over 100 million copies and been made into three major motion pictures. He was a friend of J.R.R. Tolkien.

His theological contribution in *The Great Divorce* (1946) and *Miracles* (1947) are respected by many theologians and general readers. His book *Mere Christianity* was adapted from a series of radio broadcasts from 1942 to 1944. His writings have enduring appeal.

Because he has been one of the most quoted Christian writers since he began his role as a Christian apologist, below are quotes from Lewis' writings:

Since it is so likely that children will meet cruel enemies, let them at least have heard of brave knights and heroic courage. (*On Stories: And Other Essays on Literature*)

Each day we are becoming a creature of splendid glory or one of unthinkable horror. (*Mere Christianity*)

There are only two kinds of people: those who say to God, "Thy will be done," and those to whom God says, "All right, then, have it your way." (*The Great Divorce*)

No man knows how bad he is till he has tried very hard to be good. (*Mere Christianity*)

The sun looks down on nothing half so good as a household laughing together over a meal. (*The Weight of Glory*)

The instrument through which you see God is your whole self. And if a man's self is not kept clean and bright, his glimpse of God will be blurred. (*Mere Christianity*)

A man can no more diminish God's glory by refusing to worship Him than a lunatic can put out the sun by scribbling the word "darkness" on the walls of his cell. (*The Problem of Pain*)

In our own case we accept excuses too easily; in other people's, we do not accept them easily enough. (*The Weight of Glory*)

If God forgives us we must forgive ourselves otherwise its like setting up ourselves as a higher tribunal than him. (*Collected Letters of C. S. Lewis*)

Of all the bad men, religious bad men are the worst. (*Reflections on the Psalms*)

One road leads home and a thousand roads lead into the wilderness. (*The Pilgrim's Regress*)

Christianity, if false, is of no importance and, if true, is of infinite importance. The one thing it cannot be is moderately important. (*God in the Dock*)

BILLY GRAHAM (1918-2018)

Billy Graham was an ordained Southern Baptist preacher whose career is principally known because of a series of more than 400 "Crusades" in 185 countries between 1947 and 2005. Beginning with circus tents set up in parking lots, he eventually filled stadiums with tens-of-thousands of interested listeners. The largest Crusade attracted more than a million people to one service. Many of his Crusades were broadcast on television. He hosted a radio show, "Hour of Decision," from 1950 to 1954. In October 1989, Graham became the only functioning minister to have a star on the Hollywood Walk of Fame.

Graham was widely recognized and a popular Evangelical minister who has been one of the "most admired men" in America for 55 years. He would end Crusades with an invitation for any who felt convicted and wanted to "accept Jesus Christ as your personal savior" to publicly come forward. Thousands responded to his invitation.

Graham was an adviser to several U.S. Presidents, including Dwight Eisenhower, Lyndon Johnson, and Richard Nixon, and met with many other presidents, from Harry Truman to Barack Obama.

He was friends with Martin Luther King, Jr., and once paid for King's bail after his arrest for participation in a Civil Rights demonstration (in 1963). King and Graham preached together on several occasions at Graham's invitation.

He founded the Billy Graham Evangelistic Association in 1950, originally headquartered in Minneapolis but which relocated to Charlotte, North Carolina in 1999. It is still active and publishes *Decision* magazine as its official publication, as well as *Christianity Today*, which is "a global media ministry."

Graham was regarded as America's Protestant patriarch, providing a Christian conscience to the nation. He organized and supported evangelism worldwide. He supported training conferences to increase the evangelical presence in many nations.

Graham refused to join Jerry Falwell's "Moral Majority" in 1979, explaining, "I'm for morality, but morality goes beyond sex to human freedom and social justice. …We have to stand in the middle in order to preach to all people, right and left." Graham's views about seeking salvation for all people—everywhere—motivated his worldwide ministerial efforts. He summarized his belief in a 1997 interview:

> I think that everybody that loves or knows Christ, whether they are conscious of it or not, they are members of the body of Christ… [God] is calling people out of the world for his name, whether they come from the Muslim world, or the Buddhist world or the non-believing world, they are members of the Body of Christ because they have been called by God. They may not know the name of Jesus but they know in their hearts that they need something they do not have, and they turn to the only light they have, and I think that they are saved and they are going to be with us in heaven.

Graham was diagnosed with Parkinson's disease in 1992, which led to his retirement because of failing health. Graham passed away on February 21, 2018, at which time America and the world lost an Evangelical giant. He has been seen and heard both in person and through radio and television by more people than any other Evangelical minister in history. He lived just short of a century, dying at the age of 99.

Many pastors, bishops, priests, and other leaders of different faiths had theological differences with Billy Graham, but there were almost none who disputed his greatness. He preached a message of salvation by acceptance and confession of Jesus as Savior. His beliefs were grounded in the writings of the Apostle Paul and echoed much of what Martin Luther believed about salvation. There are millions of people living today whose confidence in salvation through Jesus Christ is based on the preaching of Billy Graham. He inspired not only believers, but also other Evangelical ministers and writers.

Historical Documents

What follows are articles of belief as published by two of the most influential fathers of the Reformation.

95 Theses by Martin Luther

1. When our Lord and Master Jesus Christ said, "Repent" (Matt. 4:17), he willed the entire life of believers to be one of repentance.

2. This word cannot be understood as referring to the sacrament of penance, that is, confession and satisfaction, as administered by the clergy.

3. Yet it does not mean solely inner repentance; such inner repentance is worthless unless it produces various outward mortification of the flesh.

4. The penalty of sin remains as long as the hatred of self (that is, true inner repentance), namely till our entrance into the kingdom of heaven.

5. The pope neither desires nor is able to remit any penalties except those imposed by his own authority or that of the canons.

6. The pope cannot remit any guilt, except by declaring and showing that it has been remitted by God; or, to be sure, by remitting guilt in cases reserved to his judgment. If his right to grant remission in these cases were disregarded, the guilt would certainly remain unforgiven.

7. God remits guilt to no one unless at the same time he humbles him in all things and makes him submissive to the vicar, the priest.

8. The penitential canons are imposed only on the living, and, according to the canons themselves, nothing should be imposed on the dying.

9. Therefore the Holy Spirit through the pope is kind to us insofar as the pope in his decrees always makes exception of the article of death and of necessity.

10. Those priests act ignorantly and wickedly who, in the case of the dying, reserve canonical penalties for purgatory.

11. Those tares of changing the canonical penalty to the penalty of purgatory were evidently sown while the bishops slept (Matt. 13:25).

12. In former times canonical penalties were imposed, not after, but before absolution, as tests of true contrition.

13. The dying are freed by death from all penalties, are already dead as far as the canon laws are concerned, and have a right to be released from them.

14. Imperfect piety or love on the part of the dying person necessarily brings with it great fear; and the smaller the love, the greater the fear.

15. This fear or horror is sufficient in itself, to say nothing of other things, to constitute the penalty of purgatory, since it is very near to the horror of despair.

16. Hell, purgatory, and heaven seem to differ the same as despair, fear, and assurance of salvation.

17. It seems as though for the souls in purgatory fear should necessarily decrease and love increase.

18. Furthermore, it does not seem proved, either by reason or by scripture, that souls in purgatory are outside the state of merit, that is, unable to grow in love.

19. Nor does it seem proved that souls in purgatory, at least not all of them, are certain and assured of their own salvation, even if we ourselves may be entirely certain of it.

20. Therefore the pope, when he uses the words "plenary remission of all penalties," does not actually mean "all penalties," but only those imposed by himself.

21. Thus those indulgence preachers are in error who say that a man is absolved from every penalty and saved by papal indulgences.

22. As a matter of fact, the pope remits to souls in purgatory no penalty which, according to canon law, they should have paid in this life.

23. If remission of all penalties whatsoever could be granted to anyone at all, certainly it would be granted only to the most perfect, that is, to very few.

24. For this reason most people are necessarily deceived by that indiscriminate and high-sounding promise of release from penalty.

25. That power which the pope has in general over purgatory corresponds to the power which any bishop or curate has in a particular way in his own diocese and parish.

26. The pope does very well when he grants remission to souls in purgatory, not by the power of the keys, which he does not have, but by way of intercession for them.

27. They preach only human doctrines who say that as soon as the money clinks into the money chest, the soul flies out of purgatory.

28. It is certain that when money clinks in the money chest, greed and avarice can be increased; but when the church intercedes, the result is in the hands of God alone.

29. Who knows whether all souls in purgatory wish to be redeemed, since we have exceptions in St. Severinus and St. Paschal, as related in a legend.

30. No one is sure of the integrity of his own contrition, much less of having received plenary remission.

31. The man who actually buys indulgences is as rare as he who is really penitent; indeed, he is exceedingly rare.

32. Those who believe that they can be certain of their salvation because they have indulgence letters will be eternally damned, together with their teachers.

33. Men must especially be on guard against those who say that the pope's pardons are that inestimable gift of God by which man is reconciled to him.

34. For the graces of indulgences are concerned only with the penalties of sacramental satisfaction established by man.

35. They who teach that contrition is not necessary on the part of those who intend to buy souls out of purgatory or to buy confessional privileges preach unchristian doctrine.

36. Any truly repentant Christian has a right to full remission of penalty and guilt, even without indulgence letters.

37. Any true Christian, whether living or dead, participates in all the blessings of Christ and the church; and this is granted him by God, even without indulgence letters.

38. Nevertheless, papal remission and blessing are by no means to be disregarded, for they are, as I have said (Thesis 6), the proclamation of the divine remission.

39. It is very difficult, even for the most learned theologians, at one and the same time to commend to the people the bounty of indulgences and the need of true contrition.

40. A Christian who is truly contrite seeks and loves to pay penalties for his sins; the bounty of indulgences, however, relaxes penalties and causes men to hate them – at least it furnishes occasion for hating them.

41. Papal indulgences must be preached with caution, lest people erroneously think that they are preferable to other good works of love.

42. Christians are to be taught that the pope does not intend that the buying of indulgences should in any way be compared with works of mercy.

43. Christians are to be taught that he who gives to the poor or lends to the needy does a better deed than he who buys indulgences.

44. Because love grows by works of love, man thereby becomes better. Man does not, however, become better by means of indulgences but is merely freed from penalties.

45. Christians are to be taught that he who sees a needy man and passes him by, yet gives his money for indulgences, does not buy papal indulgences but God's wrath.

46. Christians are to be taught that, unless they have more than they need, they must reserve enough for their family needs and by no means squander it on indulgences.

47. Christians are to be taught that they buying of indulgences is a matter of free choice, not commanded.

48. Christians are to be taught that the pope, in granting indulgences, needs and thus desires their devout prayer more than their money.

49. Christians are to be taught that papal indulgences are useful only if they do not put their trust in them, but very harmful if they lose their fear of God because of them.

50. Christians are to be taught that if the pope knew the exactions of the indulgence preachers, he would rather that the basilica of St. Peter were burned to ashes than built up with the skin, flesh, and bones of his sheep.

51. Christians are to be taught that the pope would and should wish to give of his own money, even though he had to sell the basilica of St.

Peter, to many of those from whom certain hawkers of indulgences cajole money.

52. It is vain to trust in salvation by indulgence letters, even though the indulgence commissary, or even the pope, were to offer his soul as security.

53. They are the enemies of Christ and the pope who forbid altogether the preaching of the Word of God in some churches in order that indulgences may be preached in others.

54. Injury is done to the Word of God when, in the same sermon, an equal or larger amount of time is devoted to indulgences than to the Word.

55. It is certainly the pope's sentiment that if indulgences, which are a very insignificant thing, are celebrated with one bell, one procession, and one ceremony, then the gospel, which is the very greatest thing, should be preached with a hundred bells, a hundred processions, a hundred ceremonies.

56. The true treasures of the church, out of which the pope distributes indulgences, are not sufficiently discussed or known among the people of Christ.

57. That indulgences are not temporal treasures is certainly clear, for many indulgence sellers do not distribute them freely but only gather them.

58. Nor are they the merits of Christ and the saints, for, even without the pope, the latter always work grace for the inner man, and the cross, death, and hell for the outer man.

59. St. Lawrence said that the poor of the church were the treasures of the church, but he spoke according to the usage of the word in his own time.

60. Without want of consideration we say that the keys of the church, given by the merits of Christ, are that treasure.

61. For it is clear that the pope's power is of itself sufficient for the remission of penalties and cases reserved by himself.

62. The true treasure of the church is the most holy gospel of the glory and grace of God.

63. But this treasure is naturally most odious, for it makes the first to be last (Matt. 20:16).

64. On the other hand, the treasure of indulgences is naturally most acceptable, for it makes the last to be first.

65. Therefore the treasures of the gospel are nets with which one formerly fished for men of wealth.

66. The treasures of indulgences are nets with which one now fishes for the wealth of men.

67. The indulgences which the demagogues acclaim as the greatest graces are actually understood to be such only insofar as they promote gain.

68. They are nevertheless in truth the most insignificant graces when compared with the grace of God and the piety of the cross.

69. Bishops and curates are bound to admit the commissaries of papal indulgences with all reverence.

70. But they are much more bound to strain their eyes and ears lest these men preach their own dreams instead of what the pope has commissioned.

71. Let him who speaks against the truth concerning papal indulgences be anathema and accursed.

72. But let him who guards against the lust and license of the indulgence preachers be blessed.

73. Just as the pope justly thunders against those who by any means whatever contrive harm to the sale of indulgences.

74. Much more does he intend to thunder against those who use indulgences as a pretext to contrive harm to holy love and truth.

75. To consider papal indulgences so great that they could absolve a man even if he had done the impossible and had violated the mother of God is madness.

76. We say on the contrary that papal indulgences cannot remove the very least of venial sins as far as guilt is concerned.

77. To say that even St. Peter if he were now pope, could not grant greater graces is blasphemy against St. Peter and the pope.

78. We say on the contrary that even the present pope, or any pope whatsoever, has greater graces at his disposal, that is, the gospel, spiritual powers, gifts of healing, etc., as it is written. (1 Cor. 12:28)

79. To say that the cross emblazoned with the papal coat of arms, and set up by the indulgence preachers is equal in worth to the cross of Christ is blasphemy.

80. The bishops, curates, and theologians who permit such talk to be spread among the people will have to answer for this.

81. This unbridled preaching of indulgences makes it difficult even for learned men to rescue the reverence which is due the pope from slander or from the shrewd questions of the laity.

82. Such as: "Why does not the pope empty purgatory for the sake of holy love and the dire need of the souls that are there if he redeems an infinite number of souls for the sake of miserable money with which to build a church?" The former reason would be most just; the latter is most trivial.

83. Again, "Why are funeral and anniversary masses for the dead continued and why does he not return or permit the withdrawal of the endowments founded for them, since it is wrong to pray for the redeemed?"

84. Again, "What is this new piety of God and the pope that for a consideration of money they permit a man who is impious and their enemy to buy out of purgatory the pious soul of a friend of God and do not rather, because of the need of that pious and beloved soul, free it for pure love's sake?"

85. Again, "Why are the penitential canons, long since abrogated and dead in actual fact and through disuse, now satisfied by the granting of indulgences as though they were still alive and in force?"

86. Again, "Why does not the pope, whose wealth is today greater than the wealth of the richest Crassus, build this one basilica of St. Peter with his own money rather than with the money of poor believers?"

87. Again, "What does the pope remit or grant to those who by perfect contrition already have a right to full remission and blessings?"

88. Again, "What greater blessing could come to the church than if the pope were to bestow these remissions and blessings on every believer a hundred times a day, as he now does but once?"

89. "Since the pope seeks the salvation of souls rather than money by his indulgences, why does he suspend the indulgences and pardons previously granted when they have equal efficacy?"

90. To repress these very sharp arguments of the laity by force alone, and not to resolve them by giving reasons, is to expose the church and the pope to the ridicule of their enemies and to make Christians unhappy.

91. If, therefore, indulgences were preached according to the spirit and intention of the pope, all these doubts would be readily resolved. Indeed, they would not exist.

92. Away, then, with all those prophets who say to the people of Christ, "Peace, peace," and there is no peace! (Jer. 6:14)

93. Blessed be all those prophets who say to the people of Christ, "Cross, cross," and there is no cross!

94. Christians should be exhorted to be diligent in following Christ, their Head, through penalties, death and hell.

95. And thus be confident of entering into heaven through many tribulations rather than through the false security of peace (Acts 14:22)

67 ARTICLES BY ULRICH ZWINGLI

The articles and opinions below, I, Ulrich Zwingli, confess to have preached in the worthy city of Zurich as based upon the Scriptures which are called inspired by God, and I offer to protect and conquer with the said articles, and where I have not now correctly understood said Scriptures I shall allow myself to be taught better, but only from said Scriptures.

1. All who say that the Gospel is invalid without the confirmation of the Church err and slander God.

2. The sum and substance of the Gospel is that our Lord Jesus Christ, the true Son of God, has made known to us the will of his heavenly Father, and has with his innocence released us from death and reconciled God.

3. Hence Christ is the only way to salvation for all who ever were, are and shall be.

4. Who seeks or points out another door errs, yes, he is a murderer of souls and a thief.

5. Therefore all who consider other teachings equal to or higher than the Gospel err, and do not know what the Gospel is.

6. For Jesus Christ is the guide and leader, promised by God to all human beings, which promise was fulfilled.

7. That he is an eternal salvation and head of all believers, who are his body, but which is dead and can do nothing without him.

8. From this follows first that all who dwell in the head are members and children of God, and that it is the church or communion of the saints, the bride of Christ, Ecclesia catholica.

9. Furthermore, that as the members of the body can do nothing without the control of the head, so no one in the body of Christ can do the least without his head, Christ.

10. As that man is mad whose limbs (try to) do something without his head, tearing, wounding, injuring himself; thus when the members of Christ undertake something without their head, Christ, they are mad, and injure and burden themselves with unwise ordinances.

11. Hence we see in the clerical (so-called) ordinances, concerning their splendor, riches, classes, titles, laws, a cause of all foolishness, for they do not also agree with the head.

12. Thus they still rage, not on account of the head (for that one is eager to bring forth in these times from the grace of God,) but because one will not let them rage, but tries to compel them to listen to the head.

13. Where this (the head) is hearkened to one learns clearly and plainly the will of God, and man is attracted by his spirit to him and changed into him.

14. Therefore all Christian people shall use their best diligence that the Gospel of Christ be preached alike everywhere.

15. For in the faith rests our salvation, and in unbelief our damnation; for all truth is clear in him.

16. In the Gospel one learns that human doctrines and decrees do not aid in salvation.

ABOUT THE POPE.

17. That Christ is the only eternal high priest, from which it follows that those who have called themselves high priests have opposed the honor and power of Christ, yes, cast it out.

ABOUT THE MASS.

18. That Christ, having sacrificed himself once, is to eternity a certain and valid sacrifice for the sins of all faithful, from which it follows that the mass is not a sacrifice, but is a remembrance of the sacrifice and assurance of the salvation which Christ has given us.

19. That Christ is the only mediator between God and us.

ABOUT THE INTERCESSION OF THE SAINTS.

20. That God desires to give us all things in his name, whence it follows that outside of this life we need no mediator except himself.

21. That when we pray for each other on earth, we do so in such manner that we believe that all things are given to us through Christ alone.

ABOUT GOOD WORKS.

22. That Christ is our justice, from which follows that our works in so far as they are good, so far they are of Christ, but in so far as they are ours, they are neither right nor good.

CONCERNING CLERICAL PROPERTY.

23. That Christ scorns the property and pomp of this world, whence from it follows that those who attract wealth to themselves in his name slander him terribly when they make him a pretext for their avarice and willfulness.

CONCERNING THE FORBIDDING OF FOOD.

24. That no Christian is bound to do those things which God has not decreed, therefore one may eat at all times all food, from which one learns that the decree about cheese and butter is a Roman swindle.

ABOUT HOLIDAY AND PILGRIMAGE.

25. That time and place is under the jurisdiction of Christian people, and man with them, from which is learned that those who fix time and place deprive the Christians of their liberty.

ABOUT HOODS, DRESS, INSIGNIA.

26. That God is displeased with nothing so much as with hypocrisy; from which is learned that all is gross hypocrisy and profligacy which is mere show before men. Under this condemnation fall hoods, insignia, plates, etc.

ABOUT ORDER AND SECTS.

27. That all Christian men are brethren of Christ and brethren of one another, and shall create no father (for themselves) on earth. Under this condemnation fall orders, sects, brotherhoods, etc.

ABOUT THE MARRIAGE OF ECCLESIASTS.

28. That all which God has allowed or not forbidden is righteous, hence marriage is permitted to all human beings.

29. That all who are known as clergy sin when they do not protect themselves by marriage after they have become conscious that God has not enabled them to remain chaste.

ABOUT THE VOW OF CHASTITY.

30. That those who promise chastity [outside of matrimony] take foolishly or childishly too much upon themselves, from which is learned that those who make such vows do wrong to the pious being.

ABOUT THE BAN.

31. That no special person can impose the ban [excommunication] upon any one, except the Church, that is the [full] congregation of those among whom the one to be banned dwells, together with their watchman, i.e., the pastor.

32. That one may ban only him who gives public offence.

ABOUT ILLEGAL PROPERTY.

33. That property unrighteously acquired shall not be given to temples, monasteries, cathedrals, clergy or nuns, but to the needy, if it cannot be returned to the legal owner.

ABOUT MAGISTRY.

34. The spiritual (so-called) power has no justification for its pomp in the teaching of Christ.

35. But the laity has power and confirmation from the deed and doctrine of Christ.

36. All that the spiritual so-called state claims to have of power and protection belongs to the laity, if they wish to be Christians.

37. To them, furthermore, all Christians owe obedience without exception.

38. In so far as they do not command that which is contrary to God.

39. Therefore all their laws shall be in harmony with the divine will, so that they protect the oppressed, even if he does not complain.

40. They alone may put to death justly, also, only those who give public offence (if God is not offended let another thing be commanded).

41. If they give good advice and help to those for whom they must account to God, then these owe to them bodily assistance.

42. But if they are unfaithful and transgress the laws of Christ they may be deposed in the name of God.

43. In short, the realm of him is best and most stable who rules in the name of God alone, and his is worst and most unstable who rules in accordance with his own will.

ABOUT PRAYER.

44. Real petitioners call to God in spirit and truly, without great ado before men.

45. Hypocrites do their work so that they may be seen by men, also receive their reward in this life.

46. Hence it must always follow that church-song and outcry without devoutness, and only for reward, is seeking either fame before the men or gain.

ABOUT OFFENCE.

47. Bodily death a man should suffer before he offend or scandalize a Christian.

48. Whoever through stupidness or ignorance is offended without cause, he should not be left sick or weak, but he should be made strong that he may not consider as a sin that which is not a sin.

49. Greater offence I know not than that one does not allow priests to have wives, but permits them to hire prostitutes. Out upon the shame!

ABOUT REMITTANCE OF SIN.

50. God alone remits sin through Jesus Christ, his Son, and alone our Lord.

51. Who assigns this to created beings detracts from the honor of God and gives it to him who is not God; this is real idolatry.

52. Hence the confession which is made to the priest or neighbor shall not be declared to be a remittance of sin, but only a seeking for advice.

53. Works of penance coming from the counsel of human beings (except excommunication) do not cancel sin; they are imposed as a menace to others.

54. Christ has borne all our pains and labor. Therefore whoever assigns to works of penance what belongs to Christ errs and slanders God.

55. Whoever pretends to remit to a penitent being any sin would not be a vicar of God or St. Peter, but of the devil.

56. Whoever remits any sin only for the sake of money is the companion of Simon and Balaam, and the real messenger of the devil personified.

ABOUT PURGATORY.

57. The true divine Scriptures know nothing about purgatory after this life.

58. The sentence of the dead is known to God only.

59. And the less God has let us know concerning it, the less we should undertake to know about it.

60. That mankind earnestly calls to God to show mercy to the dead I do not condemn, but to determine a period of time therefore (seven years for a mortal sin), and to lie for the sake of gain, is not human, but devilish.

ABOUT THE PRIESTHOOD.

61. About the form of consecration which the priests have received recent times the Scriptures know nothing.

62. Furthermore, they [the Scriptures] recognize no priests except those who proclaim the word of God.

63. They command honor should be shown, i.e. e., to furnish them with food for the body.

ABOUT THE CESSATION OF MISUSAGES.

64. All those who recognize their errors shall not be allowed to suffer, but to die in peace, and thereafter arrange in a Christian manner their bequests to the Church.

65. Those who do not wish to confess, God will probably take care of. Hence no force shall be used against their body, unless it be that they behave so criminally that one cannot do without that.

66. All the clerical superiors shall at once settle down, and with unanimity set up the cross of Christ, not the money-chests, or they will perish, for I tell you the ax is raised against the tree.

67. If any one wishes conversation with me concerning interest, tithes, unbaptized children or confirmation, I am willing to answer.

Let no one undertake here to argue with sophistry or human foolishness, but come to the Scriptures to accept them as the judge (for the Scriptures breathe the Spirit of God), so that the truth either may be found, or if found, as I hope, retained. Amen.

Thus may God rule.

500 Years Later:
Christianity's Past to Present

October 29, 2017 was Reformation Sunday.[18] It is the Sunday closest to the date Martin Luther nailed his 95 Theses to the door of the Wittenberg Castle church. The document raised questions and propositions for debate. It was intended to lead to a meaningful discussion among Catholics, in the hope it would cause a reform to the institution.

The institution did not accept the invitation to meaningfully discuss the issues raised, and instead of reflecting on their own conduct, they condemned Martin Luther. Martin Luther was a devout Catholic. His questions were sincere. His loyalty to the institution was unaffected by the errors he saw in the scandalous selling of indulgences to finance projects in Rome.

Rome believed itself above criticism. They assumed their historic control was a right conferred by God. Therefore, the sincerity of Martin Luther and the legitimacy of his questions and propositions meant nothing to the institution. They branded Luther a heretic and threatened his life. This was the worst possible approach for Catholicism and the best possible result for Christianity.

Cardinal Timothy Dolan, Archbishop of New York has recently acknowledged that the Catholic Church was plagued with generalized corruption at the time of Luther "which we cannot deny." He described the effect Luther had: "It was the striking of a match, creating a bonfire —the flames of which are still burning."

Luther's flame burns still because it was grounded in Christian sincerity, founded on legitimate criticism of institutional corruption,

---

[18] This section was originally published as a DenverSnuffer.com blog post, titled "Reformation Sunday," on October 28, 2017.

and advocated by a man whose faith led him on a quest to find and acknowledge truth despite all opposition encountered. The result was a society divided into camps that vilified or praised, threatened or protected, believed or condemned him. The ideas he advocated have literally changed the world. Those he persuaded have grown in numbers over the past 500 years.

Reformation Sunday should not pass without reflecting on the changes Martin Luther brought about to the world today. Although a flawed man, he was nonetheless an instrument in God's hand to change our world for the better. If you own a Bible you can read in your native language, you owe a debt to Martin Luther. If you are either Catholic or Protestant, your church today is a result of changes caused by Martin Luther's flames. Catholicism was reformed and Protestant churches came into existence as the result of Martin Luther.

CHRISTIANITY'S PRESENT

And this gospel of the kingdom
will be proclaimed throughout the whole world
as a testimony to all nations,
and then the end will come.

Matthew 24:14 ESV

THE RESTORATION BEGINS
1820 A.D.

REFORM WAS NOT ENOUGH

The Protestant Fathers could protest against institutional Christian corruption. They could reform and improve Christianity. They could publish the Scriptures and allow the common man to read the words of Christ, prophets, and apostles for the first time. What they could not do was restore again what had been lost.

Between the close of the New Testament and the 16th century, Christianity had not merely declined, it had perished. It had become an institutionalized belief system with fixed forms of conducting that system. Professional clergy, supported by the tithes and offerings of the believers, was universally accepted before and after the Reformation.

Churches owned property and exercised control. There was no separation between Christianity's right to *preach* morality and the right to *enforce* morality. It had never been done, and therefore, the Protestant Reformation fathers assumed that was altogether proper.

What changed was not persecution and abuse. Only the identity of the denomination changed. Whereas Catholic abuses, burnings, killings, and rule ended in areas controlled by newly rebelling denominations, in its place, Lutheran abuses, burnings, killings, and rule assumed that prerogative.

The new sects did not know how to behave any better than the Catholics they rejected. During the Peasant Rebellion, Martin Luther concluded that the peasants "would not listen; they would not let anyone tell them anything; their ears must be unbuttoned with bullets, till their heads jump off their shoulders." He instructed, "On the obstinate, hardened, blinded peasants, let no one have mercy, but let everyone, as he is able, hew, stab, slay, lay about him as though among mad dogs…so that peace and safety may be maintained."

Ulrich Zwingli was similarly disposed, as was John Calvin. Calvin wanted Michael Servetus executed for "blasphemy" but thought he ought to be beheaded rather than burned. Servetus did not believe in infant baptism or the Trinity.

John Knox believed in killing Catholics and thought religious freedom belonged only to those who believed as he did. He has been called the Apostle of Murder. Because of his role in the murder of Cardinal Beaton, John Knox was sentenced to years as a galley slave.

In short, Reform was unable to escape the low and un-Christian condition the Reformers inherited from their Catholic predecessor.

It would take generations following the Reformation before the development of benign Christian thought would begin to change Christianity to be more Christian. Reforming is not the same as restoring. And without Christ's direct involvement, there was no way to recover what was lost.

Protestant Reformer John Wesley reflected on one of the results of losing original Christianity. In Wesley's sermon, "The More Excellent Way," he explained,

> The cause of this [decline of spiritual gifts following Constantine] was … "the love of many," almost of all Christians, so called, was "waxed cold." The Christians had no more of the Spirit of Christ than the other Heathens. The Son of Man, when he came to examine his Church, could hardly "find faith upon earth." This was the real cause why the extraordinary gifts of the Holy Ghost were no longer to be found in the Christian Church; because the Christians were turned Heathens again, and had only a dead form left.

Once Christianity died, it needed to be reborn. And for that, something more than earnest desire was needed. It required God to be directly involved.

ESSENTIAL MISSING PARTS

A great deal of good was accomplished by the Protestant fathers, but some things required for original Christianity could not be reformed back into existence. It is not possible to reform a corrupt institution and recover the original. Wishing, studying, hoping, and working to recover original Christianity is a task beyond the ability of theologians. For that, it requires God and someone who is sent by God to do the work.

New World Reformer Roger Williams was considered a dangerous heretic who fled from the colony of Massachusetts when facing arrest and imprisonment for his beliefs. He founded Providence, Rhode Island where he established the First Baptist Church in America. Williams became convinced that there was no possibility for recovering original Christianity without God's direct involvement. He wrote, "Christianity fell asleep in the bosom of Constantine, and the laps and bosoms of those Emperors who professed the name of Christ." This sober reflection led to his conviction that freedom of conscience was necessary to allow every soul to search for and accept all truth they could find. He declared, "There is no regularly constituted church of Christ on earth, nor any person qualified to administer any church ordinances; nor can there be until new apostles are sent by the Great Head of the Church for whose coming I am seeking."

Without God directing a restoration of the original faith, it had been lost and could not be recovered. There was too much that had been lost and too little that had been kept. The conclusion Roger Williams reached was the correct and inevitable outcome from the beginning of the Reformation. Reform could and should lead to restoration—if God would return the essential missing parts.

EARLY ATTEMPTS AT RESTORING

If Roger Williams was willing to wait for a restoration, Thomas Campbell wanted to cause one. A Scottish Presbyterian minister who migrated to the United States in 1807, Thomas disagreed with Presbyterian teachings that led to a split between him and that church.

He published a tract in 1809, titled "Declaration and Address of the Christian Association of Washington."

The 4th and 5th parts of his tract included:

> 4: That this society by no means considers itself a church…nor do the members, as such, consider themselves as standing connected in that relation…but merely as voluntary advocates for church reformation; and, as possessing the powers common to all individuals, who may please to associate in a peaceable and orderly manner…

> 5: That this society, formed for the sole purpose of promoting simple evangelical Christianity, shall…[not] inculcate any thing of human authority, of private opinion, or inventions of men, as having any place in the constitution, faith, or worship, of the Christian church—or, any thing, as matter of Christian faith, or duty, for which there cannot be expressly produced a thus saith the Lord either in express terms, or by approved precedent.

Thomas Campbell hoped to recover apostolic Christianity and regarded all of the historic Christian creeds, starting with the Nicene Creed, as unnecessary and divisive. He thought the Bible was clear enough to render creeds unnecessary. Campbell's motto was: "Where the Scriptures speak, we speak; where the Scriptures are silent, we are silent."

This view was a direct affront to historic Christianity because all denominations—Catholic and Protestant—accepted the creeds. Rejection of the creeds was rejection of historic Christianity itself. Therefore, Thomas Campbell was a heretic.

Alexander, the son of Thomas Campbell, followed his father into the Presbyterian ministry. He also became disillusioned with Presbyterian inadequacies and pettiness and left Scotland for America. By the time father and son were reunited, they both had rejected traditional historic Christianity and welcomed restoring the primitive Christianity of the New Testament.

The Campbells hoped to recover the original by subtracting errors. Their calculation was that by eliminating every superfluous thing, what remained would be the original. These mathematics could not, however, recover anything lost. For that, things necessarily had to be added. And adding could only come from God.

GOD SPEAKS AGAIN

While Alexander Campbell was wanting to restore primitive Christianity, a 14-year-old boy went alone into the woods to ask God which church to join. Like Moses who saw a bright bush that seemed afire but was not consumed and like Paul on the road to Damascus who heard a voice and saw a light, Joseph Smith encountered a pillar of fire and learned that God had a work for him to do.

In the years that followed, Joseph Smith said angels appeared to him, gave him an ancient book that he translated "by the gift and power of God" into the Book of Mormon, founded a church, organized two cities, and was killed at age 38.

Joseph Smith declared God told him Christianity was lost to apostasy, but God was restoring it again. Smith testified Jesus Christ appeared to him on several occasions to restore not only lost truths but also the authority to minister ordinances.

Joseph said on multiple occasions that his religion was "truth" and that all truth, wherever found, was part of the gospel of Jesus Christ.

Unlike the Protestant fathers, Joseph Smith produced new Scriptures and recorded revelations from God in the first-person voice of Jesus Christ. The missing "Thus saith the Lord" from the Campbellite movement was supplied through Joseph.

Whereas missing parts of original Christianity could not be recovered in either Protestantism or the Campbellite Restoration, Joseph Smith claimed it was possible to recover everything lost from Christianity through modern revelation.

Smith attracted tens-of-thousands of followers, and those who believed
Joseph Smith's claims were nicknamed "Mormons." A complete
restoration began but was not finished in Joseph Smith's lifetime. He
produced more Scripture than any prophet or apostle of the Bible. He
provided prophecies about events to happen prior to Christ's return in
glory. Many of these prophecies have been fulfilled, and many are yet
to be fulfilled. The tens-of-thousands inspired by his message gathered
into a community expecting to establish a last days' Zion.

However, his followers were often the source of his persecution. His
death was the result of a conspiracy of former followers and angry
outsiders. His death left the prophesied last days' Zion to be something
another generation would later fulfill.

Following the death of Joseph Smith, Mormons splintered into
different groups, each affirming that God favored their claims to be the
lawful successor possessing the restored gospel. The largest faction
followed Brigham Young into the western wilderness to the Salt Lake
Valley, where they are still headquartered today. There are currently
almost 100 groups claiming Joseph Smith as their founder. They
oppose one another, and most have taken the step of excommunicating
all other Mormons.

All "Mormons" accept the Book of Mormon as a volume of Scripture.
It has an account of the resurrected Jesus Christ appearing to people in
the Americas as part of His "other sheep" mentioned in the New
Testament.

Joseph Smith was not a Protestant nor a reformer, but he instead
claimed to be the restorer of the original Christianity. Joseph Smith's
claims are based on his testimony that God opened the heavens and
spoke to mankind again.

CAMPBELLITES AND MORMONS INTERSECT

Because both Campbellites and Mormons shared the ideal of restoring
a pure religion, they were destined to intersect. Campbellite ministers
Parley Pratt and Sidney Rigdon began the contact. Rigdon was a

dynamic preacher and trusted follower of Alexander Campbell. Rigdon met the first Mormon missionaries as they passed through Ohio and was impressed enough with their message and the Book of Mormon to investigate the claims.

He traveled to New York, met Joseph Smith, and was entirely satisfied. He not only joined the movement but quickly became one of the leaders of the new Mormon movement.

By the time Rigdon returned to Ohio, he was as fervent a Mormon as he had previously been a Campbellite. His charisma and eloquence quickly multiplied converts. The center of Mormonism moved from upper New York to Kirtland, Ohio.

But Mormon success in Ohio came at the expense of the Campbellites and provoked Alexander Campbell. The Mormon-Campbellite intersection turned into an outright collision.

Alexander Campbell wrote one of the earliest and most scathing reviews of the Book of Mormon in 1831, titled *Delusions: An Analysis of the Book of Mormon: With an Examination of its Internal and External Evidences, and a Refutation of its Pretenses to Divine Authority.* Campbell's attack was written the year after the Book of Mormon was first printed. He wrote: "Smith, its real author, as ignorant and impudent a knave as ever wrote a book, betrays the cloven foot in basing his whole book upon a false fact, or a pretended fact, which makes God a liar." He claimed both Smith and his followers were deluded by false spirits.

Joseph Smith responded,

> ...while he is breathing out scurrility he is effectually showing the honest, the motives and principles by which he is governed, and often causes men to investigate and embrace the book of Mormon, who might otherwise never have perused it.

Smith continued:

> I wish to inform him further, that as he has, for a length of time, smitten me upon one cheek, and I have offered no resistance, I

have turned the other also, to obey the commandment of our Savior; and am content to sit awhile longer in silence and see the great work of God roll on, amid the opposition of this world in the face of every scandal and falsehood which may be invented and put in circulation.

Mormonism benefited from the attention Campbell brought it. It did "roll on, amid the opposition" and grew throughout Joseph Smith's lifetime. Mormon converts came from Canada, the United Kingdom, and Europe during Smith's lifetime.

Early Campbellite converts greatly influenced Joseph Smith. Rigdon's leadership changed Mormonism. When it began, Mormonism was modeled after the Book of Mormon. Rigdon changed the priority to one of recovering the New Testament church. Mormonism became preoccupied with organizational structure and administrative control. Even while Joseph Smith was still alive, his teachings and revelations became secondary, and the church structure became primary. With presidents, apostles, seventies, bishops, elders, priests, teachers, and deacons, Mormons began to hold rank and position with titles and governing prerogatives that came to define the religion. Authority in Mormonism, like in Roman Catholicism, became so central that revelation and God's voice grew increasingly distant. A central hierarchy would doom Mormonism to the same destiny as Catholicism.

MORMONISM: DECLINE AND FALL

Mormonism started and—in the last years of Joseph Smith's life— returned to restoring a religion older than Christianity. The Apostle Paul wrote to the Galatians that *God...preached before the gospel unto Abraham.* Joseph Smith was recovering that gospel, which was also known to and practiced by Adam and the patriarchs. He continually made additions, expansions, and development of the religion from revelations given by Christ. He hoped that the fullness of the gospel and the fullness of the priesthood could be regained.

In January 1841, Christ promised He would restore the lost fullness but commanded a temple be built for that restoration. The Lord said the Mormons had sufficient time to build His holy house, but if they disobeyed the commandment, they would be rejected.

The Mormons disobeyed. Instead of the temple, they diverted resources and instead built a Masonic Hall, brick homes, and improved their personal property. Three-and-a-half years later, Joseph Smith was killed, and the unfinished temple was built only to the second floor, less than half of the planned structure. The Mormon city of Nauvoo, however, had been built into a prosperous community.

As soon as Joseph Smith was killed, the expanding religion he founded began to both contract and splinter. Internal disagreements divided the Mormons. Of the approximate 15,000 people Joseph gathered, only about half followed Brigham Young to the Salt Lake wilderness. Other factions left for Wisconsin and Texas, and some remained in the Midwest, years later reorganizing in Missouri.

Since the murder of Joseph Smith and his brother Hyrum, all the Mormon sects have either abandoned or outright rejected much of what Joseph Smith began. Only the sect Brigham Young led kept building temples but hardly knew how to use them or how rites were to be organized. Young borrowed more heavily from Masonry ritual than had Joseph Smith in order to finish out a Mormon temple ritual.

Brigham Young characterized himself as a "Yankee guesser" rather than a prophet like Joseph Smith. But he ruled over followers by claiming to have priesthood keys that authorized him to dictate. He instituted plural wives, claimed apostates should be slain, and led a reign of terror in the intermountain West. His violent teaching culminated in the murder of over 200 men, women, and children at Mountain Meadows. The Mountain Meadows Massacre aroused national anger, and the U.S. Army was dispatched to Utah in 1858 to unseat Brigham Young as the territorial governor.

Other Mormons reorganized in Missouri in 1860 and were the second most successful sect. They began to languish in the 1960s, and today they hardly believe the Book of Mormon and entertain doubts about Joseph Smith.

Small polygamist groups splintered from Brigham Young's Mormons. They claim to have preserved Joseph Smith's original teachings, but they are uniformly authoritarian and often violate marriage and child-protection laws in their perverse beliefs and practices.

What began as a noble endeavor to recover God's original pure religion and to have Jesus Christ come to visit with believers in a House built for God degenerated quickly following the death of Joseph Smith.

Today Mormonism is divided into competing factions that no longer hope to recover the fullness of the gospel and fullness of the priesthood. Mormon meetings, conferences, and preaching focus more on hierarchies, authority, and "keys" than on Heaven.

Mormonism fell victim to this preoccupation much more quickly than Catholicism. When the New Testament apostles and witnesses died, it took three centuries for Christianity to embrace a central hierarchy. When Joseph and Hyrum Smith were murdered, it only took from June 27th to August 8th for an elected body (headed by Brigham Young) to gain control. Three years later, Brigham Young was elected president, gaining sole management over his people. Both in 1844 and 1847, no voice from Heaven guided Mormonism as they elected replacement leaders. Hierarchy displaced revelation and heavenly guidance. Mormon sects today show more signs of decay than of life.

So much has been lost that it requires another restoration to return to the religion begun by Joseph Smith.

THE RESTORATION CONTINUES TODAY

Restoration and apostasy are constants. One or the other is underway at all times. There is never stasis for Christ's Gospel.

Apostasy loses, deducts, and subtracts truth. That process of losing light changes truth to error. To prevent salvation, it is not necessary for religion to become utterly corrupt; it is only necessary to change the ordinances and break the covenant. *Restoration* removes errors, recovers lost truths, and returns a connection to Heaven.

In apostasy, God's voice is quiet as men who pretend to speak for God multiply. In restoration, God speaks again.

Whenever restoration is underway, there are new additions to Scripture, recovered ordinances, and active expansion of mankind's understanding of God.

The objective of restoration is to create covenant people. It is not just to help believers become "born again" but to go beyond that to reconnect them to the family of God. There are Christian ordinances that go beyond faith, repentance, and baptism. These must be restored in their complete vigor and value.

Restoration always fulfills prophecy.

There was a restoration when Joseph Smith was alive. It recovered a great deal of what had been lost. However, it did not complete the required work to fulfill all the prophecies and promises of Christ to the Fathers. The final restoration Christ foretold will occur in a single generation prior to His return in glory.

Joseph Smith restored but also prophesied the failure of his effort and the rejection by the Gentiles of the fullness of the restoration. The Gentiles have rejected the fullness, and each generation since Joseph Smith's death has rejected ever more of the restoration. The leaders of various Mormon factions have actively rejected increasingly greater parts of what God began through Joseph.

Restoration and salvation go hand-in-hand. But restoration requires the Lord to send His messenger to deliver His words. Without a messenger delivering the Lord's message, His sheep cannot hear His voice.

There is a lot of work still necessary to be done by God's people. That work is now underway, and His voice can be heard. In September 2017 in Boise, Idaho, a conference of believers accepted a new covenant and became the first people since the restoration began in Joseph Smith's day to accept the Book of Mormon as a covenant.

The people who accepted that covenant are now publishing new Scripture, adding to the body of Christian teachings, and accepting more of Christ's gospel. They understand that as long as they remain faithful, God will continue to endow them with greater understanding.

Anyone can receive the blessings that only come from hearing and heeding the Master's voice. A new dispensation requires a new baptism. Baptism is available for all who have faith and repent.

In the past, God's active voice was replaced by institutions that quickly fell into inevitable corruption. To avoid that, these believers do not have an institution; they have only shared beliefs and ordinances that unite their hearts. They allow all to belong to or fellowship with any group they choose because baptism is offered freely to all. They pay no ministers, and therefore, profiting from preaching has ended among them.

If you believe in Jesus Christ and acknowledge Him as the Son of God who taught truth and died to save mankind from sin and death, then you should act on that by being baptized in His name. His doctrine is simple: Believe in Him, repent of your sins, be baptized for the remission of your sins, and He will send the Holy Ghost to guide you.

Christ's Restoration is underway, and He is preparing people for His return in glory. You can and should be restored to His household of faith so you will be ready for His return.

Key Figures in the Restoration

The following is a series of short biographies of "Restoration"
Christians who lived from 1763 A.D. to 1877 A.D.

Thomas Campbell (1763-1854)
& Alexander Campbell (1788-1866)

Thomas and Alexander Campbell were father and son. Both were originally Presbyterians, both became convinced that the religion was incomplete, and both collaborated on founding one of the most powerful movements in American religious history.

Thomas Campbell was a Presbyterian minister, educated in Scotland, that migrated from Ireland to the United States in 1807. After arriving in America, he split with the Presbyterians over Calvinist doctrine and the Eucharist. He lost his ministerial credentials after publishing a tract in 1809 that was critical of the faith. In response, he organized the Christian Association of Washington, a congregationally-governed church.

Thomas Campbell wanted to completely restore apostolic Christianity and believed Christian creeds were unnecessary and divisive. The Bible was clear enough that creeds were unnecessary. His motto was, "Where the Scriptures speak, we speak; where the Scriptures are silent, we are silent." His son, Alexander, observed, "It requires but little reflection to discover that the fiercest disputes about religion are about what the Bible does not say, rather than about what it does say." For all other Christian denominations—Catholic and Protestant—it was the creeds of historic Christianity that defined them as "Christian." Rejection of the creeds was revolutionary and un-welcomed. This desire to return to the original apostolic Christianity was "Restorationist" and a move beyond Protestantism.

Alexander Campbell intended to follow his father into the Presbyterian ministry and studied at the University of Glasgow, but he became disillusioned with what he regarded as theological pettiness in the religion. By the time he joined his father in America, both father and son had diverged from traditional Christianity, and both welcomed the Restoration concept.

Both Campbells sought to return to the original, primitive form of Christianity. Their movement was nicknamed by critics as "Campbellites," and later their ministries resulted in congregations today identified as the "Churches of Christ," "Christian Churches," "Evangelical Christian Church in Canada," and "Disciples of Christ." They practiced baptism by immersion and adopted the name of "Christian" as their only proper name.

Alexander Campbell converted and trained Sidney Rigdon, who would later convert to the Mormon movement led by Joseph Smith. In response to the loss of congregants to Mormonism, he authored the earliest anti-Mormon book (*Delusions: An Analysis of the Book of Mormon*) in 1832, only two years after the Book of Mormon was published).

Alexander Campbell regularly debated clergy from other faiths on such topics as baptism, infant baptism, socialism and Christianity, Roman Catholicism, and the Restoration movement. Some of these were transcribed and received international attention.

Alexander Campbell longed for Christian unity under a "restored" original. He explained, "I have no idea of adding to the catalogue of new sects. I labor to see sectarianism abolished and all Christians of every name united upon the one foundation upon which the apostolic church was founded."

SIDNEY RIGDON (1793-1876)

Sidney Rigdon was originally a Baptist minister who later became a follower of Alexander Campbell and a Campbellite preacher. He was a dynamic leader whose forceful oratory persuaded those audiences who heard him preach.

In the fall of 1830, Rigdon met the first four missionaries sent out by the newly created "Mormonite" movement (as it was then called). He read the Book of Mormon the missionaries were distributing, and he was baptized. Because of his conversion and the respect he held among Campbellites, he led hundreds to convert to the new Mormonite movement. Shortly afterward, in December of 1830, he traveled to New York to meet Joseph Smith.

Because of Rigdon's background, education, and oratory, Joseph Smith enlisted his help with his movement. Rigdon became a scribe, counselor, and fellow president with Smith over the church when a "First Presidency" was organized.

Rigdon shared in persecutions with Joseph Smith—he was tarred and feathered by a mob in 1832 and imprisoned in Missouri in 1838. When Smith ran for the office of the President of the United States in 1844, Rigdon ran as his Vice-President.

Rigdon attempted to lead the Mormon church following the deaths of Joseph and Hyrum Smith, but he was defeated in an election in August 1844 by Brigham Young and the Twelve. Subsequent to his defeat, Young viewed Rigdon as a potential competitor and had him excommunicated from the church the following month, September 1844.

Rigdon was accused of having co-written the Book of Mormon, but he denied the claim and explained it was in print before he first saw the text.

Rigdon agreed with Campbell's contention that a New Testament form of Christianity was not practiced by existing denominations. In Rigdon's view, however, the original church could not be spontaneously reestablished but required God to confer authority to proceed. Rigdon saw in Joseph Smith an ingredient missing from Campbell's movement: Priesthood authority from God. Rigdon's conversion to Mormonism alienated him from Alexander Campbell, who criticized both Mormonism and Rigdon and resented the many Campbellites led into Mormonism by Rigdon.

Rigdon participated in a heavenly vision with Joseph Smith in which the condition of mankind in the afterlife was revealed. The vision is known as Doctrine & Covenants section 76. The lengthy vision describes three levels of afterlife for man following the resurrection. These are identified as the Telestial (lowest), Terrestrial (middle), and Celestial (highest). The lengthy vision relates in part the following:

We, Joseph Smith, Jun., and Sidney Rigdon, being in the Spirit on the sixteenth day of February, in the year of our Lord one thousand eight hundred and thirty-two—

By the power of the Spirit our eyes were opened and our understandings were enlightened, so as to see and understand the things of God—Even those things which were from the beginning before the world was, which were ordained of the Father, through his Only Begotten Son, who was in the bosom of the Father, even from the beginning; Of whom we bear record; and the record which we bear is the fulness of the gospel of Jesus Christ, who is the Son, whom we saw and with whom we conversed in the heavenly vision.

For while we were doing the work of translation, which the Lord had appointed unto us, we came to the twenty-ninth verse of the fifth chapter of John, which was given unto us as follows—Speaking of the resurrection of the dead, concerning those who shall hear the voice of the Son of Man: And shall come forth; they who have done good, in the resurrection of the just; and they who have done evil, in the resurrection of the unjust.

Now this caused us to marvel, for it was given unto us of the Spirit. And while we meditated upon these things, the Lord touched the eyes of our understandings and they were opened, and the glory of the Lord shone round about.

And we beheld the glory of the Son, on the right hand of the Father, and received of his fulness; And saw the holy angels, and them who are sanctified before his throne, worshiping God, and the Lamb, who worship him forever and ever. And now, after the many testimonies which have been given of him, this is the testimony, last of all, which we give of him: That he lives! For we saw him, even on the right hand of God; and we heard the voice bearing record that he is the Only Begotten of the Father—That by him, and through him, and of him, the worlds are and were created, and the inhabitants thereof are begotten sons and daughters unto God. And this we saw also, and bear record, that an angel of God who was in authority in the presence of God, who rebelled against the Only Begotten Son whom the Father loved and who was in the bosom of the Father, was thrust down from the presence of God and the Son, And was called Perdition, for the heavens wept over him—he was Lucifer, a son of the morning. And we beheld, and lo, he is fallen! is fallen, even a son of the morning!

Following his excommunication, Rigdon never returned to the faction led by Brigham Young but instead made two attempts to organize a Church of Christ, both of which failed (one before his death, and the other shortly after).

JOSEPH SMITH, JR. (1805-1844)

Roger Williams believed the Protestant Reformation could not fix Christianity. He taught that a Restoration would be necessary and could only happen if Jesus Christ sent another apostle to reestablish the original Christian church. Joseph Smith claimed that Jesus Christ had indeed visited him and given him authority to restore the original Christian church.

Smith grew up in a poor New England family and received only a limited education. He claimed that God the Father and Jesus Christ visited him in 1820; that John the Baptist visited both him and Oliver Cowdery, conferring the authority to baptize; and that other angels visited him, conveying heavenly information and authority.

Smith was a controversial figure while alive. Editorial pages in the United States and Britain praised or condemned him, and he was often the target of newspaper cartoon caricatures. Despite the controversy, he attracted tens of thousands of followers. He is regarded as a prophet of God by his followers and regarded as everything from a cynical manipulator to a deluded simpleton by his critics.

Smith was the first religious figure to publish new Scriptures since Mohammed and was frequently compared to Mohammed. Smith added other volumes of Scripture to the Bible: the Book of Mormon, the Doctrine and Covenants, and (posthumously) the Pearl of Great Price.

Smith solved problems that were inherent in the Protestant Reformation. Protestantism is predicated on Catholic failure, apostasy, and error. But if Catholicism erred and Protestantism grew from and is dependent upon Catholicism for its Scriptures, creeds, and fundamental theology, how can an error be "reformed" back to a whole and correct original? If men failed to preserve the original, how can they reclaim from a broken part the whole original? And if the original body of beliefs *can* be reclaimed, how can Protestants ever obtain the original *authority*? It cannot be derived from Catholicism, since the Roman Catholic Church refused to convey authority to the Protestants. Joseph Smith claimed to have reestablished the original Christian church, with authority from Heaven and increased knowledge required for salvation. His efforts produced, he believed, something other than Catholicism and Protestantism; it was a Restoration of Jesus Christ's church.

Over 80 different sects claim Joseph Smith as their founder. The largest of these is headquartered in Salt Lake City, Utah. None of them have retained the original teachings nor been faithful to the church model that Joseph Smith established.

Joseph was opposed, mobbed, imprisoned, tarred and feathered, and sentenced to die by a Missouri Military court-martial. Much of the persecution he faced came from disaffected former-Mormon believers. It was a conspiracy between renegade former-Smith-believers and local anti-Mormons that led to his murder in Carthage, Illinois on June 27, 1844. His brother, Hyrum Smith, was also slain in the same attack.

Smith's claims can be summarized by a testimony he declared jointly with fellow Mormon leader, Sidney Rigdon, of Jesus Christ:

> *The Lord touched the eyes of our understandings and they were opened, and the glory of the Lord shone round about. And we beheld the glory*

of the Son, on the right hand of the Father, and received of his fulness; And saw the holy angels, and them who are sanctified before his throne, worshiping God, and the Lamb, who worship him forever and ever.

And now, after the many testimonies which have been given of him, this is the testimony, last of all, which we give of him: That he lives! For we saw him, even on the right hand of God; and we heard the voice bearing record that he is the Only Begotten of the Father—

That by him, and through him, and of him, the worlds are and were created, and the inhabitants thereof are begotten sons and daughters unto God.

BRIGHAM YOUNG (1801-1877)

Brigham Young was a carpenter, joiner, and glazier who converted to Mormonism in 1832 and later became a member of the twelve apostles of the Church of Latter Day Saints (now known as The Church of Jesus Christ of Latter-day Saints).

As a member of the twelve, Young was a missionary who traveled in the United States and England, bringing others into the faith. He remained faithful when other apostles left the faith and the church. Following the murder of Joseph and Hyrum Smith, Young campaigned for the twelve apostles to be elected to serve as the highest leadership body. Winning that vote, he and his fellow apostles proceeded to stabilize the society, and they organized a departure from Nauvoo, Illinois to the American West.

Young and fellow apostles led approximately 16,000 Latter-day Saints to the Salt Lake basin and colonized an intermountain area from Mexico to Canada. He was responsible for founding over 200 settlements, many of which continue as cities today in Mexico, Arizona, Utah, Nevada, Idaho, Wyoming, Montana, and Canada. That accomplishment could only have been done by a man of practical wisdom. He solved problems and seemed comfortable in the role given to him by the people he led. He oversaw construction of an entire society out of a barren wilderness.

Young practiced and publicly advocated polygamy. He had 20 wives and fathered 47 children. For him, polygamy was an essential, saving practice. He taught, "Now if any of you will deny the plurality of wives, and continue to do so, I promise that you will be damned." He claimed polygamy was taught to him by Joseph Smith, although Joseph Smith publicly condemned the practice and had those who practiced it brought before the Nauvoo High Council for misconduct.

Responding to criticism about the practice, Young advocated giving the vote to women in order to counter his critics. Utah was among the first territories to grant women the right to vote in 1870.

Brigham Young was elected as the church's president in 1847 and remained in that role until his death in 1877. He was also elected as the Territorial Governor from 1851 to 1858. While he was governor and president, the church and state of territorial Utah combined under Young's complete dominance. His fiery rhetoric during a revival period of 1856-57 (referred to as the "Mormon Reformation") led to violence as he advocated the practice of "blood atonement" for sins. During the Reformation, he said,

> I will tell you what this people need, with regard to preaching; you need, figuratively, to have it rain pitchforks, tines downwards, from this pulpit, Sunday after Sunday. Instead of the smooth, beautiful, sweet, still, silk-velvet-lipped preaching, you should have sermons like peals of thunder, and perhaps we then can get the scales from our eyes.

And rain pitchforks in sermons it did. He and other leaders were indirectly responsible for the Mountain Meadows Massacre, where over 120 members of a passing wagon train were killed on their way to California. This led to President Buchanan sending the U.S. Army to seat a new governor. Although no longer in control of the governorship, he nevertheless controlled his territory until his death.

The respect Young had from his followers was not merely based on deference to the church founded by Joseph Smith; he was also a charismatic leader who dispensed practical advice. He warned, "He who takes offense when no offense is intended is a fool, and he who takes offense when offense is intended is a greater fool." He also said, "If you have a bad thought about yourself, tell it to go to hell because that is exactly where it came from."

Although he is viewed today as insensitive to women, he had high regard for the accomplishments of women who served in a critical role for society. "If I had a choice of educating my daughters or my sons because of opportunity constraints, I would choose to educate my daughters." He also said, "You educate a man; you educate a man. You educate a woman; you educate a generation."

Brigham Young also warned about the deference Mormon leaders were given. He said,

> I am more afraid that this people have so much confidence in their leaders that they will not inquire for themselves of God whether they are led by Him. I am fearful they settle down in a state of blind self-security, trusting their eternal destiny in the hands of their leaders with a reckless confidence that in itself would thwart the purposes of God in their salvation, and weaken that influence they could give to their leaders, did they know for themselves, by the revelations of Jesus, that they are led in the right way. Let every man and woman know, by the whispering of the Spirit of God to themselves, whether their leaders are walking in the path the Lord dictates, or not. This has been my exhortation continually.

Brigham Young University in Provo, Utah was named after him and is supported by the church he led for 31 years as its president. His statue is on the Capitol Rotunda in Washington, DC.

The Stumbling Blocks of Modern Christianity

Part I. The Nature of God

What Manner of Being?

When Christ appeared to His disciples after His resurrection, they thought He was a ghost or spirit. He corrected this misunderstanding:

> *And as they thus spake, Jesus himself stood in the midst of them, and saith unto them, Peace be unto you. But they were terrified and affrighted, and **supposed that they had seen a spirit**. And he said unto them, Why are ye troubled? and why do thoughts arise in your hearts? Behold my hands and my feet, that it is I myself: **handle me, and see; for a spirit hath not flesh and bones, as ye see me have.** And when he had thus spoken, he shewed them his hands and his feet. And while they yet believed not for joy, and wondered, he said unto them, Have ye here any meat? And they gave him a piece of a broiled fish, and of an honeycomb. And **he took it, and did eat before them.*** (Luke 24:36-43 KJV, emphasis added)

The testimonies of those who saw the risen Lord confirm He was not a "spirit" but composed of "flesh and bone" and could (and did) ingest food, just like a man of flesh and blood would likewise do. These marks on His body of "flesh and bone" are intended as an identifier of the Savior. Isaiah confirms His wounds are for our benefit and salvation.[19] They will certify Him as the Messiah when He returns:

> *And one shall say unto him, What are these wounds in thine hands? Then he shall answer, Those with which I was wounded in the house of my friends.* (Zechariah 13:6 KJV)

---

[19] See Isaiah 53:5.

A modern revelation on March 7, 1831 explains this future event more fully:

> *And then shall the Lord set his foot upon this mount, and it shall cleave in twain, and the earth shall tremble, and reel to and fro, and the heavens also shall shake. And the Lord shall utter his voice, and all the ends of the earth shall hear it; and the nations of the earth shall mourn, and they that have laughed shall see their folly. And calamity shall cover the mocker, and the scorner shall be consumed; and they that have watched for iniquity shall be hewn down and cast into the fire. And then shall the Jews look upon me and say: What are these wounds in thine hands and in thy feet? Then shall they know that I am the Lord; for I will say unto them: These wounds are the wounds with which I was wounded in the house of my friends. I am he who was lifted up. I am Jesus that was crucified. I am the Son of God. And then shall they weep because of their iniquities; then shall they lament because they persecuted their king.* (D&C 45:48-53)

On the day of His resurrection, Christ spent several hours walking on the road to Emmaus with two disciples. The men regarded Him as a "stranger," with no particular distinction between Him and other mortals as they walked together for hours. He taught them from the Hebrew Scriptures about the mission of the Messiah, requiring Him to suffer and die. They implored Him to remain for dinner, which He did. When He blessed and "brake bread"—a clearly physical act by a clearly physical being—they recognized Him as Jesus.[20]

Christ *lost* His body of "flesh and bone" in the Council of Nicaea when He became "homoousios" (of one substance with the Father) instead of "homoios" (distinct from, but similar to the Father). And thus the Son of Man (as Christ identified Himself)[21] was transformed by the arguments of men into something altogether "other" from those who descended from Adam. With that development in 325 A.D., the "Trinity" sprang into existence as a fundamental belief of Historic Christianity. This dramatic departure in the definition of God really

---

[20] See Luke 24:13-31.
[21] See Mark 14:21; Matthew 26:24; Luke 22:22; John 3:13, among others.

marks the departure of the original or "primitive Christianity" from the later "Historic Christianity" that replaced the original.

Fishermen and laborers who saw Christ and testified and described Him as a man were shunned in favor of the philosophies of men who had not seen Him. But the philosophers controlled Christianity and could dictate all of its terms. The newly re-created image was unlike man, thus causing a contradiction in God's original description of Himself.[22] Indeed, how *two beings* could be *one* renders Christ "incomprehensible." This admission was added by another council that adopted the Athanasian Creed, which states in part:

> That we worship one God in Trinity, and Trinity in Unity; Neither confounding the persons, nor dividing the substance. For there is one Person of the Father, another of the Son and another of the Holy Spirit. But the Godhead of the Father, of the Son, and of the Holy Spirit is all one, the glory equal, the majesty co-eternal. Such as the Father is, such is the Son and such is the Holy Spirit. The Father uncreated, the Son uncreated, and the Holy Spirit un-created. The Father incomprehensible, the Son incomprehensible, and the Holy Spirit incomprehensible. The Father eternal, the Son eternal, and the Holy Spirit eternal. And yet they are not three eternals, but one eternal. As also there are not three uncreated nor three incomprehensibles, but one uncreated and one in-comprehensible.

Whereas Christ said "life eternal" is to "know Him,"[23] Historic Christianity decreed, in effect: "Don't even try to know Him. You can never comprehend Him." John's testimony promised men could see and know Christ because we are like Him: *Now are we the sons of God, and it doth not yet appear what we shall be: but we know that, when he shall appear, we shall be like him; for we shall see him as he is* (1 John 3:2 KJV). But Historic Christianity's creeds imposed a barrier upon knowing Him and, therefore, a barrier upon "life eternal" for Christians.

---

[22] Compare Genesis 1:26.
[23] See John 17:3.

Creedal Historic Christianity is like the New Testament Samaritans whom Christ rebuked saying: *Ye worship ye know not what: we know what we worship: for salvation is of the Jews* (John 4:22 KJV). The philosophers of Historic Christianity are like the pagans on Mars Hill whose beliefs were denounced by Paul as "superstitious":

> *And they took him, and brought him unto Areopagus, saying, May we know what this new doctrine, whereof thou speakest, is? For thou bringest certain strange things to our ears: we would know therefore what these things mean. (For all the Athenians and strangers which were there spent their time in nothing else, but either to tell, or to hear some new thing.) Then Paul stood in the midst of Mars' hill, and said, Ye men of Athens,* **I perceive that in all things ye are too superstitious**. *For as I passed by, and beheld your devotions, I found an altar with this inscription, TO THE* **UNKNOWN** *GOD. Whom therefore ye ignorantly worship, him declare I unto you. God that made the world and all things therein, seeing that he is Lord of heaven and earth, dwelleth not in temples made with hands; Neither is worshipped with men's hands, as though he needed any thing, seeing he giveth to all life, and breath, and all things; And* **hath made of one blood all nations of men for to dwell on all the face of the earth**, *and hath determined the times before appointed, and the bounds of their habitation; That they should seek the Lord, if haply they might feel after him, and find him, though he be not far from every one of us: For in him we live, and move, and have our being; as certain also of your own poets have said, For* **we are also his offspring. Forasmuch then as we are the offspring of God**, *we ought not to think that the Godhead is like unto gold, or silver, or stone, graven by art and man's device. And the times of this ignorance God winked at; but now commandeth all men every where to repent.* (Acts 17:19-30 KJV, emphasis added)

Men are of one blood, and all are the offspring of God. God is, therefore, knowable and wants for mankind to know Him. Christ said, *And this is life eternal, that they might know thee the only true God, and Jesus Christ, whom thou hast sent* (John 17:3 KJV).

Christ "lost His body" as a result of the post-Nicaea church philosophers who twisted the Scriptures to fit their incorporeal idol.

That was neither part of the New Testament teachings nor how Christ was understood in early Christianity. The post-Nicaea concern was over polytheism. They abhorred the idea of multiple gods, thinking it a pagan idea. Israel had "one God" and not several. Therefore, the idea of the Trinity allowed them (and Historic Christianity ever after) the pretense of monotheism despite the separate beings of God the Father and His Son, Jesus Christ.

The "oneness" of God the Father and Christ does not consist, as the Historic Christian creeds suggest, in these being one person of one substance, uncreated, incomprehensible and altogether "other than mankind." Christ explained His "oneness" with the Father in His intercessory prayer in John 17. Speaking about the immediate disciples who were with Him when He prayed, He petitioned that, *Holy Father, keep through thine own name those whom thou hast given me, that they may be one, as we are* (John 17:11 KJV). The disciples were not of one substance with Christ, nor uncreated, nor incomprehensible—but were separate, individual men. Yet they were to be "one" just as the Father and Son are likewise "one." Christ's prayer also referred to future believers who would accept the testimonies of the apostles. Concerning them Christ also prayed, *Neither pray I for these alone, but for them also which shall believe on me through their word; That they all may be one; as thou, Father, art in me, and I in thee, that they also may be one in us: that the world may believe that thou hast sent me* (John 17:20-21 KJV).

Do you believe on the apostles' testimonies? Are you therefore "one" with other believers? Did you merge into the bodies of other believers in order to become "one" with them? Are you the same substance as your minister or priest? If by belief in the same testimony as other Christians you can become "one" with them, then Christ and the Father can likewise be "one" without disturbing their entirely separate existence from one another.

This is not a heresy and not a recent invention. In The Epistle of Ignatius to the Smyrnaeans, he relied on what would later become New Testament Scripture (as well as common sense) to explain that Christ came into the world as a mortal man, although He had been created by the Father and acknowledged by Him as His Only Begotten Son. Here is Ignatius' explanation:

The Word, when His flesh was lifted up, after the manner of the brazen serpent in the wilderness, drew all man to Himself for their eternal salvation. And I know that He was possessed of a body not only in His being born and crucified, but I also know that He was so after His resurrection, and believe that He is so now. When, for instance, He came to those who were with Peter, He said to them, "Lay hold, handle Me, and see that I am not an incorporeal spirit." "For a spirit hath not flesh and bones, as ye see Me have." And He says to Thomas, "Reach hither thy finger into the print of the nails, and reach hither thy hand, and thrust it into My side;" and immediately they believed that He was Christ. Wherefore Thomas also says to Him, "My Lord, and my God." And on this account also did they despise death, for it were too little to say, indignities and stripes. Nor was this all; but also after He had shown Himself to them, that He had risen indeed, and not in appearance only, He both ate and drank with them during forty entire days. And thus was He, with the flesh, received up in their sight unto Him that sent Him, being with that same flesh to come again, accompanied by glory and power. For, say the holy oracles, "This same Jesus, who is taken up from you into heaven, shall so come, in like manner as ye have seen Him go unto heaven." But if they say that He will come at the end of the world without a body, how shall those "see Him that pierced Him," and when they recognize Him, "mourn for themselves"? For incorporeal beings have neither form nor figure, nor the aspect of an animal possessed of shape, because their nature is in itself simple.[24]

The idea that Christ is now and will be a physical being when He returns in glory was a fundamental teaching of the New Testament and early Christians. Do not allow the false reasoning of Historic Christian philosophers to change the person of our Lord into an imaginary idol invented by those who hijacked Christianity and changed it into a political, economic, and social industry. Ignatius regarded any who taught to the contrary to be damned: "…but blasphemes my Lord, not owning Him to be God incarnate."[25] He declared:

[24] Chapters II and III, long version as found in *Ante-Nicene Fathers*, Vol. 1, p. 89; Edited by Alexander Roberts & James Donaldson, Hendrickson Publishing, Fourth Printing, 2004.
[25] Ibid., Chapter V

Let no man deceive himself. Unless he believes that Christ Jesus has lived in the flesh, and shall confess His cross and passion, and the blood which He shed for the salvation of the world, he shall not obtain eternal life.[26]

This was important precisely because understanding the correct doctrine is required before it is possible to know God. It is as if Ignatius took aim at the heretical and false doctrine in Historic Christian creeds that God is incomprehensible:

Do ye, therefore, notice those who preach other doctrines, how they affirm that the Father of Christ cannot be known, and how they exhibit enmity and deceit in their dealings with one another.[27]

Because they deny Christ is a person of flesh and bone, "they make a jest of the resurrection. They are the offspring of that spirit who is the author of all evil."[28]

Truth comes by the revelation of Heaven. Men corrupt it, and it ceases to have the same authority and effect as it would if believed. All men are required to repent and return to God. Part of that repentance will require Historic Christians to forsake the abominable creeds adopted by false priests and come to know Christ Jesus, who was sent by the Father into the world as a man, who lived, died, was resurrected, and will return again in glory.

ETERNAL LIFE: KNOWING GOD

Christ explained "eternal life" as knowing Him: *And this is life eternal, that they might know thee the only true God, and Jesus Christ, whom thou hast sent* (John 17:3 KJV).

The writers of the New Testament knew Christ. They were taught by Him, or He appeared to them. Prior to His death, Christ promised He

---

26 Ibid., Chapter VI
27 Ibid.
28 Ibid., Chapter VII

would continue to be known because He and His Father would take up their abode with others in the future.

> *Judas saith unto him, not Iscariot, Lord, how is it that thou wilt manifest thyself unto us, and not unto the world? Jesus answered and said unto him, If a man love me, he will keep my words: and my Father will love him, and we will come unto him, and make our abode with him.* (John 14:22-23 KJV)

This promise was intended to be taken literally.

In addition to His followers, the antagonist (Saul) was also visited after Christ's resurrection. Christ approached him on the road to Damascus,[29] and He later took up His abode with Paul, who was then caught up to Heaven and taught "unspeakable things" of the mysteries of God.[30]

A modern prophet explained that Christ's promise to "take up his abode" with men is not merely figurative or in the heart, but is indeed a personal appearance in which the believer comes to know his Lord: *John 14:23—The appearing of the Father and the Son, in that verse, is a personal appearance; and the idea that the Father and the Son dwell in a man's heart is an old sectarian notion, and is false* (D&C 130:3).

Christ appeared to Joseph Smith, and he testified of the appearing:

> *I saw a pillar of light exactly over my head, above the brightness of the sun, which descended gradually until it fell upon me. It no sooner appeared than I found myself delivered from the enemy which held me bound. When the light rested upon me I saw two Personages, whose brightness and glory defy all description, standing above me in the air. One of them spake unto me, calling me by name and said, pointing to the other—*

> *"This is My Beloved Son. Hear Him!"* [31]

---

[29] See Acts 9:1-22.
[30] See 2 Corinthians 12:1-5.
[31] Joseph Smith History (JS-H) 1:16-17

In another appearance to both Joseph Smith and Sidney Rigdon, they jointly testified:

> ...the Lord touched the eyes of our understandings and they were opened, and the glory of the Lord shone round about.
>
> And we beheld the glory of the Son, on the right hand of the Father, and received of his fulness; And saw the holy angels, and them who are sanctified before his throne, worshiping God, and the Lamb, who worship him forever and ever. And now, after the many testimonies which have been given of him, this is the testimony, last of all, which we give of him: That he lives! For we saw him, even on the right hand of God; and we heard the voice bearing record that he is the Only Begotten of the Father—
>
> That by him, and through him, and of him, the worlds are and were created, and the inhabitants thereof are begotten sons and daughters unto God. (D&C 76:19-24)

Christianity was never intended to be controlled by pastors, ministers, priests, bishops, or even apostles. Christianity was intended to be alive, with Christ directly involved with His followers. But the creeds of Historic Christianity have impeded the relationship between a God who wants to be known and religious institutions who preach He is unknowable.

The entire message of Joseph Smith can be reduced to one verse in the Bible: *If any of you lack wisdom, let him ask of God, that giveth to all men liberally, and upbraideth not; and it shall be given him* (James 1:5 KJV). Joseph believed this and asked. God answered. Christians can all do the same. *But let him ask in faith, nothing wavering. For he that wavereth is like a wave of the sea driven with the wind and tossed* (ibid., v.6).

God has the capacity to answer all prayers addressed to Him. And He will send no one away empty-handed.

> Ask, and it shall be given you; seek, and ye shall find; knock, and it shall be opened unto you: For every one that asketh receiveth; and he that seeketh findeth; and to him that knocketh it shall be opened. Or what man is there of you, whom if his son ask bread, will he give him a

stone? Or if he ask a fish, will he give him a serpent? If ye then, being evil, know how to give good gifts unto your children, how much more shall your Father which is in heaven give good things to them that ask him? (Matthew 7:7-11 KJV)

TRINITARIAN IMPEDIMENT

The doctrine of the Trinity that was settled, if not created, in the Council of Nicaea is an impediment and not an advantage to knowing God. If "life eternal" is to "know God" (as John declared), then of what value is a doctrine that makes God "incomprehensible"?

Even theologian James R. White from the Christian Research Institute makes damning admissions as he labors to defend the Nicene Creed.[32] He explains that "every time they came up with a statement that was limited solely to biblical terms," it was unclear. They invented and used new terminology because "they needed to use a term that could not be misunderstood"—meaning that they had to go outside the Scriptures because the Scriptures failed to say what they wanted to be said. He elaborates that "they sought to clarify biblical truth." He does not want to admit their extra-biblical creed was a departure, and he struggles to claim the council was only accomplishing a limited and clarifying task.

What if instead of debating and focusing on "substance" (or the material of which God is composed), the debate did confine itself solely to biblical terms? Nicene terminology debated the terms **homoousios** and **homoiousios** to resolve their extra-biblical debate. The **heteroousios** term was easily defeated.

These terms mean:

- Homoousios: of the same identical substance.
- Homoiousios: of similar substance.
- Heteroousios: of a different substance.

---

[32] See "What Really Happened at Nicea?" CRI Statement DN-206.

Why focus on "substance" at all? What in the New Testament makes that a Christian concern? The only time "substance" enters into the picture is when a very physical Jesus Christ accomplishes very physical acts during His ministry. Touching the eyes and healing;[33] breaking apart loaves of bread;[34] handling a bowl, water, and towel and touching feet;[35] or when He was resurrected, allowing the disciples to handle His physical body to confirm it was Him.[36] These physical descriptions of a Being composed of material substance, like us, are in the Bible precisely to inform us of Christ's physical nature. All the biblical texts were discarded because they were insufficient to describe the kind of "substance" the theologians wanted to adopt.

The quest for singular and unknowable "substance" for God was because of the Christian embarrassment at their loss of monotheism. If Christ and the Father were different in any way from one another, then the monotheistic tradition of apostate Judaism would be lost. Earliest Judaism had a Divine Council with a Father who presided, a Divine Son, and angelic hosts. Their theology changed dramatically during the Second Temple period, which has been regarded by many scholars as a time of Jewish apostasy.

Like so many other false notions, however, this one is also solved by the Bible. Christ declared plainly how the Father and the Son were "one":

> *Neither pray I for these alone, but for them also which shall believe on me through their word;* ***That they all may be one; as thou, Father, art in me, and I in thee, that they also may be one in us:*** *that the world may believe that thou hast sent me. And the glory which thou gavest me I have given them;* ***that they may be one, even as we are one:*** *I in them, and thou in me, that they may be made perfect in one; and that the world may know that thou hast sent me, and hast loved them, as thou hast loved me.* (John 17:20-23 KJV; emphasis added)

The disciples were not of the identical substance. Peter was separate from John, who were both different beings than Andrew. Yet they were

---

[33] See John 9:6.
[34] See Matthew 14:19.
[35] See John 13:5.
[36] See Luke 24:39.

to be "one" in the same way the Son and the Father are "one." Or in other words, the unity of the Godhead is not clarified by a discussion on "substance" and is utterly confused by making them identical "substance" so as to avoid polytheism. The Godhead is "one" because they are united in purpose, accomplishing the same work jointly, and abiding by the identical principles of truth and righteousness. In that way, men can likewise become "godly" by uniting in God's purpose, working jointly to save the souls of men, and abiding the same standards of truth and righteousness.

Trinitarian theology is not an advantage to Christian orthodoxy. It is an impediment to understanding and knowing God. It alienates you from the Godhead, with whom you are intended to become "one." And above all else, even the defenders of Trinitarianism admit it is extra-biblical and cannot be proven if the discussion is limited solely to the Bible.

Life eternal is to know Jesus Christ and His Father who sent Him. You cannot know an unknowable god. Trinitarianism was defended by Athanasius at Nicaea and advocated by him afterwards. He developed a follow-on creed to help further explain what was done to the orthodox god at Nicaea. Here is what he claimed they accomplished with their creedal explanation of god: "The Father incomprehensible, the Son incomprehensible, and the Holy Spirit incomprehensible...As also there are not three...incomprehensible, but one uncreated and one incomprehensible."

The Orthodox Christian god is one great "incomprehensible" and unknowable being who cannot be defined if you limit the description solely to the Bible. If you are an Orthodox Christian, that ought to trouble you.

Christians have become like the Samaritans whom Christ told worshiped *they know not what* (John 4:22 KJV) or the pagans Paul addressed on Mars Hill who did not know what or who they worshiped.[37]

---

[37] See Acts 17:22-23.

False traditions cannot save you, however sincerely you may hold them. Knowing God, however, is life eternal.

PART II. BIBLIOLATRY

Christians universally claim that the canon of Scripture is closed. According to the tradition, God finished revealing things, and the single means of knowing God's will, gaining authority, and obtaining salvation is fully documented in the Scriptures. This is the "sola scriptura" belief (i.e., the Scriptures alone save).

This is not true. Even the Scriptures do not make such a claim. All the Christian apologists who cite the various Old and New Testament verses to support this claim rely on convoluted interpretation. They also ignore the promises in Scripture that God will continue to speak[38] and will send prophets.[39] One of the principles of Biblical hermeneutics is that interpretation of Scripture is best accomplished by using the newest to understand the oldest. The passages of the Old Testament quoted in the New Testament mean what the New Testament claims because the New Testament is more recent. If this principle were not used, then you could question many of the ways Old Testament meanings get assigned by New Testament writers, because they are counter-intuitive or even apparently contradictory to the original Old Testament text.

For example, the Isaiah text in 7:14 (read apart from the New Testament claims) apparently means that a young virgin will not have time to conceive a child and give birth (approximately 9 months) before the kings of both Damascus and Samaria are overthrown.[40] But according to the New Testament, this is a Messianic passage foretelling the virgin birth of Christ.[41] Therefore, Christians universally claim the virgin birth of Christ was foretold by Isaiah 7:14.

---

[38] See James 1:5-6; Joel 2:28-32.
[39] See Revelation 11:3; Zechariah 4:14.
[40] See Isaiah 7:5-16.
[41] See Matthew 1:23.

If you accept the rule of interpreting Scripture by using the most recent revelation to assign meaning to all earlier Scripture, then the meaning of the Bible ought to be reckoned by using the Book of Mormon and revelations to Joseph Smith. Christians are unwilling to do this, and when considering a new revelation, they apply their rules of interpretation in the reverse. It is hypocritical. Moreover, if the same test were applied in like manner using the Old Testament, then Christianity would fail for lack of support.

Consider what the Book of Mormon has to say about this Bibliolatry:

Many of the Gentiles shall say: A Bible! A Bible! We have got a Bible, and there cannot be any more Bible. But thus saith the Lord God: O fools, they shall have a Bible; and it shall proceed forth from the Jews, mine ancient covenant people. And what thank they the Jews for the Bible which they receive from them? Yea, what do the Gentiles mean? Do they remember the travails, and the labors, and the pains of the Jews, and their diligence unto me, in bringing forth salvation unto the Gentiles? O ye Gentiles, have ye remembered the Jews, mine ancient covenant people? Nay; but ye have cursed them, and have hated them, and have not sought to recover them. But behold, I will return all these things upon your own heads; for I the Lord have not forgotten my people.

Thou fool, that shall say: A Bible, we have got a Bible, and we need no more Bible. Have ye obtained a Bible save it were by the Jews? Know ye not that there are more nations than one? Know ye not that I, the Lord your God, have created all men, and that I remember those who are upon the isles of the sea; and that I rule in the heavens above and in the earth beneath; and I bring forth my word unto the children of men, yea, even upon all the nations of the earth? Wherefore murmur ye, because that ye shall receive more of my word? Know ye not that the testimony of two nations is a witness unto you that I am God, that I remember one nation like unto another?

Wherefore, I speak the same words unto one nation like unto another. And when the two nations shall run together the testimony of the two nations shall run together also. And I do this that I may prove unto many that I am the same yesterday, today, and forever; and that I speak forth my words according to mine own pleasure. And because that I have spoken one word ye need not suppose that I cannot speak another; for my work is not yet finished; neither shall it be until the end of man, neither from that time henceforth and forever.

Wherefore, because that ye have a Bible ye need not suppose that it contains all my words; neither need ye suppose that I have not caused more to be written. For I command all men, both in the east and in the west, and in the north, and in the south, and in the islands of the sea, that they shall write the words which I speak unto them; for out of the books which shall be written I will judge the world, every man according to their works, according to that which is written. For behold, I shall speak unto the Jews and they shall write it; and I shall also speak unto the Nephites and they shall write it; and I shall also speak unto the other tribes of the house of Israel, which I have led away, and they shall write it; and I shall also speak unto all nations of the earth and they shall write it. And it shall come to pass that the Jews shall have the words of the Nephites, and the Nephites shall have the words of the Jews; and the Nephites and the Jews shall have the words of the lost tribes of Israel; and the lost tribes of Israel shall have the words of the Nephites and the Jews. And it shall come to pass that my people, which are of the house of Israel, shall be gathered home unto the lands of their possessions; and my word also shall be gathered in one. And I will show unto them that fight against my word and against my people, who are of the house of Israel, that I am God, and that I covenanted with Abraham that I would remember his seed forever. (2 Nephi 29:3-14)

Christians do not actually worship Christ. If they did, they would be eager to hear any word that proceeds from His mouth. But instead, they mute Christ, insist they can employ the words of a book as their salvation, and render Christ silent. This is idolatry, and they would rather worship their idol—the book—than the God who died, rose again, and lives still.

If He lives, then He can speak. He does speak. Christians are just not listening.

Part III: Paid Clergy

Today, the best estimate is that there are over 40,000 different "Christian" denominations or sects. No one knows for sure because there is no organized database that identifies them all. Many are as small as a single congregation. The total number of "Christians" is estimated at over 2.2 billion.

Jesus Christ is *the same yesterday, today and forever* (Hebrews 13:8 KJV). God has made a point of explaining that He does not change.[42] The pace at which "Christian" sects are dividing appears to be accelerating. The disagreements between "Christian" sects are pronounced enough that many of them claim they alone are "true" and only they can save your soul. They denounce other denominations as false, their followers unsaved or, worse, damned and followers of the devil.

The Scriptures claim there is *one Lord, one faith, and one baptism* (Ephesians 4:5 KJV). Christians should compare what they see in "Christianity" of today with what the Scriptures teach. How can messages from the various sects conflict so greatly that the Christian world is divided into more than 40,000 different bodies?

Christianity was never to be "preached" by just anybody willing to make a claim to be preaching the truth. A true messenger must be "sent" by God.[43] That does not mean they have some sentimental inclination to proclaim a message. It means that God sent them.

Paul was sent by God, and he explained the criteria. The qualifications have never changed, been rescinded, or superseded. The unchangeable God requires the same today as anciently.

How can an unchangeable God—who is the same yesterday, today, and forever—be guiding these conflicting and contentious Christian denominations? The answer is simple: He is not.

The Christian sects are led by hireling priests who stir up conflict that prevents Christian believers from agreeing with one another. They

---

[42] See Malachi 3:6.
[43] See Romans 10:14-15.

flatter their congregations and keep them content. "Christians" are fed a weekly dose of vanity and lies by men and women expecting to be paid (by their followers) for their preaching. If you removed the profits from Christian churches, you would quickly see the pulpits abandoned by the hucksters employed there. If no one were paid to preach, conflicts would quickly end between the rank-and-file Christians.

MORMONISM:
A CASE STUDY IN CHRISTIAN APOSTASY

CHRISTIAN APOSTASY

Irenaeus lived approximately 130 A.D. to 202 A.D. The exact dates of his life are not known, nor is the exact date he wrote his greatest work, a five-book series titled *Against Heresies*. His outline of heretical teachings is known to have been composed late in the second century. Until the discovery of the gnostic gospels at Nag Hammadi in 1945, it was from *Against Heresies* that most information about the gnostics was learned.

Irenaeus provides us with a glimpse into the state of Christianity less than a century after the death of the apostles. What is revealed through that glimpse is a bizarre bunch of conflicting views. Many of the teachings he condemned are so alien to today's Christians that we would regard them as perverse aberrations. Yet they competed in the early Christian marketplace for converts and claimed to be a true reflection of Christ's teachings.

Christ foretold there would be "children of the wicked one" who would be planted among His "wheat" while they both grew together.[44] Likewise, the apostle Paul was astonished at how quickly the church at Galatia was corrupted with perverse teachings,[45] and he predicted the entire falling away (apostasy) of the Christian church.[46]

While the apostles were alive and preaching, Christians divided themselves into contentious factions. Some followed one teacher, others another, and they emphasized their disagreements rather than their common beliefs.[47] "Ministers of Satan" were actively teaching

---

[44] See Matthew 13:24-30,36-43.
[45] See Galatians 1:6-7.
[46] See 2 Thessalonians 2-3.
[47] See 1 Corinthians 1:11-13.

inside the earliest bodies of Christians,[48] and Paul lamented that "all of Asia" had fallen into error and rejected his teaching.[49] John warned of false spirits and false apostles who were spreading falsehoods that misrepresented Christ,[50] and by Nicaea in 324 A.D., the denial of Christ coming into the flesh was so widely accepted that a newly adopted and false teaching of the "Trinity" completed the overthrow of true doctrine regarding Christ who lived as a man in the flesh among us. Even if falsehoods supplanted Christianity, John's vision foretells that God's patience will finally come to an end and the religions that worship devils and gold and silver and idols will be destroyed.[51]

MORMON APOSTASY

If Christians were to examine the history of Mormonism, they would better understand how unclean spirits and false prophets overtook Christianity.[52] Joseph Smith began Mormonism under the influence of one spirit, but upon his death, Brigham Young followed under the influence of another. As a true shepherd would,[53] Joseph gave his life for the sheep. Brigham Young declared he would flee and never surrender his life, a sign of a false shepherd.[54] He proclaimed he was unwilling to lay down his life as Joseph did:

> But woe, woe to that man who comes here to unlawfully interfere with my affairs. Woe, woe to those men who come here to unlawfully meddle with me and this people. I swore in Nauvoo, when my enemies were looking me in the face, that I would send them to hell across lots, if they meddle with me; and I ask no more odds of hell today. (July 26, 1857)

> A mob killed Joseph and Hyrum in jail, notwithstanding the faith of the State was pledged to protect them. ...I have broken no law,

---

48 See 2 Corinthians 11:13-15.
49 See 2 Timothy 1:15.
50 See 1 John 4:1-2.
51 See Revelation 9:20.
52 See Revelation 16:13; also 2 Timothy 11:13-15.
53 See John 10:11.
54 See John 10:12-13.

and under the present state of affairs, I will not suffer myself to be taken by any United States officer, to be killed as they killed Joseph. (August 12, 1857)

Do you expect to stand still, sit still, or lie still, and untimely let them take away my life? I have told you a great many times what I have to say about that. I do not profess to be so good a man as Joseph Smith was. I do not walk under their protection nor into their prisons, as he did. (August 9, 1857)

Brigham Young advocated controlling people by holding economic power over them. He explained how he envisioned keeping people in line and subordinate to him by getting them to consecrate their property to the church he led:

If any man is in darkness through the deceitfulness of riches, it is good policy for him to bind up his wealth in this Church, so that he cannot command it again, and he will be apt to cleave to the kingdom. If a man has the purse in his pocket, and he apostatizes, he takes it with him; but if his worldly interest is firmly united to the Kingdom of God, when he arises to go away, he finds the calf is bound, and, like the cow, he is unwilling to forsake it. (April 6, 1852)

Brigham Young defied the U.S. Government when its representatives were critical of his authoritarian rule in the Territory of Utah:

What says the United States? "Let us send a governor there; let us send our judges there." But what do they cry? "We have no influence or power, for there are other men there who rule, and we cannot help it; they have the reins of government and turn the people whithersoever they will, and we cannot help ourselves." What did a gentleman say to [U.S. President] Mr. Fillmore? Said he, "You need not send anybody there, for Brigham Young is Governor, and he will govern the people all the time; and there is no other man that can govern them." If there is any truth in this, it is, he will do so as long as the Lord lets him. (October 3, 1852)

On June 9, 1853, he threatened in a public discourse to kill any apostates or non-believers who opposed him. Beginning in 1855, God's wrath at Brigham Young and his followers became evident in a series of natural disasters that caused famine and severe hardships. In response to these afflictions, Young increased his threatening and began a bloody period known as the "Mormon Reformation." The Mountain Meadows Massacre happened as a result, at least in part, of the fiery rhetoric Brigham Young preached during the Mormon Reformation.

Like the early Christians who were overcome by deceiving spirits,[55] Mormonism was overcome by the lusts, appetites, and ambitions of Young, who was animated by a very different spirit than Joseph Smith. The result of leading by that spirit is aptly described in the Book of Mormon:

> *For the time speedily shall come that all churches which are built up to get gain, and all those who are built up to get power over the flesh, and those who are built up to become popular in the eyes of the world, and those who seek the lusts of the flesh and the things of the world, and to do all manner of iniquity; yea, in fine, all those who belong to the kingdom of the devil are they who need fear, and tremble, and quake; they are those who must be brought low in the dust; they are those who must be consumed as stubble; and this is according to the words of the prophet.* (1 Nephi 22:23)

LDS Mormonism has not only been "built up to get gain" but is a multi-billion dollar empire:

- They have undertaken a trillion-dollar development for housing in Florida that will employ a population of 500,000 people on 133,000 acres.

- They have built a two- to five-billion dollar shopping mall/ condominium housing/office complex across the street from their Salt Lake City temple (the total cost depends on whether the retail establishment alone or the entire project is valued).

---

[55] See Mark 13:5-6; 2 Timothy 3:13; 1 Corinthians 15:33-34; Ephesians 5:5-6.

- They are now finalizing a similarly ambitious project in downtown Philadelphia, adjacent to the temple the LDS Church completed in September 2016.

Millions of faithful Mormons are entirely oblivious to the dramatic gulf between the Scriptures, revelations, and teachings of the founder Joseph Smith and the replacement religion created through Brigham Young. That transition mirrors what happened to early Christianity. By the time only one Christian orthodox faith survived, it was also making merchandise of men's souls. The description of Babylon the great whore in John's revelation accurately describes both the false Christian religious empire founded in Rome in the fourth century and the false Mormon empire founded by Brigham Young in the late 1840s:

> *The merchandise of gold, and silver, and precious stones, and of pearls, and fine linen, and purple, and silk, and scarlet, and all thyine wood, and all manner vessels of ivory, and all manner vessels of most precious wood, and of brass, and iron, and marble, and cinnamon, and odours, and ointments, and frankincense, and wine, and oil, and fine flour, and wheat, and beasts, and sheep, and horses, and chariots, and slaves, and souls of men.* (Revelation 18:12-13 KJV)

Christianity did not survive the second century. Mormonism did not survive its third decade. The answer to the question, "Why?" is the same: Both became more interested in economic gain, power over the flesh, popularity in the eyes of the world, and the lusts of the flesh and the things of the world than in practicing and preserving the faith taught by Christ. The Book of Mormon describes these corrupting influences infecting churches.[56]

Christ's religion requires sacrifice. Its reward is later, after this world. In this world, if one practices the faith taught by Christ, *we are of all men most miserable* (1 Corinthians 15:19 KJV).

How can we support with our donations the false ministers who preach for hire and neglect the poor among us? How can we assume we will be saved by the smooth things we hear from our hireling priests?[57] How

---

[56] See 1 Nephi 22:23.
[57] See Isaiah 30:10.

second hand exclusively and stone the prophets in their turn. The new church, in spite of whatever human goodness it may foster, can be henceforth counted on as a staunch ally in every attempt to stifle the spontaneous religious spirit, and to stop all later bubblings of the fountain from which in purer days it drew its own supply of inspiration. Unless, indeed, by adopting new movements of the spirit it can make capital out of them and use them for its selfish corporate designs![58]

Mormonism was founded in 1830 by Joseph Smith who claimed that ten years prior to founding a church he had been visited by God the Father and Jesus Christ. In the intervening years between the first visit and the time a church was organized, Joseph claimed to have been visited by an angelic messenger who delivered to him a new volume of Scripture, known as the Book of Mormon. He claimed to have received revelations before founding the church and then many more after its organization.

Whether you believe Joseph Smith's claims or not, he and his followers give a unique opportunity to witness how founding a religion sets in motion a series of predictable events that happen every time a new religion begins. Perhaps the best way to decipher the transition of Christianity from the original primitive Christianity to its replacement (Historic Christianity) is to study Mormonism. Similar to the way the primitive Christian church passed away after the death of the apostles, Mormonism passed away following the deaths of Joseph and Hyrum Smith. The same process was at work in both.

Primitive Christianity and Mormonism set out to change the world, and after some initial progress, both enjoyed worldly success. Their success diverted attention from saving souls to managing people and property. Paul observed, *The love of money is the root of all evil* (1 Timothy 6:10 KJV).

A new religion is not profitable for the first believers. They are persecuted. They sacrifice their lives and property to follow what they

---

[58] *The Varieties of Religious Experience*, The Gifford Lectures on Natural Religion delivered at Edinburgh in 1901-1902, Lectures XIV and XV: The Value of Saintlessness.

believe to be God's burden laid on them. Because of their sacrifices, they have faith and know they please God. Without sacrifice, it is impossible to obtain the faith required for salvation. Founders make sacrifices; successors enjoy the fruit of those sacrifices.

In time, the founding gives way to popular approval. John Wesley observed that the price that is paid for popular acceptance is the loss of the Spirit:

> It does not appear that these extraordinary gifts of the Holy Ghost were common in the Church for more than two or three centuries. We seldom hear of them after that fatal period when the Emperor Constantine called himself a Christian; …From this time they almost totally ceased; …The Christians had no more of the Spirit of Christ than the other heathens. …This was the real cause why the extraordinary gifts of the Holy Ghost were no longer to be found in the Christian Church; because the Christians were turned Heathens again, and had only a dead form left. Churches all come to depend on money for survival.[59]

Churches, like the men who belong to them, are vulnerable to the "love of money," which leads to "all evil." People can have the gifts of the Spirit or they can acquire riches in this world, but they cannot have both. Catholicism grew wealthy from the offerings of its members. When it owned most of the European lands and ruled over all people within Roman Catholic boundaries, it was cold, corrupt, violent, and cruel. The transition from persecuted minority to dangerous majority took three centuries. With that status, the original was lost.

Mormonism followed the same path and achieved the same end in less than half the time. If a Christian wants to know how primitive Christianity was lost to apostasy, the history of The Church of Jesus Christ of Latter-day Saints is where it can be found. Mormon beliefs are so unstable that they now "unequivocally condemn" 10 of the first 11 of their church presidents, including Brigham Young, John Taylor, and David O. McKay.

---

[59] John Wesley, Sermon 89: "The More Excellent Way"

In order to progress forward, we must go back. Since we have no way to recover enough information to understand Christianity's trek from Jerusalem to Rome, Mormonism allows Christians a view into the transition from Nauvoo to Salt Lake. Both paths followed the same tragic topography.

CHRISTIANITY'S PROMISE

*Therefore the Lord, the Lord Almighty,
the Mighty One of Israel, declares:*

*"Ah! I will vent my wrath on my foes
and avenge myself on my enemies.
I will turn my hand against you;
I will thoroughly purge away your dross
and remove all your impurities.
I will restore your leaders as in days of old,
your rulers as at the beginning.
Afterward you will be called
the City of Righteousness,
the Faithful City."*

Isaiah 1:24-26 KJV

The Restoration Continues
Moving Forward from Today

Condemnation

God prepared the world for half a millennium before He called Joseph Smith to formally begin a restoration. God sent an angel to give Joseph an assignment when he was still a youth:

> He was a messenger sent from the presence of God to me and that his name was Nephi, that God had a work for me to do, and that my name should be had for good and evil among all nations, kindreds, and tongues, or that it should be both good and evil spoken of among all people. (*JS, History*, 1838–1856, vol. A-1, created 11 June 1839–24 Aug. 1843)

Joseph received two promises about the work he would perform. The first was that he would have both good and bad spoken of him among all nations.

Later he was given the priesthood authority by another angel. This authority allowed him to preach repentance and baptism. The second promise was that this priesthood authority to preach repentance and perform baptism "shall never be taken again from the earth until the sons of Levi do offer again an offering unto the Lord in righteousness."

Eventually, the Lord offered many other conditional opportunities to mankind through Joseph Smith, but those required the people to rise up to live God's commandments. God explained, *I, the Lord, am bound when you do what I say, but when you do not what I say you have no promise* (D&C 82:10).

By 1830, the Book of Mormon was in print, and several revelations from God had provided instructions and commandments for believers to follow. God expected more from those who were converted by the message He gave to Joseph Smith.

The first edition of the Book of Mormon contained numerous scribal errors. The original was hand-copied, and the printer used that duplicate copy. But that copy had an average of 1½ copy errors per page. Although Joseph Smith attempted to correct these printing mistakes in subsequent editions, he never finished that work. Book of Mormon transmission errors remain in the text today.

In September 1832, less than two years after the Book of Mormon was printed, the believers were condemned for their carelessness in respecting God's revelations. God expected careful, respectful fidelity, and believers were careless and inattentive. As a result, the believers were condemned and warned:

> *Your minds in times past have been darkened because of unbelief, and because you have treated lightly the things you have received, which vanity and unbelief have brought the whole church under condemnation. And this condemnation rests upon the children of Zion, even all, and they shall remain under this condemnation until they repent and remember the new covenant, even the Book of Mormon, and the former commandments which I have given them, not only to say but to do according to that which I have written, that they may bring forth fruit meet for their Father's kingdom. Otherwise, there remains a scourge and a judgment to be poured out upon the children of Zion.* (D&C 84:54-58)

After the Book of Mormon was published, Joseph Smith taught and led believers for 14 more years. He accomplished many remarkable things but was never able to inspire his followers to repent and remove the Lord's condemnation.

The Restoration intends to fully restore the great promises given by God to the fathers, including Adam, Noah, Abraham, Isaac, Jacob, and Joseph. But those blessings require people to live up to God's teachings and commandments. It is not enough to call upon God as our Lord and Savior. He requires us to live up to His commandments. As Christ warned His followers: *And why call ye me, Lord, Lord, and do not the things which I say?* (Luke 6:46 KJV). A lone prophet-restorer cannot do what is required. No individual has built a city of Zion.

Joseph Smith began the Restoration, but it lapsed into condemnation within two years after it began. God expected more than people were willing to do.

The foundation provided by Joseph—including the Book of Mormon and authority to preach repentance and baptize—has remained. But breathing life back into the Restoration requires a new generation who are willing to follow God—people who will awaken to their awful state and arise by repenting and following God faithfully.

REJECTION

Those who believed the message God provided through Joseph Smith remained condemned for 185 years. During that time, God was still patient with them, giving them opportunity to repent and return. And while Joseph lived, they received a flood of revelation, teaching, commandments, and restored ordinances.

But believers constantly fell into conflicts with one another and with Joseph. Close friends and church leaders betrayed Joseph and fellow believers. Internal conflicts, disobedience, and rebellion caused them to be driven out of settlements in Ohio, Missouri, and Illinois. After expulsion from one Missouri location, the Lord said, *Behold, I say unto you, there were jarrings, and contentions, and envyings, and strifes, and lustful and covetous desires among them; therefore by these things they polluted their inheritances* (D&C 101:6). After polluting their inheritance, by the inspiration of God there were mobs that drove them out. God's judgments may seem harsh, but they are designed to help mankind wake-up and return to God.

In January 1841, a new community of believers gathered along the Mississippi River in Illinois. There were a few years of peace for Joseph and those believers. Although they had experienced violence and opposition before, God provided them with another chance in Illinois.

This proved to be the last chance given them by God to remove the condemnation, and if they failed, they risked outright rejection by God. The Lord told those believers,

But I command you, all ye my saints, to build a house unto me; and I grant unto you a sufficient time to build a house unto me; and during this time your baptisms shall be acceptable unto me. But behold, at the end of this appointment your baptisms for your dead shall not be acceptable unto me; and if you do not these thing at the end of the appointment you shall be rejected as a church, with your dead, saith the Lord your God.

...if they will not hearken to my voice, nor unto the voice of these men whom I have appointed, they shall not be blest, because they pollute mine holy grounds, and mine holy ordinances, and charters, and my holy words which I give unto them. And it shall come to pass that if you build a house unto my name, and do not do the things that I say, I will not perform the oath which I make unto you, neither fulfill the promises which ye expect at my hands, saith the Lord. For instead of blessings, ye, by your own works, bring cursings, wrath, indignation, and judgments upon your own heads, by your follies, and by all your abominations, which you practice before me, saith the Lord. (D&C 124:31-32;46-48)

They failed to meet God's standard. They disobeyed God's commandments. They did not build the temple required. Once again they fell into "jarrings, and contentions, and envyings, and strifes, and lustful and covetous desires," including widespread secret adultery that Joseph Smith publicly condemned and fought to expose. Joseph had many people excommunicated for their secret adulteries and their taking of multiple wives.

Joseph Smith and his brother were killed because of conspiracies between disbelievers and apostates within the fold. This brought upon all the believers the promised "cursings, wrath, indignation, and judgments" because of their widespread disobedience. After Joseph was killed, a man who practiced adultery in secret, Brigham Young, was elected to lead.

These people were driven out of Illinois, scattered, and split into competing denominational factions because some were unwilling to tolerate adultery and lying. Yet the Book of Mormon and authority to preach repentance and baptism still remained.

It would be left for some future generation to remember, repent, awake, and rise up to receive the full measure of the promises given to Abraham, Isaac, Jacob, and Joseph.

THREE GREAT THINGS LEFT UNDONE

The Restoration of the gospel began with Joseph Smith. But he was martyred before his dispensation fully restored Zion. Revelation foretells what the Lord will restore before His return. There are three great things left undone.

First, faithful followers of the Lord must build a temple for the Lord so He can return and restore His presence. This temple is to be a tabernacle for Him, located in *an Holy City, that my people may gird up their loins, and be looking forth for the time of my coming; for there shall be my tabernacle, and it shall be called Zion, a New Jerusalem.* (Moses 7:62)

Joseph Smith built a temple in Kirtland, Ohio—but infighting and conflicts among his people drove him out of that city by a murderous mob of former church members. He relocated and tried again to build a temple in Independence, Missouri and then Far West, Missouri. But the people failed to build a temple in either place.

The last spot Joseph attempted to build the "foundation of Zion" temple was in Nauvoo, Illinois. Before that temple was completed, Joseph Smith was killed, and Nauvoo's besieged citizens driven out of Illinois.

After Joseph Smith died, there was no one left able to understand—much less complete—the restoration work. The scattered factions who believed God began a restoration through Joseph Smith have been unable to preserve it. Generation after generation they have allowed the Lord's vineyard to become cumbered with bitter fruit.[60] One perverse sect practiced the abomination of adultery as a sacrament. When their leaders were imprisoned and the government confiscated their property,

---

[60] See the "Allegory of the Olive Trees" in Jacob 5 in the Book of Mormon.

they finally abandoned polygamy. This resulted in still more splinter groups that wanted to continue the abomination of having multiple wives. The Mormon factions all failed to preserve, or even comprehend, the Restoration.

The temple will be where God intends to accomplish a second great event. It will be in His temple where the Lord will confer "the fullness of the priesthood." When Joseph Smith died, the "fullness of the priesthood" was unfulfilled and poorly understood. Because many people equate "priesthood" with authority, all the many churches that claim Joseph Smith as their founder falsely claim they hold that "fullness of the priesthood" authority.

The "fullness of the priesthood" is not merely authority. It requires knowledge of the full truth about God's work. Revelation must restore understanding of the past, present, and future. God explained to Joseph that *truth is knowledge of things as they are, and as they were, and as they are to come; and whatever is more or less than this is the spirit of that wicked one who was a liar from the beginning* (D&C 93:24-25).

Restoring the fullness will involve *a revelation from God, from the beginning of the world to the ending thereof* (2 Nephi 27:7). It remains the second of three great future accomplishments that did not happen during Joseph Smith's lifetime.

The third remaining work is a "New Jerusalem"—a community devoted to living God's commandments and welcoming His return.

Until a proper temple is built for the Lord to dwell within, the fullness of the priesthood has been restored, and a holy city is gathered, the Restoration begun by Joseph remains unfinished. However, these three events were promised by God to the ancient covenant fathers, and they are certain to happen.

ABANDONMENT AND RENEWAL

Restoring ended when Joseph Smith was killed. His death began a steady loss of light and truth. But the prophecies and covenants of God assured the patriarchal fathers, from Adam to Abraham, that a full restoration would happen.

In the years before his death, Joseph worked on a new version of the Bible—not a translation from Greek and Hebrew, but an inspired, revelatory commentary that added lost material and clarified ambiguous passages. He was commanded to do this work, which was called "the fullness of the Scriptures." The "fullness of the Scriptures" was never published during Joseph's lifetime.

On July 17, 1840, four years before his death, Joseph Smith explained, "God had often sealed up the heavens because of covetousness in the Church. Said the Lord would cut his work short in righteousness and except the church receive the fullness of the Scriptures that they would yet fall." Following that warning, there was a mission to raise money to publish Scriptures. In October 1840, a letter in the newspaper, *Times and Seasons*, asked for support to publish "the new translation of the Scriptures." The publication was to include a corrected edition of the Book of Mormon and the Joseph Smith Translation of the Bible. All efforts failed to put the Joseph Smith Translation into print, and Joseph died without it being published.

In January 1841, the Lord commanded a temple be built, but when Joseph was killed in June 1844, it was less than half completed. Without the temple, Joseph Smith could not finish an educational ceremony intended for the temple. Brigham Young gained control of the Restoration and admitted the temple rites were incomplete. He said Joseph Smith told him, "Bro. Brigham, this is not arranged right, but we have done the best we could under the circumstances in which we are placed…"

On January 13, 1856, Brigham Young explained it would require a resurrected Joseph Smith to return before the temple rites could be properly arranged. "After Joseph comes to us in his resurrected body, he will more fully instruct us concerning the baptism for the dead and the sealing ordinances." Young explained, "I tell you there will not be much of this done until Joseph comes."

After Brigham Young died, his successor, John Taylor, explained on October 12, 1883 that the death of Joseph Smith interrupted the Restoration, including sorting out and correcting temple ceremonies. Taylor said:

> The reason why things are in the shape they are is because Joseph felt called upon to confer all ordinances connected with the priesthood. He felt in a hurry on account of a certain premonition that he had concerning his death, …Had Joseph Smith lived he would have had much more to say on many of those points which he was prevented from doing by his death.

Other than the LDS Church, all the splintered restoration groups completely discontinued temple rites. During the 1800s, the LDS acknowledged their temple ordinances were unfinished and needed much more for completion. Eventually, they abandoned any idea of *finishing* temple rites and began claiming they *had* the "fullness." Even so, the LDS incomplete rites have been revised, cut, and shortened to remove controversial materials.

If the restoration work is to be completed, it will not happen in any of the existing corporate "Mormon" organizations. They are not capable of continuing the Restoration. Moving forward will require believers to acknowledge that the religion has been adrift and is incomplete—or in other words, they must acknowledge an apostasy.

Continuing the Restoration has been left for others who are willing to face the disappointments of history. These others are now working to participate in moving along the unfinished work.

In 1831, Joseph Smith warned that "except the church [receive] the fullness of the Scriptures that they would yet fall." Fullness of the Scriptures included the Book of Mormon, the revelations, and most importantly, a new, inspired Bible with many revisions. In September 1832, less than one year later, believers were condemned by the Lord and commanded to *repent and remember the new covenant, even the Book of Mormon and the former commandments which I have given them, not only to say, but to do according to that which I have written* (D&C 84:57). This was not merely failing to obey what was written; believers also failed to accurately preserve the revelations God had provided, and therefore, their Scriptures were corrupted.

But repentance did not happen, and the fullness was not completed.

After 182 years, a few people were inspired to recover and reclaim the former commandments and Book of Mormon. After 185 years, a body of believers repented, presented their Scriptures to the Lord, and asked God to remove the condemnation. God approved their work and removed their condemnation. God also committed to covenant with them and restore promises given to the patriarchal fathers.

Corrected and completed Scriptures have now been published and are accurate as far as it is possible to presently recover. These new Scriptures prune away the uninspired alterations men have made. They are truer to the Restoration and the Lord's intent than any other Scriptures available today.

This new edition of Scripture is a witness to the whole world. It is a sign that the moment has arrived when things prophesied in Scripture will occur in a single generation. Mankind doesn't have to accept the witness; they don't even have to notice the witness. God is only obligated to send the witness. Once He sends the witness, God has done His part.

Although previous Scriptures were titled the Old Testament, New Testament, and Doctrine and Covenants, the new Scriptures are titled:

- The Old Covenants,
- The New Covenants, and
- Teachings & Commandments.

The Old Covenants contains those covenants God made with Adam, Enoch, Noah, Abraham, and Moses. The new title more accurately reflects the record.

The New Covenants include both the New Testament and the Book of Mormon. Joseph Smith intended to publish them together in a single volume. Both books contain covenants established through Jesus Christ during His lifetime and immediately following His resurrection.

The Teachings & Commandments includes the revelations given to Joseph Smith, as well as revelations from today. Joseph's revelations were first published in 1833 and titled "Book of Commandments." An expanded volume, the "Doctrine and Covenants," was published in 1835. The name-change referred to "doctrine," meaning the Lectures on Faith, and "covenants," meaning the revelations to Joseph Smith. All the Mormon institutions removed the "doctrine"—the Lectures on Faith. The "doctrine" has now been restored in the "Teachings & Commandments." The new name reflects the content: "teachings," which instruct and invite, and "commandments," which are required of mankind and are necessary for salvation. Teachings & Commandments is a living, expanding canon. People with a living covenant with God always have an open canon, and they expect additional revelation and Scripture.

The hand of the Lord was present helping those involved in the process of preparing the new Scriptures. These Scriptures were the first step to resuming the Restoration. Upon taking that step, God responded and established a new covenant with His people today.

REMEMBERING REMNANTS

The message of the Restoration was first given to the Gentiles with the obligation to seek out two remnants of God's people. The first remnant is the people who descended from the Jews.

While living among the Jews, Jesus Christ said He had other sheep to visit: *And other sheep I have which are not of this fold: them also I must bring, and they shall hear my voice; and there shall be one fold, and one shepherd* (John 10:16 KJV)

After His resurrection, Christ visited the Americas to teach His "other sheep" who were not at Jerusalem, He referred to those people and their posterity as "a remnant of the house of Jacob." He called them His people. They are the second remnant.

The Restoration began with Gentiles but imposed upon them the obligation to seek out and attempt to recover both remnants of His sheep: His covenant people.

Despite that obligation, a Hebrew translation of the Book of Mormon was neglected until the LDS Church put one into print in 1981, which it subsequently withdrew from print. Six years later, the RLDS sect printed one. Both of these include the textual errors that provoked condemnation from the Lord in 1832.

The Restoration has renewed, and people obtained a covenant from the Lord in 2017. They have not forgotten the two remnants. Using the corrected, recovered, and accepted Scriptures, both a Jewish-friendly English version is now in print, and a Hebrew-language translation is being prepared for publication. These will be taken to Jewish communities in North America, Europe, and the Middle East for distribution. This is being done as part of God's agenda to fulfill the promises He made to the patriarchal fathers.

Today, little thought is given to the promises made to Abraham, Isaac, and Jacob. Little is even known about the promises God made to Adam, Enoch, and Noah. But God never forgets His word. He has said about His promises: *Though the heavens and the earth pass away, these words shall not pass away, but shall be fulfilled* (T&C 43:3).

The new Scriptures restore information about God's earlier promises and add promises to people living today.

Zion and the New Jerusalem will include Gentiles, remnants who descend from the original American peoples, and remnants of the Jews. The people who obtained a covenant from the Lord in 2017 are working actively to invite the remnants of former covenant people to awaken and arise.

God promised the patriarchal fathers there would be a New Jerusalem established in the Americas, and the Jews would return to old Jerusalem. In May 1948, the nation of Israel was recognized, but Jerusalem was divided. In 1967, Israel obtained possession of East

Jerusalem during the Six-Day War. In December of 2017, the United States recognized Jerusalem as the capital of Israel.

There will be a temple built in old Jerusalem. There will also be a temple built in Zion, on the American continent:

> *It shall come to pass in the last days, that the mountain of the Lord's house shall be established in the top of the mountains, and shall be exalted above the hills; and all nations shall flow unto it. And many people shall go and say, Come ye, and let us go up to the mountain of the Lord, to the house of the God of Jacob; and he will teach us of his ways, and we will walk in his paths: for out of Zion shall go forth the law, and the word of the Lord from Jerusalem.* (Isaiah 2:2-3 KJV)

God has promises to keep. He is keeping them right now, and will continue until all God's covenant with the patriarchal fathers has been fully vindicated.

ZION

God promised Enoch there would be a community of believers in the last days whom God would prepare to welcome the return of Enoch's people. The New Testament writer, Jude, mentioned that promise: *Enoch also, the seventh from Adam, prophesied of these, saying, Behold, the Lord cometh with ten thousands of his saints, to execute judgment upon all* (Jude 1:14-15 KJV).

A more complete account of God's promise was restored to the Scriptures through Joseph Smith. God declared:

> *As I live, even so will I come in the last days, in the days of wickedness and vengeance, to fulfill the oath which I have made unto you concerning the children of Noah. And the day shall come that the earth shall rest. But before that day, the heavens shall be darkened, and a veil of darkness shall cover the earth; and the heavens shall shake, and also the earth. And great tribulations shall be among the children of men, but my people will I preserve. And righteousness will I send down out of Heaven. Truth will I send forth out of the earth to bear testimony of*

my Only Begotten, his resurrection from the dead, yea, and also the resurrection of all men. And righteousness and truth will I cause to sweep the earth as with a flood, to gather out my own elect from the four quarters of the earth unto a place which I shall prepare, a holy city, that my people may gird up their loins and be looking forth for the time of my coming. For there shall be my tabernacle, and it shall be called Zion, a New Jerusalem. And the Lord said unto Enoch, Then shall you and all your city meet them there, and we will receive them into our bosom. And they shall see us, and we will fall upon their necks, and they shall fall upon our necks, and we will kiss each other; and there shall be my abode. And it shall be Zion which shall come forth out of all the creations which I have made. (Genesis 4:22 RE)

Zion will be an actual location and a place of actual gathering.

No religious institution has the capacity to accomplish Zion. It will be a new society, a new way of thinking, a different way of interacting, an entirely new law, a form of government not presently existing, an order of living that alters everything, and a form of righteousness that is only possible in a society with a new structure ordered by God.

Zion will be produced by a journey begun in equality and pursued by equals, with no man demanding submission. Persuasion, meekness, unfeigned love, and pure knowledge are the only tools that can produce Zion. An hierarchy makes Zion impossible.

God alone will establish Zion. His instructions will lead us, teach us, command us, and guide us, but we have to consent.

The counterpart to Zion is the world—called "Babylon" in the Scriptures. Babylon is doomed, but Zion will survive. The wicked in Babylon will destroy one another until all governments will come to a full end. Commerce will fail. And therefore, Zion must be people of one heart, one mind, living in righteousness, with no poor among them. As the last days darken to fulfill the prophesies of Scripture, Zion alone will not take up arms against their neighbor.

God is laying the groundwork for Zion: He provided a new covenant in 2017, inspired the publication of new Scriptures in 2019, has commissioned work that invites the remnants of His earlier covenant people to awaken and arise, and He has promised a temple, a New Jerusalem, and Zion.

In the Book of Matthew, Christ prophesied a single generation would see all these things happen:

> *This generation in which these things shall be shown forth shall not pass away until all I have told you shall be fulfilled. Although the days will come that heaven and earth shall pass away, yet my words shall not pass away, but all shall be fulfilled.* (Matthew 11:8 RE; see also Matthew 24:34-35 KJV)

All three things needed to finish the Restoration—building an accepted temple for the Lord, obtaining "the fullness of the priesthood," and establishing the New Jerusalem—are or soon will be underway. Under God's direction and with His help, a small body of believers is laboring to accomplish these very things, and if they follow God's direction, they will vindicate God's promises to the covenant fathers.

The Restoration will at last be completed.

God's Work Among His Children

God's Mysteries

There is a great difference between recognizing the "signs of the times" and knowing the detail of how prophecy will be fulfilled. An example of the difference is found in Matthew. Matthew 2:1-18 tells of "wise men" who studied the Scriptures, watched the signs in the heavens, recognized a "star" that testified of the birth of the Messiah or newborn "king of the Jews," traveled a great distance (perhaps as long as two years) to worship Him, facilitated fulfilling prophecy by their presence in Jerusalem, and were visited by God in a dream. Here is the account:

> *Now when Jesus was born in Bethlehem of Judea in the days of Herod the king, behold, there came wise men from the east to Jerusalem, Saying, Where is he that is born King of the Jews? for we have seen his star in the east, and are come to worship him. When Herod the king had heard these things, he was troubled, and all Jerusalem with him. And when he had gathered all the chief priests and scribes of the people together, he demanded of them where Christ should be born. And they said unto him, In Bethlehem of Judea: for thus it is written by the prophet, And thou Bethlehem, in the land of Juda, art not the least among the princes of Juda: for out of thee shall come a Governor, that shall rule my people Israel.*
>
> *Then Herod, when he had privily called the wise men, inquired of them diligently what time the star appeared. And he sent them to Bethlehem, and said, Go and search diligently for the young child; and when ye have found him, bring me word again, that I may come and worship him also. When they had heard the king, they departed; and, lo, the star, which they saw in the east, went before them, till it came and stood over where the young child was.*
>
> *When they saw the star, they rejoiced with exceeding great joy. And when they were come into the house, they saw the young child with Mary his mother, and fell down, and worshipped him: and when they*

had opened their treasures, they presented unto him gifts; gold, and frankincense, and myrrh.

And being warned of God in a dream that they should not return to Herod, they departed into their own country another way.

And when they were departed, behold, the angel of the Lord appeareth to Joseph in a dream, saying, Arise, and take the young child and his mother, and flee into Egypt, and be thou there until I bring thee word: for Herod will seek the young child to destroy him. When he arose, he took the young child and his mother by night, and departed into Egypt: And was there until the death of Herod: that it might be fulfilled which was spoken of the Lord by the prophet, saying, Out of Egypt have I called my son.

Then Herod, when he saw that he was mocked of the wise men, was exceeding wroth, and sent forth, and slew all the children that were in Bethlehem, and in all the coasts thereof, from two years old and under, according to the time which he had diligently inquired of the wise men. Then was fulfilled that which was spoken by Jeremy the prophet, saying, In Rama was there a voice heard, lamentation, and weeping, and great mourning, Rachel weeping for her children, and would not be comforted, because they are not. (Matthew 2:1-18 KJV)

Despite all the wise men were able to know, they did not know where to find the newborn king. They mistakenly went to Herod's people to inquire about Christ's birth. They did not know, and God did not reveal to them, that Christ would be born in Bethlehem. It is unlikely they would have willingly acted to fulfill the Jeremiah 31:15 slaughter of children. Yet Matthew credits their involvement with fulfilling this prophecy. Can men unwittingly fulfill prophecy? Can anyone—even wise men who are well studied in Scripture and prophecy—ever fully understand prophecy? One of the lessons from this scriptural account is that all "wise men" whose diligence and faithfulness lead them to understand God's hand is at work may still not understand how or where God will act. There remain "mysteries" which God will accomplish but men cannot understand beforehand.

If the wise men knew He had been born but could not identify where Christ's birth happened despite all else they were able to do, then how can anyone know how God will accomplish His "strange act" in the last days?

Remember the modern-day caution in D&C 101:93-95:

> *What I have said unto you must needs be, that all men may be left without excuse; That wise men and rulers may hear and know that which they have never considered; That I may proceed to bring to pass my act, my strange act, and perform my work, my strange work, that men may discern between the righteous and the wicked, saith your God.*

Prophecies are not given to know details beforehand. They are given so that when they are fulfilled, one may understand that God knows the end from the beginning.[61]

JOHN THE BAPTIST

John the Baptist was the last messenger sent by God in the dispensation of Moses.[62] He represented the end of one dispensation and the beginning of another. He overthrew the kingdom of the Jews and wrested all the authority that remained with the Jews that had come from the original commission delivered through Moses. John the Baptist's message was to repent, warning that the "Kingdom of Heaven" was at hand.[63] The Jews were concerned at his message and sent representatives to inquire from him about the authority he had to start something new.[64]

John the Baptist's authority to baptize was recognized and accepted by Jesus Christ. He came to John and submitted to baptism because only by so doing would Jesus follow the requirements of righteousness.[65]

---

[61] See Isaiah 48:3-5.
[62] See John 1:6.
[63] See Matthew 3:2.
[64] See John 1:21-25.
[65] See Matthew 3:14-16.

John was sent by God,[66] and his right and authority was undisputed by both Jesus and the early Christians. Ignatius wrote about Christ's baptism: "[He] was baptized by John, that He might ratify the institution committed to that prophet."[67] And Christ "was baptized by John, that all righteousness may be fulfilled."[68]

Jesus posed the question to Jewish leaders of John the Baptist's authority. He asked, *The baptism of John, whence was it? from heaven, or of men?*—a question that the Jewish leaders knew if they answered would expose the problem of rejecting John. Continuing, *And they reasoned with themselves, saying, If we shall say, From heaven; he will say unto us, Why did ye not then believe him?* (Matthew 21:25 KJV). They concluded that they could not answer this question.

Jesus Christ described John the Baptist in these words: *Among those that are born of women there is not a greater prophet than John the Baptist* (Luke 7:28 KJV). Jesus also said of him: *He was a burning and a shining light* (John 5:35 KJV).

John was born to a Levite father,[69] but he was taken into the Judaean wilderness and hidden there to protect him from the authorities.[70] When he returned from the wilderness, he came dressed in camel hair, wearing a leather girdle, and eating locusts and wild honey.[71] These details suggest he lived without employment, home, or wealth, surviving on what God provided, as if Christ had John in mind when He taught the Sermon on the Mount:

> *And why take ye thought for raiment? Consider the lilies of the field, how they grow; they toil not, neither do they spin: And yet I say unto you, That even Solomon in all his glory was not arrayed like one of these. Wherefore, if God so clothe the grass of the field, which today is, and to morrow is cast into the oven, shall he not much more clothe you, O ye of little faith? Therefore take no thought, saying, What shall we eat? or, What shall we drink? or, Wherewithal shall we be clothed? (For*

---

[66] See John 1:6.
[67] Epistle of Ignatius to the Ephesians, Chapter XVIII.
[68] Epistle of Ignatius to the Smyrnaeans, Chapter I.
[69] See Luke 1:5.
[70] Ibid., vs. 80.
[71] See Matthew 3:4.

after all these things do the Gentiles seek:) for your heavenly Father knoweth that ye have need of all these things. But seek ye first the kingdom of God, and his righteousness; and all these things shall be added unto you. Take therefore no thought for the morrow: for the morrow shall take thought for the things of itself. Sufficient unto the day is the evil thereof. (Matthew 6:28-34 KJV)

These things, which describe the life of John the Baptist, seem to us both fanatical and impractical. When cast out of the Garden, mankind was doomed to obtain bread by the sweat of our labor.[72] We are commanded to labor for our support[73] and not steal,[74] nor expect another man's bread to be given to us.[75] If a man will not labor, he should not eat what others produce through their labor.[76] Yet John seems to have abandoned everything to serve God, and in turn, he lived only on what God provided for him.

Would we have recognized and accepted John as a messenger sent by God? How would we have determined that this "homeless" man was "sent by God"? If he had no pulpit, how could we know that, for a brief time, he alone could perform an ordinance required for salvation? If he was not part of the established system of religion, why would we give him any heed? If there was an existing temple, a presiding high priest, a governing board in the Sanhedrin, and established synagogues where Scripture was recited and messages were delivered each week, why would we expect John to be more relevant to our salvation than the religious system in place? If the entire religious landscape was attributed to Moses (who was known to be a prophet[77]), what makes us think we would choose to believe God sent the outsider, John? Why do we think salvation today will require anything less of a test than was required when John first appeared and began to preach? Why do we think we are any different than the Jews who rejected both John and Jesus? If our religion is a comfortable part of our lives, then what is its value?

---

[72] See Genesis 3:19.
[73] See 2 Thessalonians 3:11.
[74] See Ephesians 4:28.
[75] See 2 Thessalonians 3:8.
[76] Ibid., vs. 10.
[77] See John 9:29.

Christ described what is required to follow Him:

> *Suppose ye that I am come to give peace on earth? I tell you, Nay; but rather division: For from henceforth there shall be five in one house divided, three against two, and two against three. The father shall be divided against the son, and the son against the father; the mother against the daughter, and the daughter against the mother; the mother in law against her daughter in law, and the daughter in law against her mother in law.* (Luke 12:51-53 KJV)

And again, the Lord taught:

> *Blessed are they which are persecuted for righteousness' sake: for theirs is the kingdom of heaven. Blessed are ye, when men shall revile you, and persecute you, and shall say all manner of evil against you falsely, for my sake. Rejoice, and be exceeding glad: for great is your reward in heaven: for so persecuted they the prophets which were before you.* (Matthew 5:10-12 KJV)

If our religion does not cause others to revile us, members of our families to be offended, or help us understand the life of Christ and the prophets, it is not Christ's religion. If religion takes us to a comfortable church each week where we are assured we will be saved in Heaven, it is not truly Christian. If it does not require sacrifice, then we have nothing in common with either Christ or the prophets.

It is still possible to practice Christianity but not in comfortable pews, listening to flattery and praise. The Bible warns that the time will come when God will: *Render the hearts of this people insensitive, Their ears dull, And their eyes dim, Otherwise they might see with their eyes, Hear with their ears, Understand with their hearts, And return and be healed* (Isaiah 6:10 NAS). This happens every week in most "Christian" churches throughout the world.

Would we have recognized John the Baptist as a burning and shining light? How?

BAPTIST OR BELOVED?

The debate over who was "speaking" the testimony of Jesus Christ in the beginning of the Gospel of John has been one of the longest-standing questions in Christianity. Heracleon addressed this at about 165 A.D. He was a Gnostic and from the school of Valentinus. Valentinus was an early Gnostic who claimed to have secret knowledge that was passed from John (the Beloved). He attributed early material in the Gospel of John to John the Baptist.

Origen, who wrote early in the third century, disputed Heracleon and argued that it was John the Beloved who was responsible for the composition.[78] The debate has never ended.

The term "logos" (which is rendered as "word" in most English translations of the Gospel of John) has a PRE-Gospel of John history. The most recent use of the term, prior to the composition of the Gospel of John, was Philo of Alexandria. He was born two decades before the birth of Christ and wrote just a few years prior to the composition of John's writing. Philo considered the "logos" to be an intermediary between man and God, a Divine being that bridged the gap between fallen man and perfect God. There is a great debate over the extent to which Philo's writings influenced John's composition.

John the Beloved's composition begins by placing Christ in a pre-Earth creative role that is cosmic in scope. (This introduction was intended to alert the reader that the individual described in the text that would follow was God.) Then the often-mundane events build with proof upon proof that the "man Jesus" was indeed the cosmic creator and God in very fact. By the end of the account, the proof was assembled to demonstrate that the opening description was true beyond dispute. Christ was God.

Origen's writings make it clear that a pre-Earth existence for mankind —not just Christ, but all men—was part of early Christian belief. That belief has been lost for most Christians. Origen wrote:

---

[78] *Origen's Commentary on John*, Sixth Book, Chapter 2.

John's soul was older than his body, and subsisted by itself before it was sent on the ministry of the witness of the light…

He extends this to us all:

> …if that general doctrine of the soul is to be received, namely, that it is not sown at the same time with the body, but is before it, and is then, for various causes, clothed with flesh and blood; then the words "sent from God" will not appear to be applicable to John alone.[79]

…meaning that not only did John exist before he was flesh and blood, but all men likewise existed before they entered this world.

The pre-Earth existence of mankind is taught in the Bible. Jeremiah was told he was "ordained" before he entered his mother's womb: *Before I formed thee in the belly I knew thee; and before thou camest forth out of the womb I sanctified thee, and I ordained thee a prophet unto the nations* (Jeremiah 1:5 KJV).

Job likewise described the joy of the spirits of men when they learned of the plan for creating this world: *When the morning stars sang together, and all the sons of God shouted for joy…* (Job 38:7 KJV). And Christ's apostles inquired about the pre-birth sins of the man born blind,[80] a question that could only be asked if it were possible for him to sin before birth because he existed prior to his birth.

Although Christians today do not recognize the doctrine of pre-Earth existence of man's spirit, it once was a part of Christian belief. Like the confusion about who is speaking in the earliest verses of the Gospel of John, Christianity has lost clarity that can only be restored by another revelation from God. As Roger Williams, a late Protestant Reformer in the American Colonies, said: "The apostasy…hath so far corrupted all, that there can be no recovery out of that apostasy until Christ shall send forth new apostles to plant churches anew." He recognized that no man has authority to perform even the basic ordinances of the Gospel of Jesus Christ unless Christ has authorized that man.

---

[79] *Origen's Commentary on John*, Book II, Chapter 24.
[80] See John 9:2.

Reading the New Testament is like reading another person's mail. It was written to a specific body of believers who had been taught by those who knew Christ. Today it is just as necessary to have that same vital connection to Christ in order to be saved. How can we believe the truth if we are not taught the truth? How can we be taught the truth unless someone is sent from Christ to teach a message from Him? How can anyone pretend to teach the truth if Christ did not send them?[81]

RECONCILIATION (A LITTLE)

A joint accord has recently been reached by the Lutherans and Catholics on one issue that has divided them since Martin Luther. Luther (because he rejected Catholic authority claims) needed another basis for salvation. He identified God's grace alone as the solution. Catholicism, however, required the accoutrements it offered through its claims to priesthood authority and, by extension, authoritative ordinances. Therefore, the Catholic claims required believers to respond with suitable submission—or works—to be saved.

The accord is entitled the "Joint Declaration on the Doctrine of Justification by the Lutheran World Federation and the Catholic Church"[82] and now allows the question of grace versus works to be buried, as between Catholics and Lutherans. Harmony is found in the statement which contains these words:

> By grace alone, in faith in Christ's saving work and not because of any merit on our part, we are accepted by God and receive the Holy Spirit, who renews our hearts while equipping us and calling us to good works.

Paragraph 25 explains:

> We confess together that sinners are justified by faith in the saving action of God in Christ. By the action of the Holy Spirit in baptism, they are granted the gift of salvation, which lays the basis

---

[81] See Romans 10:14-15.
[82] See: http://www.vatican.va/roman_curia/pontifical_councils/chrstuni/documents/rc_pc_chrstuni_doc_31101999_cath-luth-joint-declaration_en.html

for the whole Christian life. They place their trust in God's gracious promise by justifying faith, which includes hope in God and love for him. Such a faith is active in love and thus the Christian cannot and should not remain without works. But whatever in the justified precedes or follows the free gift of faith is neither the basis of justification nor merits it.

It is by grace we do the required works to be saved. As explained in Philippians 2:13 KJV: *For it is God which worketh in you both to will and to do his good pleasure.* As Paul explained in Romans 6:1-2 KJV concerning those who are born again through Christ: *What shall we say then? Shall we continue in sin, that grace may abound? God forbid.* We must escape sin by the grace of God and then do the works that testify we are in possession of God's grace.

As James explained:

> *Even so faith, if it hath not works, is dead, being alone. Yea, a man may say, Thou hast faith, and I have works: shew me thy faith without thy works, and I will shew thee my faith by my works. Thou believest that there is one God; thou doest well: the devils also believe, and tremble. But will thou know, O vain man, that faith without works is dead?* (James 2:17-20 KJV)

If we are saved by the grace of God, our works will testify of that grace within us. Without the works of righteousness—put within us by being born again a new creation of Christ's—we may claim to have been saved by grace, but it is without proof.

However, what if salvation is not determined by grace alone, by works alone, or even some combination of the two? What if it comes from the ministry of one sent by God to declare salvation? And faith comes by hearing the message, like Paul taught?[83] Paul was expounding a passage from Isaiah,[84] a prophet sent by God. Paul was likewise sent with a message from God. What if the meaning is that in order to receive salvation, it is essential that the believer receive a message from a minister actually sent by God with a message for our day and time?

---

[83] See Romans 10:17.
[84] See Isaiah 53:1.

What if salvation requires the same thing now as when Isaiah preached and prophesied, and when Paul taught, and when Christ ministered to mankind? What if there is a necessary relationship between the sender of a message (God) and the speaker of the message (one sent by God) in order for the message to actually result in salvation for the hearer-believer?

Who has believed our report, indeed? And who, then, has saving faith?

This is a moment that has been 500 years in the coming, but it does not carry the certifying imprint of God's word. Instead, it carries the authority of compromise between two institutions whose link to God is borrowed from those who did speak with and for God but who have long been dead. Does living faith require a living message? If so, neither Lutheran nor Catholic institutions can save, nor can their new agreement signal anything important for anyone's salvation

CHRISTIAN REJECTION

There exists an intolerant and anti-Christian view that rejects (as "un-Christian") all those who think there is a necessary role for works in addition to faith.[85] Such a view ignores two verses penned by James and rejects three chapters of Christ's teachings.[86] Such a view also rejects Christ's own submission to the ordinance of baptism *to fulfill all righteousness* (Matthew 3:15 KJV). The dogmatic and blind guides who hold such views base their entire false construction on Paul's letter to the Ephesians that states in passing: *For by grace are ye saved through faith; and that not of yourselves: it is the gift of God: Not of works, lest any man should boast...* (Ephesians 2:8-9 KJV). It is a mistake to interpret Paul to be in conflict with Christ's Sermon on the Mount, and if there is a conflict, we ought to obey Christ.

Paul taught in Ephesus, resided there for a time, and was acquainted with the arguments going on in that community when he wrote his letter to them. The document is literally "reading someone else's mail"

---

[85] "Faith without works is dead." See James 2:20,26.
[86] See Matthew 5-7.

without the benefit of knowing the background of weeks of Paul's teaching and information related to him from visitors to the city. We cannot now have any confidence that these two verses represent Paul's understanding or even Paul's oral teachings.

What we do know for certain, however, is that Christ instructed us to be the salt of the earth[87] and light of the world.[88] It is anti-Christ to deny the obligation to be salt and to provide light. It is anti-Christ to reject Christ's admonition to let the world "see your good works" if we are to follow Him.[89]

Christ warned us to "keep the commandments." He cursed those who proclaim we are merely saved by grace and have no obligation to obey His commandments. He declared, *Whosoever therefore shall break one of these least commandments, and shall teach men so, he shall be called the least in the kingdom of heaven: but whosoever shall do and teach them, the same shall be called great in the kingdom of heaven* (Matthew 5:19 KJV).

Christ then elevated the commandment to not kill by warning Christians to "not be angry" with their brothers.[90] He explained that His followers would not even engage in Christian-giving without first forgiving all those who offended them.[91]

Christ commanded us to agree with disputants and not oppose them. We are to give what they demand of us rather than withhold even our cloak.[92]

Christ elevated the commandment against committing adultery by commanding His followers to not entertain *lust in your heart* (Matthew 5:27-28 KJV).

Christ revoked divorce as an option for His followers, except in the case of adultery.[93]

---

[87] See Matthew 5:13.
[88] Ibid., vs. 14.
[89] Ibid., vs. 16.
[90] See Matthew 5:21-22.
[91] Ibid., vs. 23-24.
[92] Ibid., vs. 25-26,39-42.
[93] Ibid., vs. 31-32.

Christ commanded us to love even our enemies and return good for evil. [94]

Christ commanded us to "be perfect" as a follower and believer in Him.[95]

This is only the first of the three chapters of Christ's instructions about what following Him requires.

James explained how a Christian is to follow Christ:

> *What doth it profit, my brethren, though a man say he hath faith, and have not works? Can faith save him? If a brother or sister be naked, and destitute of daily food, And one of you say unto them, Depart in peace, be ye warmed and filled; notwithstanding ye give them not those things which are needful to the body; what doth it profit? Even so faith, if it hath not works, is dead, being alone. Yea, a man may say, Thou hast faith, and I have works: shew me thy faith without thy works, and I will shew thee my faith by my works.* (James 2:14-18 KJV)

---

[94] Ibid., vs. 43-47.
[95] Ibid., v. 48.

GOD'S MESSAGE AND MY WITNESS

*For thou shalt be His witness unto all men
of what thou hast seen and heard.*
Acts 22:15 KJV

As one who, like the Apostle Paul, has stood in the presence of Christ, and likewise been caught up into Heaven and been taught unspeakable things, I know from the Lord's own voice my standing before Him. Whether others regard me as a "Christian," I know that Christ regards me as His devoted follower and faithful servant. I likewise comprehend His grace for others, including those who would exclude me from being defined as "Christian" and, therefore, exclude me from salvation itself.

Rather than debate, deny, or judge the "Christianity" of others using any criteria, Bible verse, or Protestant hope for salvation, I accept any person's claim to be "Christian" as welcome news. Whether they lived for the first millennium and a half of Christian history when only the Catholic Church existed, or they divide themselves into groups claiming to hold the exclusive qualifications to be saved today, I judge no man. I encourage all to hold fast to the hope of salvation offered by Christ, even if they hold beliefs by which they judge and reject me as a fellow Christian.

In the Fall of 2017, I gave three talks in the United States: 1) on September 21st in Los Angeles, California; 2) on October 19th in Dallas, Texas; and 3) on November 16th in Atlanta, Georgia. I have been sent to give these three messages. I do know God. I have been ministered to by Him, and He has prepared me to minister to others. Like Paul, who was sent by God, I will also tell you of an unchangeable God, who is the same yesterday, today, and forever. His message requires the same from you today as it did when Jesus Christ first taught in Galilee and Judea.

Each talk was delivered in a public venue that was free and open to the public, requiring no ticket, RSVP, or reservation, and no donations were solicited. Charity is wasted on hireling clergy, which should be used for the poor. Clergy ought to labor for their support, as do other Christians. The sooner we stop paying a professional clergy, the sooner Christianity will lose its animosity and improve in spirit, function, and value.

Anyone who claims to be a "Christian" may be interested in reading or hearing these three talks. The talks discuss Christian history, the Reformation, Christianity since the Reformation, the Restoration movement, and Joseph Smith as a Christian thinker and biblical preacher. *Smithsonian Magazine* identified Joseph Smith as the most significant religious figure in American history, yet he remains misunderstood by most Christians primarily because his legacy has been regarded as Mormon property. In many ways, his life mirrors the Apostle Paul. He belongs to the Christian community as much as St. Francis of Assisi, Luther, Tyndale, Wesley, Knox, Williams, and Calvin.

Because of the divisions between denominations, most believers are unwilling to consider the views held by others who practice a very different form of Christianity than themselves. Members of each Christian denomination believe that they practice the only true or correct form of Christianity, of which Jesus Christ approves. However, the divisional creeds of Christianity are largely the result of institutions who maintain loyalty from their parishioners by denouncing every other brand of Christianity as false, incomplete, or devil-inspired. Further, Christians are criticized by leaders of churches when they are willing to consider "heretical" ideas that cross boundaries of Catholic, Protestant, Jehovah's Witness, Salvation Army, Evangelical, or Mormon. Such present-day dynamics ought to lead every Christian into a more open dialogue about the history and present status of Christianity and also cause them to carefully consider all that claims to be part of the broad expanse of "Christianity."

Of all the various reformation and restoration thinkers, perhaps Joseph Smith remains the most feared by other Christian denominations, most likely due to the aggressive campaign by the Salt Lake City headquarters of the LDS Church to convert other Christians to their organization. These three talks are not an attempt to influence listeners to become members of the Salt Lake City-based church or of any other denomination. I was excommunicated from the LDS Church because of my research and candid writing about the flaws of the Mormon Church and its failure to candidly account for its history.

Whether you are a loyal member of a specific denomination or a freelance Christian without denominational affiliation, the three talks will provide information about Christianity that is designed to give you a greater reason to believe in Christ. They may also give you a greater reason to try to understand other Christians whose beliefs reckon from very different traditions than your own. It is hoped that Christians everywhere may with one mind and one mouth glorify God, even the Father of our Lord Jesus Christ.[96]

Each of the three talks is presented in its entirety in the next three chapters, followed by several subsequent lectures that build upon those first three.

---

[96] See Romans 15:6.

FIRST ADDRESS TO ALL CHRISTIANS

Cerritos Center for the Performing Arts
Los Angeles, California
September 21, 2017

I want to thank all of those who have volunteered and assisted in getting this event set up, the venue rented, the venue paid for, and this evening organized. Everything we do is done voluntarily and without compensation. We do not have an organization that gathers funds and makes it possible to purchase events like this. Everything that is done, including the online live-video broadcast over the internet this evening, is being done by volunteers who are taking the time to use their own resources to make this possible. We believe that sacrifice is necessary if a person is to have faith. You can believe a lot of things, but if you're going to have faith, it is the order of Heaven that you have to make sacrifice to demonstrate your faith.

All the videos that were just shown are on the Learn of Christ website[97] and also are available on YouTube and can be watched at any time.

It's my hope that this evening I'll give you a greater reason to have belief in Christ and have confidence in your belief in Christ.

In the book of Matthew, chapter 24 is Christ's most extensive prophecy about the future events, including the time of His Second Coming. While He gives some details in Matthew chapter 24, there is a statement that He makes about: *As the days of No[ah] were, so shall also the coming of the Son of man be* (Matthew 24:37 KJV).

He makes an analogy between the events that occurred during Noah's time and what we will see on the earth at the time of His return. Let me read you a description of the events at the time of Noah—and these are the kinds of events with which we typically associate the days of Noah:

---

[97] learnofchrist.org

And God saw that the wickedness of men had become great in the earth; and every man was lifted up in the imagination of the thoughts of his heart, being only evil continually.

… The earth was corrupt before God, and it was filled with violence. And God looked upon the earth, and, behold, it was corrupt, for all flesh had corrupted its way upon the earth. And God said unto Noah: The end of all flesh is come before me, for the earth is filled with violence, and behold I will destroy all flesh from off the earth. (Moses 8:22,28-30)

Ominous. Terrible. Reason for concern. And that's what we generally think of. But there's another side to that. That other side includes, obviously, Noah. You can't have the days of Noah without having **a Noah**. Another contemporary who lived at the same time with Noah was Enoch, who built a city of righteousness where people gathered together to worship the only true God, who were then in turn taken up to Heaven. That group of people, taken up to Heaven, are going to return with the Lord when He comes again in glory. Book of Jude— there is only one chapter in there. *Enoch also, the seventh from Adam, prophesied of these, saying, Behold, the Lord cometh with ten thousands of his saints* (Jude 1:14 KJV). There were those that were taken up into the heavens numbering in the tens of thousands who will return with Him.

So, if there is reason for pessimism when Christ predicts that as it was in the days of Noah, so shall it be at the time of His return, there's also extraordinary reason for optimism because we are going to see things like Noah and his family, that included Shem—who would be renamed Melchizedek, about whom the apostle Paul had a great deal to say in the book of Hebrews, comparing that man, a son of Noah, to the Lord Himself. (Actually, we ought to flip that. He compares the Lord Himself to that man.) And then there is Enoch. And so, while we tend to look at the prophecy Christ gave concerning His coming negatively, about how far degenerate the world is going to go, those are the "tares" ripening.

Christ said, "We're not going to uproot the tares, bind them in bundles, and burn them until the wheat also becomes ripe." You're here, you're Christian, and God would like you to be wheat. He would like you to ripen in righteousness while the world ripens in iniquity.

Almost a little over 2000 years ago, roughly, something happened that changed the course of history. Christ was resurrected. We have—in one generation of people—a series of testimonies about Christ and His life, death, and resurrection. The authors of those testimonies do not spare themselves from their embarrassing behavior. Christ was taken captive in the Garden, and many of those who followed Him fled immediately. (Peter took a little time to knock off a servant's ear, which Christ healed and rebuked Peter and told him to put away his sword.)

By the time He gets to being tried, there are only two who hung around for the trial; and on the cross, the only ones who followed Him who remained were women,[98] and they stood at the feet of the cross until He passed. Upon His death, there's no mention of a disciple being involved in His burial. They were cowering. They were hiding. And these were they who spent their time with Him as His chosen disciples.

Everything changed on the first day of the week when something turned cowards into men who would be willing to die for the testimony that they had that He is risen! That testimony changed the world; it changed their lives. They no longer lived as though their Master had been defeated in death. They lived as though their Master had triumphed over death, because He had. Multiple witnesses telling the same story: Abject defeat, fear, and cowardice followed by triumphant, confident, defiant belief in a risen Lord, many of whom would go to their own deaths rather than to deny their testimony that Christ lives.

You have every reason to have confidence in the fact of the resurrection of the Lord. The lives of those disciples are abundant testimony of the fact of His resurrection.

---

[98] Women are mentioned and named, but the solitary male mentioned was John (see John 19:25-27). The others "stood afar" off (see Luke 23:49).

And then we have His greatest persecutor, Saul, on the road to Damascus, being confronted by the Lord Himself, calling him and saying, It's hard for you to kick against the pricks. *Why persecutest thou me?* (Acts 26:14 KJV). And look at the change that happened in the life of Paul, ultimately leading to his death in Rome—again, as a witness and a testimony of Him in whom he had confidence of a glorious resurrection. And so, 2000 years ago, an event occurred that changed the world.

About 1900 years ago, the ministry of that generation of believers and witnesses drew to an end, and the apostles then had their voices silenced. It would take until 1675 years ago before there was an attempt to stabilize and define what it meant to be a Christian. Between the time of the death of the apostles and the council at Nicaea, there is an interlude in which Christianity assumed extraordinarily divergent forms of Christian belief, many of which were completely contradictory of one another. If you read the ante-Nicene (the "prior to" Nicaea) fathers of Christianity, the debates, the contradictions, the descriptions, the content of Christian belief was remarkably unstable, unsteady, and had very different, irreconcilable versions. 1675 years ago now, the Nicene Council made an attempt to redefine what it meant to be Christian and to stabilize the conflicting Christianities into something that would be singular and, therefore, define what it would mean to be an orthodox Christian. Coming out of Nicaea is a creed, the Nicene Creed, but it would take until about 1550 A.D. before the efforts to suppress divergent forms of Christianity succeeded far enough that we had our orthodox Christian faith in a reasonably stable form.

It was about a thousand years ago now when what is called the Great Schism occurred, in which the east and the west divided between the church centered in Rome (the Roman Catholic or Universal Church) and the Eastern Orthodox Church. They divided from one another and no longer shared communion, hierarchy, or their faith in Christ together. It was 500 years ago when Martin Luther posted the 95 Theses and set in motion the series of events that were discussed in the videos shown just before this talk.

I assume all of you regard yourselves as Christians. I regard myself as a Christian. Today there are approximately 40,000 different Christian denominations. If you go back only 500 years, most of what you regard as Christianity (and in all probability, the form of Christianity in which you believe) would not have existed. If you go back earlier still, whatever it is that you hold as your Christian belief, even the current form of Catholicism that's practiced, would be regarded as heretical by the Roman Catholic hierarchy itself.

Only 500 years ago, the only authorized forms of the Bible were printed in Latin, and they were the exclusive property of a Catholic clergy that taught in Latin—a group of people who were told what to do and how to regard Christianity. Unfortunately, for almost every one of us, the form of Christianity that we hold in our hearts and that we look to in faith, believing that it has the power to save us would be regarded throughout almost all of Christian history as heresy, as false, as damnable.

One of the Protestant fathers was Roger Williams. He was a firebrand; he was kicked out of the Massachusetts colony; he was considered dangerous (as dangerous in the Massachusetts setting as Martin Luther was considered dangerous in Roman Catholic Germany). Roger Williams is actually the one who founded the First Baptist Church.

It was mentioned that I was raised within a Baptist family. I made an attempt to get baptized. I had conviction when I was ten years old, but the minister didn't think that I was a suitable candidate. Apparently I wasn't much of a character at ten years old—at least in the eyes of a Christian Baptist minister attempting to evaluate the worthiness of a soul for baptism—and so he punted, and by the time I got to high school, the last thing I wanted to do was to be baptized.

I got baptized for the first time into the Mormon church, and I've apparently earned the same sort of reception from them as I did from the Baptist minister when I was ten. I've been regarded as unsuitable material, I guess, because when it comes to the history of Christianity and of the various denominations, what churches want are apologists. They want people to defend whatever it is they're doing, however aberrant, however unjustifiable, however flimsy the basis upon which what they teach is grounded—they want apologists. And the role of the apologist is to defend at all costs.

It was mentioned that I'm an attorney; I practice law. I mean, I actively go into the courtroom, and I defend cases at the trial level and at the appellate level. The job of an attorney is an advocate; it's to present persuasively your side of the argument. However, attorneys are only licensed to practice law if they behave ethically. One of the ethics that is binding upon an attorney is that if the court poses a question to you that exposes a weakness in your position or a fact that you dislike because it harms your position, you are ethically obligated to disclose —honestly and forthrightly—to the court the true answer to the question that is put to you. Christian apologists have no such ethical constraint. They do not need to tell you the weaknesses. They do not need to disclose to you honestly what the problems are.

I was excommunicated from the LDS Church because I evaluated their history, concluded that there were indefensible positions, and preferred to state honestly what I believe to be the truth rather than to support a distortion that is unjustified in fact, in truth, and in all honesty. I suppose, in that respect, that a lawyer comes off rather better than lawyers normally do, because legal ethics govern my thinking on how we ought to treat any discussion of our Christian faith or any discussion of what the truth is.

Well, Roger Williams (the founder of the First Baptist Church), as a refugee went and helped found Rhode Island and continued his preaching and reached this conclusion. This is a quote from Roger Williams:

> There is no regularly constituted church of Christ on earth, nor any person qualified to administer any church ordinances, nor can there be until new apostles are sent by the great head of the church for whose coming I am seeking.

I think Roger Williams was telling the truth, and I think Roger Williams foretold what was actually in the heart of God and what God ultimately intended to do.

As I mentioned, the days of Noah have to include Noah and have to include Enoch. Or in other words, in addition to all of the wretchedness that we look forward to, the world disintegrating and devolving into, there will be an opposition to that, a hand sent from God in the form of prophets, apostles, someone with a message.

When I use the word "apostle," I mean the word in the same sense in which it is used in the New Testament; that is, someone coming to deliver a message from God to those to whom He speaks. I'm not talking about some officious chap claiming a title as his rightful inheritance, as is done in Mormonism. I'm not talking about someone who "calls" themselves. I'm talking about someone to whom God speaks and says, "Go tell the people thus."

I think there has been one such man who came about 200 years ago. His life was brief. After 38½ years, he was slain, largely because of the conspiracy of followers. Shortly before his death, he said to those who were among his followers, "You don't know me, you never knew my heart." They would conspire to kill him after they had conspired to put him in jail. And they use his name now as if invoking it gives them the same kind of moral authority that a man who gave up his life and a man who suffered in prison had as moral authority in following and sacrificing to obey God. The man about whom I'm speaking is Joseph Smith, and I would ask you to please not associate that name with the Mormon church, but to allow him to stand on his own and to consider what he had to say independent of what they say he said.

There are remarkable similarities between the struggle from 1900 years ago until 1550 years ago in the Christian tradition (before it adopted a settled—although corrupted—form) and the last 160 years of Mormonism following the death of Joseph Smith. Christians could profit from the study of the more recent events involving Joseph Smith to gain insight into the earlier Christian experience.

The Apostle Paul asked questions of critical importance to Christians immediately after his declaration that says this: *Whosoever shall call upon the name of the Lord shall be saved* (Romans 10:13 KJV). Immediately following that, he poses this series of questions. He does that in order to demonstrate to the satisfaction of anyone who comes across this material that they can have confidence in him, in what he's saying, and in what source he draws his information and his inspiration from. The overwhelming majority of Protestant Christians believe and rely on this statement: *Whosoever shall call upon the name of the Lord shall be saved.* But what of the critically important questions he then asks: *How then shall they call on him in whom they have not believed? and how shall they believe in him of whom they have not heard? and how shall they hear without a preacher? And how shall they preach, except they be sent?* (ibid. vs.14,15).

There's a difference between belief and unbelief. Belief means that you have a body of correct information from which to draw in reaching your conviction concerning the gospel of Jesus Christ. Unbelief simply means that you're drawing upon information that is either incomplete, inaccurate, or outright false.

So, with those questions in mind:

- How shall they call on Him in whom they have not believed?
- And how shall they believe in Him of whom they have not heard?
- And how shall they hear without a preacher?
- And how shall they preach except they be sent?

Who can send? In the Apostle Paul's series of declarations, WHO? Who can send? How can they be sent? There were no theological seminaries. There were no doctorates of theology. There was no doctorate of divinity.

It's the Catholics who believe and rely on Paul's questions to justify their claims. They claim to have an unbroken line of authority traceable to Peter to whom the keys of the kingdom were given by Christ. If you are a Protestant, do the keys of the kingdom matter? If you are a Catholic, what ARE the keys of the kingdom given Peter, and how confident are you that those can be transferred at all, since Peter got them from Christ directly? And if they can be transferred, how confident are you that they have survived intact today?

Protestants and Catholics must both face the question of whether salvation can be obtained apart from the Roman Catholic Church, but

Paul asserts a different point and asks a different question. Catholics and Protestants alike recognize Paul's authority and right to claim that he represented Christ. Paul's conversion, however, was not based on Peter. It was not based on a preacher who was sent to him. It was not dependent upon the keys of the kingdom given to Peter. Paul asserted he was an apostle, but his calling did not come because of a transfer of authority to him by Peter. He was called by God. He begins the first few words of his epistle to the Galatians: *Paul, an apostle, (not of men, neither by man, but by Jesus Christ, and God the Father, who raised him from the dead;)... (Galatians 1:1 KJV).*

Was Paul therefore *sent*? By *whom* was he sent? You think it obvious no doubt, but the principle is critical to finding true faith in Jesus Christ. He is the same yesterday, today, and forever. If Paul was an apostle because Christ sent him—not men or man—then for a preacher to be sent to preach the truth, the same should be required today as then. If Christ does not require the same, then Christ has changed—and we know that cannot be true, for He is the same forever. If, therefore, a preacher must be sent, and Christ must do the sending, then the only preacher you should heed must be one who declares plainly that he has been sent by God. That was the claim of Joseph Smith. It was a claim that ultimately cost his life. It was a claim that, given the hardship through which he passed and the perils that he faced and the betrayals that happened and the lies that have been told by people who have profited by using his name, it is a claim that I believe, and I accept.

Another example of one who was sent by God is John the Baptist, who is clearly identified in these words: *There was a man sent from God, whose name was John* (John 1:6 KJV). Christ's apostles likewise were sent by Him, according to the New Testament. Christ said, *I have chosen you, and ordained you, that ye should go and bring forth fruit, and that your fruit should remain* (John 15:16 KJV). Everyone sent by Christ to preach in the New Testament was given their message from Him. They were sent by Him. Joseph Smith declared he was likewise sent. I would invite you to investigate his claim and see whether it persuades you.

I say these words advisedly, and I want you to take them seriously: Today all Christian churches have become corrupt. They love money and acquiring financial security and church buildings more than caring for the poor and the needy, the sick and the afflicted. The institutions claiming to be the church of God are all polluted by the cares of the world.

I want you to understand what I mean by that. During the apostolic era, there was no such thing as a Christian church building. Christians met in homes. They did not collect and compensate ministers. They gathered money, and they used it to help the poor and the needy among them.

As soon as you get a church building, I regret to inform you, you'll have to hire a lawyer. In what name are you going to take title to your building? How are you going to hide title or hold title and deal with succession? What form will the organization take? Do you intend to qualify for tax deductibility? If so, do you intend to file as a charitable institution, as an eleemosynary institution, as an educational institution? (Those are all words that you find in 501(c) of the Internal Revenue Code.) And what do you do if you want to hire and fire a minister, and you want to dispossess the one you fired and put into possession the successor in the building—what rights, who's on the board, and who possesses the right to deal with that? As soon as you own property, the cares of this world invade. It's unavoidable.

If you meet in homes (as the early Christians did) and if you gather your tithing (one tenth of your surplus after you've taken care of all your responsibilities/all your needs—whatever's left over, one tenth of that is your tithe)—after you gather your tithe, then you ought to look at your brothers and your sisters who are there in your meeting, and you ought to help those who have needs: health needs, education needs, transportation needs, food needs, or who have children that need care. Christians should take care of the poor among them, and no one should be looking at the flock and saying, "I need your money to support myself." Christian charities should be used to take care of the poor among you and not to engage in acquiring the cares of this world. This is why all Christian churches have become corrupt. They love money and acquiring financial security and church buildings more than caring for the poor and the needy, the sick and the afflicted.

I speak as part of a very tiny movement, but we're worldwide. We are a very small group of people—scattered from Japan to Europe, scattered from Australia to Canada, a small group of people—but we're trying to practice authentic Christianity in the form that it was originally intended to be practiced, meeting in homes. I met earlier today with a group of people from this local area, and there are a number in this local area who believe as I do. We celebrated the sacrament as a group together, and we reaffirmed one another in our faith.

Jesus Christ taught many principals, truths, precepts, and commandments, but He only taught one doctrine. I'm going to read you Christ's doctrine:

> *Behold, verily, verily, I say unto you, I will declare unto you my doctrine. And this is my doctrine, and it is the doctrine which the Father hath given unto me; and I bear record of the Father, and the Father beareth record of me, and the Holy Ghost beareth record of the Father and me; and I bear record that the Father commandeth all men, everywhere, to repent and believe in me. And whoso believeth in me, and is baptized, the same shall be saved; and they are they who shall inherit the kingdom of God. And whoso believeth not in me, and is not baptized, shall be damned.*

> *Verily, verily, I say unto you, that this is my doctrine, and I bear record of it from the Father; and whoso believeth in me believeth in the Father also; and unto him will the Father bear record of me, for he will visit him with fire and with the Holy Ghost. And thus will the Father bear record of me, and the Holy Ghost will bear record unto him of the Father and me; for the Father, and I, and the Holy Ghost are one.*

> *And again I say unto you, ye must repent, and become as a little child, and be baptized in my name, or ye can in nowise receive these things. And again I say unto you, ye must repent, and be baptized in my name, and become as a little child, or ye can in nowise inherit the kingdom of God.*

Verily, verily, I say unto you, that this is my doctrine, and whoso buildeth upon this buildeth upon my rock, and the gates of hell shall not prevail against them. And whoso shall declare more or less than this, and establish it for my doctrine, the same cometh of evil, and is not built upon my rock; but he buildeth upon a sandy foundation, and the gates of hell stand open to receive such when the floods come and the winds beat upon them. (3 Nephi 11:31-40)

We believe and practice this doctrine of Christ. We practice baptism by immersion in living waters (meaning lakes, rivers, streams, and oceans) where there is life. We prefer living waters for a living ordinance. We have authority from God to perform baptism and other ordinances, such as the sacrament, but we are not jealous with our authority and are willing to share it with any man who is willing to accept and follow the doctrine of Christ.

As to the commandment to be baptized, even Jesus Christ went to be baptized by John *to fulfill all righteousness* (Matthew 3:15 KJV). *And now, if the Lamb of God, he being holy, should have need to be baptized by water, to fulfil all righteousness, O then, how much more need have we, being unholy, to be baptized, even by water!* (2 Nephi 31:5).

If any of you want to be baptized, you can request it through our website, and someone local will respond. Baptism is an ordinance between you and Christ and does not mean you are joining a formal institution, because we have no institution.

We are all equal believers accountable to God. We do try to fellowship with one another, and you would be welcome to fellowship with the few believers in this area. We own no buildings; like the early Christians, we meet in homes. We ask for tithes (or 10% of what you have left over after you've taken care of all your needs), but anything collected is then used to help anyone in the fellowship meet their needs. We hope for there to be no poor among us because we use donations to help one another.

Our numbers are small. There are a few here locally nearby, but we are worldwide. At the moment, we're composed mostly of former Mormons, and I'm really getting tired of talking to former Mormons. I would really like to talk to Baptists and to Lutherans and to Methodists —particularly if they've made Wycliffe material a matter of study—you would add so much to a discussion among fellowship groups. Mormons know a lot. But Christians know a lot about the Bible. I'd love to see a cross-fertilization of the Christian ideal, in which we can bring to you some things that we have learned about the Christian faith and, in turn, hear from you what you have to share in fellowships. We want other Christians to fellowship with us. The only thing we have to offer is Christian worship to share.

We accept the Book of Mormon but not as a book that belongs to the Mormon church or the Mormon hierarchy. We view it as a testimony of Jesus Christ. I'd invite you to read it. You don't need to go buy a copy from a Mormon. You don't need to go get one from one of us. You can go to Barnes and Noble. The copyright has expired. It is now one of the Penguin Classics. If you feel a little self-conscious about buying a Penguin Classic Book of Mormon, then get the *Adventures of Huckleberry Finn* and *War and Peace* and the Book of Mormon, and you'll look like some eclectic reader. And you needn't face the shame— the awful shame—of buying a Book of Mormon. Or you can get it on Amazon; you can do that privately.

I believe if you read the Book of Mormon and you give it a fair shot— not with the Mormon missionary, you know, coming back every few days on your door with their name tag and pressuring you, rooting for you to, "Come aboard, come aboard! We really want you within our clutches," but instead dispassionately, at your leisure, contemplating it, mulling it over to consider it carefully.

The Book of Mormon confirms that Christ was resurrected. It confirms that He had other sheep (that He mentions in the Gospel of John) to whom He said He intended to go minister. It confirms that there were scattered bodies of believers throughout the world. It confirms that Jesus Christ is the same Lord yesterday, today, and forever. It confirms that Jesus Christ is a keeper of covenants. If Christ cared enough to speak to others in times past, does He not care enough likewise to speak to us? Can He not speak in our day?

Let me read you a few lines presented as part of the very closing of the
Book of Mormon:

> *Wherefore, my beloved brethren, have miracles ceased because Christ*
> *hath ascended into heaven, and hath sat down on the right hand of*
> *God, to claim of the Father his rights of mercy which he hath upon the*
> *children of men? For he hath answered the ends of the law, and he*
> *claimeth all those who have faith in him; and they who have faith in*
> *him will cleave unto every good thing; wherefore he advocateth the*
> *cause of the children of men; and he dwelleth eternally in the heavens.*
>
> *And because he hath done this, my beloved brethren, have miracles*
> *ceased? Behold I say unto you, Nay; neither have angels ceased to*
> *minister unto the children of men. For behold, they are subject unto*
> *him, to minister according to the word of his command, showing*
> *themselves unto them of strong faith and a firm mind in every form of*
> *godliness. And the office of their ministry is to call men unto*
> *repentance, and to fulfil and to do the work of the covenants of the*
> *Father, which he hath made unto the children of men...*
>
> *And by so doing, the Lord God prepareth the way that the residue of*
> *men may have faith in Christ...*
>
> *And Christ hath said: If ye will have faith in me ye shall have power to*
> *do whatsoever thing is expedient in me. And he hath said: Repent all ye*
> *ends of the earth, and come unto me, and be baptized in my name,*
> *and have faith in me, that ye may be saved.*
>
> *And now, my beloved brethren, if this be the case that these things are*
> *true which I have spoken unto you, and God will show unto you, with*
> *power and great glory at the last day, that they are true, and if they are*
> *true has the day of miracles ceased? Or have angels ceased to appear*
> *unto the children of men? Or has he withheld the power of the Holy*
> *Ghost from them? Or will he, so long as time shall last, or the earth*
> *shall stand, or there shall be one man upon the face thereof to be saved?*
>
> *Behold I say unto you, Nay; for it is by faith that miracles are wrought;*
> *and it is by faith that angels appear and minister unto men; wherefore,*
> *if these things have ceased wo be unto the children of men, for it is*

because of unbelief, and all is vain. For no man can be saved, according to the words of Christ, save they shall have faith in his name; wherefore, if these things have ceased, then has faith ceased also; and awful is the state of man, for they are as though there had been no redemption made. (Moroni 7:27-38)

We believe we are approaching the moment at which the Lord is about to return. Read that chapter, Matthew 24. All of the signs that He speaks of will occur in one single generation. If you've not noticed, the signs have begun to appear. It means you're living within a generation in which a great deal is to occur. As it was in the days of Noah, so is it about to be. That means dreadful things are coming, on the one hand, and it means prophets are going to be among us again, people with messages that come from the Lord.

I'm not here on my own volition. I've not done anything that I've done throughout the last number of years on my own volition. I do what I do, I preach what I preach, I testify to what I testify to because, like Paul, I've been sent.

I would rather understate than overstate the case, but let me end by telling you: Christ lives. He died, and He was resurrected. I know this to be true because, like Paul, I have seen Him. I don't tell you that to make this seem sensational. I tell you that to give you cause to believe in Him. He is real.

Encountering Him as a resurrected being changed the course of history. It turned cowards into courageous, willing, and enthusiastic witnesses who faced down the Roman empire to their death. They died willingly. They died as evidence of the truth that they were testifying to. That kind of faith needs to return again to the earth. That kind of faith is possible again in our day.

Christianity has taken many turns and many different forms from the death of the apostles until now. But however you may regard yourself to be a Christian, what every one of us needs is for Heaven itself to reaffirm to us what it is that Heaven would like us, as Christians, to be and to do.

I mention that Christ gave many commandments, precepts, and teachings. He also gave a law. His law can be found in Matthew chapters 5, 6, and 7. That is how you and I should practice our Christianity.

Thank you for coming this evening. Thank you for listening. This has been streamed live over the internet. It will be available in an improved form, in which graphics are going to be inserted.

I'm going to be speaking in Dallas, Texas and then in Atlanta. All three talks will be different from one another. They're all intended to give you reason to believe in Christ, and at all three of them, I'm going to invite people to go to the website. Some people who are participants in local fellowships are here. But go to the website,[99] and if you would like to be baptized, if you would like to attend a fellowship, if you would like to meet some of these people that are essentially believers in Christ trying to practice an original and more authentic version of Christianity, and to bear with one another's burdens, and to help one another in Christian charity in an attempt that there be no poor among us, then come forward. You'll find us very welcoming. Although there are a number of believers in your area, we remain few. But we're undaunted by that, and we intend to address as many as will hear us, including this evening, by doing so on the internet so that anyone worldwide who may have an interest can tune in.

Thank you all very much for attending this evening. Let me end in the name of Jesus Christ, Amen.

---

[99] learnofchrist.org

Second Address to All Christians

J. Erik Jonsson Central Library
Dallas, Texas
October 19, 2017

No matter how interesting or uninteresting this evening proves to be, we have to vacate this place in its entirety by 8:00. And so, we'll end at 7:30 sharply, even mid-sentence, perhaps.

I hope to strengthen your belief in Christ this evening and to increase your confidence in Him as WHO and WHAT He really is. The first verse of the Bible reads: *In the beginning God created the heaven and the earth* (Genesis 1:1 KJV). When it was created, it was God's. Everything belonged to Him. Twenty-six verses later it says: *And God said, Let us make man in our image, after our likeness: and let them have dominion over...* (ibid. v.26) the creation. God, who owned the earth, gave dominion over His property to man—to the man Adam and the woman Eve.

John tells us who it was that did the creating and who it was that gave man dominion over the earth: *the Word [who] was with God...* John describes, *All things were made by him* (John 1:1-3 KJV). Christ is the light and the life of man. That's the next verse. Luke explains in the book of Acts: *...he* [meaning God] *be not far from every one of us: For in him we live, and move, and have our being...* (Acts 17:27-28 KJV).

Another prophet explained our relationship to Christ in these words:

> *That God who has created you, and has kept and preserved you...and has created you from the beginning, and is preserving you from day to day, by lending you breath, that ye may live and move and do according to your own will, and even supporting you from one moment to another...*

Ye cannot say that ye are even as much as the dust of the earth; yet ye were created of the dust of the earth; but behold, it belongeth to him who created you. (Mosiah 2:20-21,25)

We borrow from Christ the power to live and move. Christ is sustaining our lives from moment to moment. Because of this, Christ knows our every deed, even our every thought, because we use *His power* to have our being. Christ can, therefore, understand us perfectly. And at the end of all of this, Christ can, therefore, judge us perfectly, because it's not just what you do, it's why you did it—and He knows that, too, about every one of us.

Do not imagine Christ as a being who is distant from you—that's incorrect. You should envision Him as someone who is *intimate* with you.

I'm glad to return to Texas. I spent nearly two years here while I was in the military. My oldest daughter was born here in Texas, and I got a Bachelor's of Business Administration from McMurry University in Abilene. In Abilene, there were three colleges at the time, and every one of them is supported or sponsored by a religious institution. The one that I attended was sponsored by the Methodist church.

I was raised by a Baptist mother. At age 19, I joined The Church of Jesus Christ of Latter-day Saints (it's commonly called the Mormon church). After 40 years—*to the day* from the day I was baptized—I was excommunicated from the LDS Church because I wrote candidly about Mormon history and disagreed with the institution's questionable retelling of its history.

One of the things about the Bible is that the characters about whom we read are not spared. When they mess things up (committing adultery and murder, as did King David), we know about it. When errors are made and Peter denies the Lord three times before the cock crowed twice, we know about it. That's not true about Mormon history. What you get there is very sanitized and somewhat misleading—and in some places, horribly so.

If you, as a Christian, were to read what I wrote of Mormon history,[100] you would think I was a defender of the LDS Church. But because I questioned the validity of their authority claims and exposed some of their un-Christian and deplorable acts that provoked the judgments of God against them, the institution considered me an apostate. They viewed my account of history as threatening to them.

Let me be clear: I have faith in Christ and know our salvation is found **only** in Him. I also believe Joseph Smith was an authentic Christian and inspired advocate with a message from God. I do not believe the LDS Church has been faithful to the message God spoke through Joseph Smith, nor has the LDS Church told an honest account of their many failures to follow God. You do not need to join any institution— and certainly do not need to become LDS—to respect Joseph Smith or find inspiration in the Book of Mormon. I think the LDS Church is in a fallen state and growing darker year by year. But I'm not here to talk of LDS history. I mention this only so **you** can understand and know what **my** views are. We're here to reflect on Christian history and to honor the Protestant Reformation.

In 1517, Catholicism was a religious, economic, land- and military-monopoly in Europe. Market control leads to laziness, indifference to the needs of the public, and excesses. Catholicism became abusive. Cardinal Timothy Dolan, the Archbishop of New York today, commented on how the Catholic Church cannot deny it had become corrupt. Dolan said Martin Luther was responsible for the "striking of a match, creating a bonfire, the flames of which are still burning."[101]

Martin Luther[102] was not the first open critic of Catholic abuses, but he succeeded where other earlier critics were burned at the stake. Luther's timing was aided by the Gutenberg printing press, making it

---

[100] Snuffer, Denver C., Jr. *Passing the Heavenly Gift*. Salt Lake City: Mill Creek Press, 2011

[101] Adamski, Mary (2017, September 21) "The fire that Luther started." *Hawaii Catholic Herald*
http://www.hawaiicatholicherald.com/2017/09/21/mary-adamski-the-fire-that-luther-started/

[102] Martin Luther (November 10, 1483 to February 18, 1546) was a German monk who began the Protestant Reformation in the 16th century, becoming one of the most influential and controversial figures in Christian history.

possible for Martin Luther's 95 Theses to be turned into a pamphlet that turned out to be history's first bestseller. But after a millennium-and-a-half of Catholic hegemony, it was not possible for Martin Luther or the other Protestant Reformation fathers to envision Christianity as something that could exist apart from an institution.

For a millennium-and-a-half, the Christian church had a hierarchy, professional clergy, cathedrals, icons, pageantry, and provided social structure. Anything like Christianity's original, independently-functioning groups (meeting in homes and using donated resources as charity for their poor) was long forgotten. The Reformation did not attempt to restore an original Christianity. The Reformers were victims of a structure that confined even their imagination. Their aim was much lower. It sought only to reform an admittedly corrupt institution into something marginally better.

The rebellion of Martin Luther lead to the establishment of a new Christian institution that mimicked its mother. The Lutheran Church bears striking similarities to its Catholic mother. To a casual observer of a Sunday service in both of these churches, they can seem identical. The differences are not particularly cosmetic but are based on Lutheran rejection of the pope's authority.

There are three great Lutheran principals: First, grace alone; second, faith alone; third, Scriptures alone. These deprive the Catholic pope of religious significance and the Catholic rites of any claim to be the exclusive way to obtain salvation. But none of these were part of original Christianity.

As to "grace alone": In original Christianity, baptism is required for salvation. Christ's simple command to "follow me" was given repeatedly: It's recorded three times in Matthew, twice in Mark, once in Luke, and twice in John. Christ showed the way, and as part of that, He was baptized (according to His own mouth) ...*to fulfil all righteousness* (Matthew 3:15 KJV). It was only after Christ WAS baptized that the Father commended Jesus and said He was well pleased. Christ also had His disciples baptize His followers.[103]

---

[103] See John 4.

Christ spoke to Saul of Tarsus on the road to Damascus and converted Him by that contact. Following his conversion, Saul was healed of blindness, renamed Paul, and immediately baptized. Paul tied baptism to resurrection.[104] He declared that to be baptized is to *put on* Christ.[105] There is only one faith, and it is only in the one Lord whom we worship, and it requires one baptism to be included in the body of believers.[106] Peter explained that baptism saves us.[107]

Christians who follow Christ will all be baptized. If you've not been baptized or would like to be baptized again, there are those who have authority to administer the ordinance who will travel to you, or there are some locally who are available to perform the ordinance. The ordinance is free. The service is provided without any charge or expectation of any gift or donation. If you're interested, you can make a request on the website, LearnofChrist.org.

Christ taught only **one** doctrine. He taught a new law. He taught principles, precepts, parables, teachings, and commandments—but he only taught one doctrine. This is the doctrine of Christ:

> *Behold, verily, verily, I say unto you, I will declare unto you my doctrine. And this is my doctrine, and it is the doctrine which the Father hath given unto me; and I bear record of the Father, and the Father beareth record of me, and the Holy Ghost beareth record of the Father and me; and I bear record that the Father commandeth all men, everywhere, to repent and believe in me.*
>
> *And whoso believeth in me, and is baptized, the same shall be saved; and they are they who shall inherit the kingdom of God. And whoso believeth not in me, and is not baptized, shall be damned.*
>
> *Verily, verily, I say unto you, that this is my doctrine, and I bear record of it from the Father; and whoso believeth in me believeth in the Father also; and unto him will the Father bear record of me, for he will visit him with fire and with the Holy Ghost. And thus will the Father*

---

[104] See Romans 6.
[105] See Galatians 3.
[106] See Ephesians.
[107] See 1 Peter 3.

bear record of me, and the Holy Ghost will bear record unto him of the Father and me; for the Father, and I, and the Holy Ghost are one.

And again I say unto you, ye must repent, and become as a little child, and be baptized in my name, or ye can in nowise receive these things. And again I say unto you, ye must repent, and be baptized in my name, and become as a little child, or ye can in nowise inherit the kingdom of God.

Verily, verily, I say unto you, that this is my doctrine, and whoso buildeth upon this buildeth upon my rock, and the gates of hell shall not prevail against them. And whoso shall declare more or less than this, and establish it for my doctrine, the same cometh of evil, and is not built upon my rock; but he buildeth upon a sandy foundation, and the gates of hell stand open to receive such when the floods come and the winds beat upon them. (3 Nephi 11:31-40)

Accordingly, original Christianity believed and taught that baptism, not merely grace, was essential to salvation.

As to "faith alone": The original Christians not only believed in baptism, but they also believed they could progress in knowledge, obedience, and virtue. Paul denounced the idea that Christians could sin and follow God: *Shall we continue in sin, that grace may abound? God forbid. How shall we, that are dead to sin, live any longer therein?* (Romans 6:1-2 KJV). Paul envisioned the Christian as becoming a new creation through baptism, after which we walk in Christ's path with sin destroyed. *We are buried with him by baptism into death: that like as Christ was raised up from the dead by the glory of the Father, even so we also should walk in newness of life* (ibid., vs.4).

Peter taught that Christians would progress in godliness until the Christian has his or her calling and election made sure:

*..that by these [things] ye might be partakers of the **divine** nature, having **escaped** the corruption that is in the world through lust. And beside this, giving all diligence, add to your faith virtue; and to virtue knowledge; And to knowledge temperance; and to temperance patience; and to patience godliness; And to godliness brotherly kindness; and to*

*brotherly kindness charity. For if these things be in you, and abound, they make you that ye shall neither be barren nor unfruitful **in the knowledge of our Lord Jesus Christ**. But he that lacketh these things is blind, and cannot see afar off, and hath forgotten that he was purged from his old sins. Wherefore the rather, brethren, give diligence to make your calling and election sure: for if ye do these things, ye shall never fall.* (2 Peter 1:4-10 KJV, emphasis added)

As to "Scripture alone": Luther translated the Bible from a second language that was not generally spoken (that is, Latin) into the everyday language of Germany in order for the common man to read it. Given the illiteracy that had gone on for a millennium-and-a-half before Martin Luther's day and the fact that even the literate would've had to have been bilingual (because Latin had become a dead language, and they would have had to be able to read and understand that dead language), then if Scripture alone defined faith, then by definition (if that's one of the keys to defining Christianity), Martin Luther just defined the overwhelming majority (practically **all** of the Christian world) as incapable of salvation. "Scripture alone" was unavailable to them as one of the required premises of Christianity.

There was no New Testament during the era of original Christianity. The idea of compiling a New Testament originated with a second century heretic who was excommunicated for apostasy.[108] The only Scriptures used or cited during the time of original Christianity was the Old Testament, containing none of the teachings of Christ, none of the letters of Paul, Peter, James, or Jude, and none of the four Gospels. It took until the fourth century for a New Testament canon to be settled. By that time, many of the writings had been altered. Further, neither Christ nor His apostles handed out a New Testament. They testified of what they knew to be true and administered baptism as a sign of faith and repentance.

Despite this, Martin Luther was entirely correct in condemning Catholicism for its errors and excesses. Following Luther's example, other Protestant churches reformed Christianity in marginal ways. But reconsidering institutional Christianity and attempting to return to its

---

[108] Marcion of Sinope

original form was not even attempted in the Protestant Reformation. Therefore, Protestantism is only a marginal improvement from its corrupt mother-church. It has never been, nor attempted to become, original Christianity.

A return to original Christianity would require a restoration. That did not begin until God spoke to Joseph Smith in 1820,[109] but Joseph's followers also wanted an institution (and now have one of the most wealthy and self-interested institutions claiming to be a church). They are undertaking approximately a trillion-dollar real estate development as part of the Church's enterprise[110] in the state of Florida, constructing everything that will be necessary—from schools and streets, to fire stations and homes—to house over half a million people just outside of Disney World on what used to be a 133,000-acre cattle ranch. That church owns about 3% of the state of Florida.

Unlike the institutional Christianity of the 1500s, early Christians were called the *ecclesia,[111]* meaning "a congregation or an assembly." But early Christians were not institutional and certainly not hierarchical. The first century of Christianity had no formal organization and no central control. Christians met informally in small groups and worshiped together in homes or public places. In this earliest form, small groups led by both men and women who were called *deaconisse* (a word that is translated into English as either "deacon" or "deaconess"— the Greek word means "servant"), it was in these home meetings where original Christians worshiped and learned of Christ and Christianity.

Original Christians had no professional clergy. They operated in a way akin to a method described in the Book of Mormon:

> *And when the priests left their labor to impart the word of God unto the people, the people also left their labors to hear the word of God. And when the priest had imparted unto them the word of God they all returned again diligently unto their labors; and the priest, **not esteeming himself above his hearers**, for the preacher was no better*

---

109 See the Pearl of Great Price, "Joseph Smith—History."
110 (2015, October 18) "Massive Mormon ranch plan in Florida draws scrutiny." CBS News: cbsnews.com/news/massive-mormon-deseret-ranch-plan-orlando-florida/
111 or ekklesia

*than the hearer, neither was the teacher any better than the learner; and thus they were all equal, and they did all labor, every man according to his strength. And they did impart of their substance, every man according to that which he had, **to the poor**, and the needy, and the sick, and the afflicted.* (Alma 1:26-27, emphasis added)

This is how I believe Christianity ought to be practiced today, without a professional clergy diverting tithes and offerings that ought to be used to help the poor, needy, sick, and afflicted. We need to and can return to those early days of Christianity.

Justin Martyr lived from 110-165 A.D., and he wrote in the "sub-apostolic" age. His writings give us a glimpse into how Christianity functioned in its earliest days. In his *First Apology*, he describes Christian worship:

They met in homes, having no church buildings. …Before being considered a Christian, a candidate was baptized "in the name of God, the Father and the Lord of the universe, and our Savior Jesus Christ, and of the Holy Spirit." (*First Apology*, chapter LXI: Christian Baptism)

Meetings began with a prayer and "saluting one another with a kiss." Then sacrament was prepared and administered using a "cup of wine mixed with water" and bread which is blessed by "giving praise and glory to the Father of the universe, through the name of the Son and of the Holy Ghost, and offers thanks at considerable length for our being counted worthy to receive these things at His hands." (Ibid., chapter LXV: Administration of the Sacraments)

The early Christians recognized there was an obligation for "the wealthy among us [to] help the needy." Therefore, after reading Scripture and "the memoirs of the apostles or the writings of the prophets" (ibid., chapter LXVII: Weekly Worship of the Christians), donations were collected. Then the donations were distributed to help those who were poor or needy among that group of Christians.

These simple observances were resilient enough to preserve Christianity after the death of the apostles and before any great hierarchical magisterium arose. It was the power of baptism, the sacrament, Scripture study, and financial aid among believers that gave Christianity its power. But it was diffused and, therefore, incapable of destruction. When Justin Martyr was slain, the scattered Christians continued unaffected. It was just like when Peter and Paul were slain, and before them, James was killed. The power of Christianity reckoned from the vitality of its original roots. These roots were in Christ, His message, and His teachings, which were employed to relieve one another by the alms shared from rich to poor.

When a centralized hierarchy took control over Christianity, the money that was used for the poor, the widows, and the orphans was diverted to build churches, cathedrals, basilicas, and palaces. Ultimately, the wealth generated by the generosity of Christian believers became the tool used by the hierarchy to buy up armies, kings, lands, and treasures, which were used to rule and reign as a cruel master over a subjugated population made miserable by the abuse heaped on them from Rome.

Even after the Protestant Reformation, Christianity continued to be ruled by hierarchies. Cathedrals and church buildings consumed (and consume) resources that are to be used to help the poor. Christ built no building, although He accepted the temple in Jerusalem as His Father's house. Peter built no church building, nor Paul, nor James, nor John. Christianity in the hands of the Lord and His apostles needed no brick and mortar for its foundation. It was built on the hearts of believers, brought together by the charity and assistance shared between them.

Today, Christianity is not benefited—but weakened—by hierarchies, cathedrals, edifices, and basilicas housing opulence, wealth, and art. Although the prophecies foretell of a temple to God to be built in Zion and another to be built in Jerusalem, there are no other structures foretold to be built by Christians or latter-day Israel. How much stronger would Christianity be today if wealth were reserved for the poor, and hierarchies were stripped of their wealth?

We would not be under-valuing the gospel and over-valuing the churches if all donations went to aid the poor and none went to support the institutions.

We have a hard time even imagining the earliest generation of Christians. We also have a tendency to use what we're familiar with as our guide and standard in trying to understand early Christianity. It affects even how we read our Scriptures. I'd like you to try to abandon the picture that you have in your head and imagine a new picture in its place.

Early Christians were **very** diverse. There was no one in charge and no attempt to standardize Christianity. These earliest believers were divided into the following kinds of Christians:

- **Pauline Christians.** These believers were grounded in a tradition founded by the apostle Paul. They claimed to follow the Old Testament and Paul's instructions. They were located in the areas Paul served as a missionary. Paul appointed teachers who were charged with guarding the doctrine from being changed.

- **Matthean Christians.** These were followers of Matthew, centered in Antioch, who attempted to form a compromise between Jewish and non-Jewish (or Gentile) Christians. It was in Antioch that the conflicts in Jewish Christianity were worked out. You read of Matthean Christianity in the book of Acts where respect and loyalty to the Jewish temple at Jerusalem is acknowledged, but Gentile converts were welcomed.

- **Johannine Christians.** These were followers of John. These believers tried to keep an original focus on "the individual's relationship with Christ" alive. They emphasized the indwelling of Christ's spirit in each Christian. They taught and believed in the pre-Earth existence of man's spirits; before the creation, Christ was the great high priest of Heaven who would redeem the creation by His sacrifice. The strength of their teaching was focusing on the individuals' relationship with Christ and that no organization could replace that individual relationship.

The idea of the love of Christ was preserved in Johannine Christianity. Spirit, knowledge, and ritual were designed to preserve knowledge of Christ. Although lost to western Christianity, John taught that man would become divinitized (or ascend in stages of progression) **to become just like God**. His teachings have been lost, but two passages in the New Testament writings of John preserve that teaching still:

> *Behold, what manner of love the Father hath bestowed upon us, that we should be called the sons of God: therefore the world knoweth us not, because it knew him not. Beloved, now are we the sons of God, and it doth not yet appear what we shall be: but we know that, when he shall appear,* **we shall be like him**; *for we shall see him as he is. And every man that hath this hope in him purifieth himself, even as he is pure.* (1 John 3:1-3, emphasis added)

And then, in Revelation chapter 3, beginning in verse 20, it is Christ who is speaking:

> *Behold, I stand at the door, and knock: if any man hear my voice, and open the door, I will come in to him, and will sup with him, and he with me.* **To him that overcometh will I grant to sit with me in my throne,** *even as I also overcame, and am set down with my Father in his throne. He that hath an ear, let him hear what the Spirit saith unto the churches.* (Revelation 3:20-22, emphasis added)

- **Petrine Christians.** These were followers of a tradition that could be traced to Peter. These Christians emphasized authority and viewed their leaders as shepherds over exiles from Heaven. It was the Petrine tradition that lead to hierarchical control as a central feature of the later kind of Christianity that survived. Peter's original teachings evolved and changed, and Peter can't be held accountable for what occurred in a corrupted system. As it evolved, sheep—that is, believers—followed bishops, who were the successors to the apostles. These bishops were believed to hold a commission to lead the flock.

- There was also **Gnosticism** centered in Egypt. They claimed to follow John. They believed Christ and John taught hidden knowledge, and salvation was related to understanding these mysteries of God.

- There was also **Syriac Christianity**, and yet **another form of Christianity established through Thomas's teaching** in India and Asia.

Almost all knowledge of the earliest forms of Christian practices have been erased by the destruction of records. John's teaching of a pre-Earth existence for the spirit of Christ and for all mankind did not suddenly disappear. It lingered for centuries.

Origen, an early Christian,[112] claimed the original teachings of Christ included that Christ came into this world in possession of knowledge He held from before the creation of this world. Jesus had been so faithful to the *Logos*, or "word of the Father," that He was entitled to that as His name. He exemplified the word of the Father. You want to know what the Father said? Look to Christ, because everything Christ did was an example of that word of the Father. Other spirits who were less faithful—and some of whom fell away altogether—are involved also with this world.

Joseph Smith also testified that we all existed as spirits living before the creation of this world,[113] and I believe this as a teaching. Each human soul is at a different point of progression and, therefore, has different abilities to perceive the truth here.[114] Every person in the world has a distinct spiritual past that began long before the creation of this world. Salvation consists of doing what is necessary in this world to advance individual spirit progression. The greatest way to progress is to follow Christ.

Joseph Smith, like the apostle John, believed and taught that all of us existed as spirits before the creation of the world. We are spirit beings having an earthly experience. There's a veil of forgetfulness because, as physical beings, our thoughts are processed through a physical bio-mechanical connection limiting our pre-Earth memory. This limit is an important part of God's plan. If we had a perfect memory of our pre-Earth existence, we would not be required to develop faith in Christ.

---

[112] Origen of Alexandria (ca. 185 – ca. 254)
[113] See Abraham 3:22.
[114] Ibid., v.19.

But our spirits know God, and in our quiet moments, we all sense our immortality. We are here to be tested, and the test is now underway.

Early Christians were very diverse, but they agreed on two things: Christ's doctrine (which I read to you a moment ago) and Christ's law. The law of Christ is found in the Sermon on the Mount (Matthew 5-7). Once Christians have these two essential teachings in common, you **can** have differences on other issues—just like the early Christians.

Christ's apostle-witnesses, like all witnesses, testified from their own background and experience. In the courtroom, when you have witnesses testifying to some event that took place, you can have a group of people at the same place, observing the same event, and they will testify, under oath, swearing to tell the truth under penalty of perjury (they go to jail if they lie), and their stories will be markedly different from one another. That's because in this world, our orientations, our understanding, and our perceptions differ depending upon the spot we stood in at the moment we witness something.

I assume all of you think you know the difference between left and right. I was in a hospital about a week ago, going to visit a fellow who had recently had open heart surgery. And at the information desk, I'm facing her, and she's facing me, and she says to me, "You go down the hall to the right…" Umm, okay… That's your perspective. Mine is that I must go down the hall to the left. It is the opposite of what she's saying, but she's giving me the directions from the vantage point she occupies. From home plate, right field is to the batter's right. But if you're in right field, you're playing to the extreme left.

Because original Christianity was peacefully diverse, the differences found in the earliest forms are somewhat preserved in our New Testament. I got a question from the website, and I'm reading you the question that came in: "Is it possible Paul and Jesus taught two different gospel messages? There is debate such is the case. Or is it that Paul expressed the message differently than Jesus did? In other words, did Jesus elaborate more content and less terminology, justification, reconciliation, grace, et cetera, and Paul did the opposite? It seems Christ, Peter, James, John's messages were sublime and easy to understand, whereas Paul's letters are difficult to understand and require fitting the pieces together." So, let's take a look at those two witnesses.

Paul was a strict Pharisee who followed the law. Paul persecuted Jesus' followers, even assisting when Stephen was killed for his testimony of Christ.[115] He had a great many things to regret. Everything in his life before his conversion to Christ gave him a context for understanding Christ and Christ's message. Paul **wanted** grace, reconciliation, and justification because he **needed** these to have hope.

Peter was a fisherman, but he walked alongside Christ for years. He saw Christ heal the sick, heard Him bless the children, saw Him walk on water. He knew that storms were quieted by Christ's word. He saw the dead rise and stood on the Mount of Transfiguration when the Father declared Christ was His Son.

Peter was as qualified a witness as Paul to testify that Christ was the promised Messiah, but we cannot expect two witnesses with such different experiences and from such different backgrounds as Peter's and Paul's to provide us identical testimonies of Christ. Both Paul and Peter understood and explained Christianity according to their background, experiences, training, and culture. So long as they agreed on Christ's doctrine and accepted Christ's law, that was enough. They were both Christian and provided us with truth.

As the earliest forms of Christianity passed through two generations, mutual respect and acknowledgement of others' Christianity was replaced by competition and conflict. As they competed with one another, the original Christianity passed away.

There are many ironies in Christian history. Most of them are embarrassing and, therefore, not widely mentioned. (In that regard, Christian history and Mormon history share this tendency for selective recollection.) Christianity changed over the first two centuries. Change of that kind was a signal that the original had passed away. Since God is the same yesterday, today, and forever, a change to His religion suggests that God was no longer in charge. It was during this time that

---

[115] The stoning of Stephen (see Acts 6:8-8:1).

an *apostasia* (a Greek word from which we get the word "apostasy") or rebellion took place, and the foundation of Christian belief splintered.

Apostasy implies a sudden event and a deliberate rebellion. The original followers of the way taught by Christ gave way to those who wanted to have both a form of Christianity and worldly popularity. Christianity was intended to change the world, but the world changed Christianity. Christian converts of this latter time were unacquainted with the original beliefs. As groups struggled for control instead of Christian tolerance, less and less of the apostles' original teachings were retained. The debates even resulted in changing the Scriptures to support one interpretation over another. Bart Ehrman has tracked some of the changes made to what would become the New Testament texts in his book titled *The Orthodox Corruption of Scripture: The Effect of Early Christological Controversies on the Text of the New Testament*. (Interesting title: "The **Orthodox** Corruption of Scripture.")

Even the Scriptures we use today were compromised during the second and third century Christian struggles, almost following an identical pattern—which is one of the reasons why I've suggested the study of Mormonism and the history of Mormonism to Christians. Mormons have changed their Scriptures, and they've only been around 180 years. So, within a 180-year window, you can see a pattern in what has gone on in Mormonism that mirrors the research that Bart Ehrman has done in showing the orthodox corruption of Scripture.

When Christ was originally baptized, the voice that was heard from Heaven did not say, *This is my beloved Son, in whom I am well pleased* (Matthew 3:17 KJV). The **original** text says, *Thou art my Son; this day have I begotten thee*, which is a quote from Psalms 2:7.

During the second and third century debates, one of the arguments that was put forth was that Christ was just a man and not the Son of God, and He became the Son of God at His baptism when God accepted Him. None of us believe that now. We believe He is the Son of God. We've got the account in Matthew, and we've got the account in Luke. We know that He was born, and the angel Gabriel announced to Mary; we know this story, and we know His Father.

But it was being debated during the second and third century, and that verse tended to support a doctrine that was defeated as proto-orthodoxy converted into orthodoxy. They were winning the debate, and they changed the verse. However, when Paul wrote his epistle to the Hebrews, he quotes Psalms 2:7, and Paul wrote more. They just didn't get around to changing that one. (Shoot, the editors missed one!)

Over time there emerged one interpretation or faction of Christianity that became identified. It was originally proto-orthodox, and then it became orthodox as it won over time, and that became the Roman Catholic religion. "Catholic" means "universal." It means "all."

Original Christianity did not have orthodoxy or heresy; these are terms that were adopted once the proto-orthodox advocates sensed victory. They branded their view as orthodox and everything else as heretical. Once heresy was identifiable, it was suppressible—and proto-orthodoxy could persecute and suppress their competition with the confidence of sensing their complete coming victory. Those who disagreed or opposed could be excommunicated for heresy and (once they gained the confidence to do so) killed; and they were killed and their version of the Scriptures burned.

These proto-orthodox Christians decided to improve the appeal of Christianity by assuring the uneducated that there was no need to learn about Christ or His actual teaching. Men could be saved in ignorance so long as they accepted the sacraments or ordinances offered by those who had authority. Christ was displaced, and faith was replaced by allegiance to an institution. This made for lazy believers who accepted a convenient religion. Once there was a universal—or catholic—church, it owned the religion. As property of the institution, the religion was used to gain economic power and wealth, control society, and suppress anything considered a threat to its power. Even kings were subordinate to the Pontiff in Rome.

One of the most hotly-debated topics by Christians in the second and third centuries was the nature of God. That threatened open warfare in the Roman Empire once Constantine adopted Christianity as the religion of the state for the Roman Empire. He had no clue there was that much debate over the nature of God. But the views were not going to be surrendered easily.

The gospel accounts, letters of the apostles, and common-sense describe Jesus Christ as a mortal man. Jesus was carried by a pregnant woman, born after a normal period of gestation, grew through childhood into adulthood, walked, talked, ate, slept, tired, rested, suffered, bled, and died. Every action he took was human. His Father, a separate being, spoke from Heaven at Jesus' baptism—and again on the Mount of Transfiguration, where He spoke from out of a bright cloud veiling His personage from view. Nothing in the New Testament makes Christ and His Father the same personage. I want to emphasize that: **Nothing in the New Testament makes Christ and His Father the same personage.** Even His declaration that He and the Father are **one** is explained in terms that clarify they are two distinct persons:

> *Holy Father, keep through thine own name those whom thou hast given me, that they may be one, as we are...*
>
> *They are not of the world, even as I am not of the world. Sanctify them through thy truth: thy word is truth. As thou hast sent me into the world, even so have I also sent them into the world...*
>
> *Neither pray I for these alone, but for them also which shall believe on me through their word; That they **all** may be one; as thou, Father, art in me, and I in thee, that they also may be one in us: that the world may believe that thou hast sent me. And the glory which thou gavest me I have given them; **that they may be one, even as we are one**: I in them, and thou in me, that they may be made perfect in one.* (John 17:11,16-18,20-23 KJV, emphasis added)

The idea that the Father and the Son were only one in the same way mankind becomes one (or unified) by agreement and purpose was unacceptable to many of the third and fourth century Christians. The idea was regarded as polytheistic, and a tradition of monotheism—carried forward from Judaism into Christianity—made this unacceptable. The earliest Christians thought nothing was improper with the Father and Son being separate and distinct. The Old Testament begins with plural gods. I read this verse a moment ago: *Let* *us make man in **our** image* (Genesis 1:26 KJV, emphasis added). The "us" and "our" is the word Elohim, which is the plural form of the word"El: *El* being "God," *Elohim* being "Gods." Indeed, Paul contemplated a structure of Heaven that included many Lords and many Gods:

> *For though there be that are called gods, whether in heaven or in earth, (as there be gods many, and lords many,) But to us there is but one God, the Father, of whom are all things, and we in him; and one Lord Jesus Christ, by whom are all things, and we by him.* (1 Corinthians 8:5-6 KJV)

One of the disputes that was wrongly decided at the council of Nicaea (called by King Constantine to resolve Christian disputes) was the nature of God.[116] Was the Godhead (as taught by Eusebius) *homoiousios,* meaning "of a similar substance" or was God (as taught by Athanasius), instead, *homoousios,* meaning "the same identical substance" as God the Father? The counsel at Nicaea did not claim to have revelation or inspiration to answer this question. They only voted and adopted Athanasius' definition of God, giving birth to the Trinity, an orthodox teaching that has become the litmus test used ever since for determining true Christianity from heresy.

(I'm going to pause and make an aside: Original Christianity wouldn't care. If you accepted the doctrine of Christ and the law of Christ and you were baptized, you could believe in either one of these—and Paul would suggest that with time and with discussion and with fellowship, we would eventually come into the unity of faith. But the unity of faith may be a distant goal, particularly among today's Christians.)

They voted. The Trinity became the litmus test for heresy—and I believe they got it wrong at Nicaea and have been wrong ever since, because Christ taught in John 17:3, *And this is life eternal, that they might* [first] *know thee the only true God, and* [second] *Jesus Christ, whom thou hast sent.* Christ's definition of eternal life separates the Father from the Son and requires us to know both.

---

116 The Council of Nicaea took place in 325 A.D. by order of the Roman Emperor Caesar Flavius Constantine.

A new dispensation of the gospel began with Joseph Smith and continues today. There are now more revelations and more Scripture given to us by Christ. At this moment, the work of laying out and formatting all of the Scriptures—Old Testaments[117] (and the volume has the plural "Testaments" because it includes covenants made with Adam, Enoch, Noah, Abraham, and Moses—but it's what you know as the Old Testament), New Testaments[118] (again, plural because it was given first to the Jews and then taken to the Gentiles; it's a multiple covenant-making opportunity), and then a third volume called Teachings and Commandments—are being prepared for publication at present.

The Book of Mormon foretold how the Gentiles would react to new Scripture:

> *Many of the Gentiles shall say: A Bible! A Bible! We have got a Bible, and there cannot be any more Bible…*
>
> *Thou fool, that shall say: A Bible, we have got a Bible, and we need no more Bible…*
>
> *And because that I have spoken one word ye need not suppose that I cannot speak another; for my work is not yet finished; neither shall it be until the end of man, neither from that time henceforth and forever. Wherefore, because that ye have a Bible ye need not suppose that it contains all my words; neither need ye suppose that I have not caused more to be written.* (2 Nephi 29:3,6,9-10)

The new edition of Scriptures will soon be available on Amazon in an inexpensive paperback version, and a higher cost, leather-bound, onionskin print version should be available by Christmas this year.[119] They confirm that God is the same yesterday, today, and forever. The purpose of the new dispensation is to make it possible again for mankind to know both God the Father and His Son.

---

[117] The title "Old Testaments" has subsequently been changed to "The Old Covenants."

[118] "New Testaments" has likewise been changed to "The New Covenants."

[119] The Restoration Edition Scriptures are available (as a leather-bound set and in a print-on-demand paperback option) for purchase at www.scriptures.shop. They are also available online for free at www.scriptures.info.

There was a remarkable event that occurred during the last two weeks of Christ's life. And I want to read you that and then talk about it.

> *And a certain ruler asked him, saying, Good Master, what shall I do to inherit eternal life?*
>
> *And Jesus said unto him, Why callest thou me good? none is good, save one, that is, God. Thou knowest the commandments, Do not commit adultery, Do not kill, Do not steal, Do not bear false witness, Honour thy father and thy mother.*
>
> *And he said, All these have I kept from my youth up. Now when Jesus heard these things, he said unto him, Yet lackest thou one thing: sell all that thou hast, and distribute unto the poor, and thou shalt have treasure in heaven: and come, follow me.*
>
> *And when he heard this, he was very sorrowful: for he was very rich. And when Jesus saw that he was very sorrowful, he said, How hardly shall they that have riches enter into the kingdom of God!...*
>
> *Then he took unto him the twelve, and said unto them, Behold, we go up to Jerusalem, and all things that are written by the prophets concerning the Son of man shall be accomplished. For he shall be delivered unto the Gentiles, and shall be mocked, and spitefully entreated, and spitted on: And they shall scourge him, and put him to death: and the third day he shall rise again. And they understood none of these things: and this saying was hid from them, neither knew they the things which were spoken.* (Luke 18:18-24,31-34 KJV)

That incident occurred when Christ changed the trajectory of His ministry and determined to go up to Jerusalem to be killed—and He knew that's what He was doing. He invited the young man to, "dispose of your property, give it to the poor, and come and follow me."

In the Scriptures, Luke calls this fellow "a certain ruler." Matthew calls him "the young man." Mark describes him as "one who came running." John doesn't mention him at all. What if he had done as Christ invited him to do?

- He would have been with Christ during the final two weeks of His life.

- He would have seen Christ's triumphal entry into Jerusalem.

- He would have heard the crowds shout, Hosannah!

- He would have heard Christ denounce the scribes and Pharisees as hypocrites in the temple.

- He would have been there for the anointing of Christ to prepare Him for His death.

- He would have eaten dinner with Lazarus, whom Jesus had raised from the dead.

- He would have been there when the sacrament of the Lord's Supper was first introduced by Christ.

- He would have witnessed the crucifixion.

- He would have seen the resurrected Lord.

- And perhaps most importantly, **we would know His name**—because he wouldn't have been able to participate in all those events and remained unnamed in Scripture. Now, it's **possible**, had he accompanied them, that we would have another gospel—having been written by him as yet another witness of Christ's passion and resurrection. Instead, he left sorrowful because he cared for his riches.

What Christ asks of us today is no different than what Christ asked of the unnamed man who left sorrowful as he turned to head to Jerusalem. It's never convenient to follow Christ. It's never without its anxieties and its sacrifices.

There is a small group of us who believe (as we do) in an original form of Christianity. We believe in gathering tithes and donations and then using them to help people among us. We don't own any buildings, and we don't anticipate ever owning a building unless God commands that

that new temple in Zion be built by us—but that would be the only thing. We rent places like this (from people who donate to allow the rental to take place). This is being broadcast on the internet by people who have voluntarily come here, brought the resources to do it, and are broadcasting this event right now. People who came down here to prepare for this talk have paid their own way and sacrificed to do it.

The only way you can have faith is through sacrifice. You can believe a lot of things, but faith requires you to act on your belief and to act consistent with that belief, which is exactly what the young man did not do. The only reason why he came to Christ as an advisor—to ask of Him, "What can I do to inherit eternal life"—is because he had confidence that Christ could answer the question and give him the truth. He respected Christ. He believed in Him as a messenger of eternal life. But when he heard the message, he stopped short and retained whatever belief he had. He did not develop faith, because faith is acquired in one and only one way—and that is by sacrifice. I hope you do not walk away sorrowful and fail to participate in a new dispensation underway.

We're a small assembly of believers. We worship in homes. We have no buildings. And in a larger event like this, we rent the facility. Everything is done by volunteers and people that contribute. Although we're small, we are worldwide. I've come, in part, to invite you to participate with us in worshiping Christ and practicing His doctrine.

We have authority to baptize, but we're not jealous of our authority, and we'll share it with any man who accepts and practices Christianity as we do.

It may seem odd to you to consider Joseph Smith as an authentic Christian. It may seem odder still to hear me say that Mormonism has rejected Joseph, and Mormons were responsible for persecuting, rejecting, and ultimately killing him—particularly when today the LDS Church claims they have succeeded Joseph as God's vehicle for salvation. The LDS Church, like the Roman Catholic Church, has no inspiration to offer, and therefore, both rely on hollow claims to have authority. When an institution's greatest claim is in its authority, they have lost Christ's message.

Joseph Smith never finished his work. He was killed when he was 38 years old.[120] His last year of life showed he was headed in a very different direction than where the Mormon churches have now arrived. I would not make Joseph Smith responsible for what you see today in the LDS Church.

Christ came as the least, as a servant kneeling to wash feet, and as a teacher of righteousness. He invited, persuaded, and taught. He did not demand respect for His authority. He submitted to abuse, rejection, and ultimately, to being slain. He loved mankind. Those who demand that their authority be respected are anti-Christ, because they oppose the core of Christ's example. We are most Christian when we are most like Christ.

I've written a book to try and help explain Joseph Smith.[121] The title of the book is *A Man Without Doubt*. I've brought 20 copies to give away. You don't need to pay for it. No one's here to take any money for it. We don't want any money from you. But if you will read the book, it will acquaint you with Joseph Smith in a way that I think shows he is an authentic Christian. If you'd like a copy, it's yours for free. They are on the back table, and someone will show you how to get a copy.

I received some questions on the internet. There are some of you who are here and were told you can ask questions, and I want to leave a little time for that. I'm only going to answer one of the questions that came in that hasn't already been addressed in the talk. And it's an obvious question from an obvious source.

A Seventh-day Adventist inquired if I keep the Sabbath. So, that cuts right to the rub, doesn't it? The answer is: Yes, I keep the Sabbath. But let me explain to you why I keep the Sabbath as I do.

In the creation, God had a plan for six days of labor and one day of rest, and that one day of rest was to be continually observed (and it would later be memorialized in the law of Moses). But on the day of

---

[120] Joseph Smith and his brother, Hyrum Smith, were killed by a mob in Carthage, Illinois, on June 27, 1844.

[121] Snuffer, Denver C., Jr. *A Man Without Doubt*. Salt Lake City: Mill Creek Press, 2016.

rest, Adam and Eve managed to get the boot out of the Garden of Eden, and so instead of a day of rest, they were laboring. The reckoning of the week was disturbed by the fact that we lost the first one, and the calendar resulted in a day's disparity. Christ was resurrected on what was called the "first day of the week," because it was the first day of the week as it was reckoned according to the fall of Adam. But Christ's atonement was intended to **fix the fall of Adam**, to put everything back right again, to repair the damage that had been done. And therefore, when Christ was resurrected, His resurrection coming (as it was) one day late was actually just on time, and He repaired not only the damage done in the original Fall, but He repaired the Sabbath as well. Hence the observance of the day of Resurrection as the day of rest —called the first day of the week instead of the seventh because that's how time had been reckoned from the fall of Adam until the resurrection of Christ.

I observe the Sabbath as the day on which Christ was resurrected, as a symbol of his repair of the premature Fall and the loss of the **original** day of rest, going back to the time of Adam and Eve. But yes, I keep the Sabbath.

Now having said that, the original Christians would let you worship on Saturday and would let me worship on Sunday, because as long as you keep the doctrine of Christ and you accept the law of Christ, we'll figure it out together over time, and eventually one will persuade the other—not, perhaps, by argument and debate but by the quiet example that persuades the heart that there's something more to be preferred in one than in the other.

Before asking you if you have any questions, we have fourteen minutes before we have to wrap this up because we need to vacate this entire place on time, as I mentioned when we began.

Let me end by saying that I do believe in the potential for the unity of Christians coming together in one faith. I suspect that, sitting here in this room, if every one of you were asked, "Are you a Christian?" every one of you would respond, "Yes." And I suspect if I asked you to explain what denomination you were that probably every one but you would tell you what's wrong with your particular version of

Christianity. I don't think the measure of your Christianity is determined by whether or not I want to judge, condemn, dismiss, belittle, or complain about your version. The authenticity of your Christianity is reckoned in your heart and in your relationship with God—and if that's authentic and if that's sincere, how dare anyone question that! If I think I know more than you, and I have a better view of Jesus Christ and His atonement than do you, then I ought to assume the burden of persuading you. I ought to meekly tell you why you ought to have greater faith in something else. But to demand and to insist and to belittle and to complain—quite frankly, that's exactly where early Christianity wound up when Christians were killing Christians because of doctrinal disputes. What kind of nonsense is that? Let's not go there. Let's accept one another as Christians if any one of us says that they are a Christian. And then, if you think you can improve their understanding, have at it. But let's not dismiss, belittle, or discard.

LIVE AUDIENCE QUESTION AND ANSWER SESSION

Do we have a microphone for people that are going to ask questions? Oh, yeah! Does anyone want to ask a question, because we can always end eleven minutes early.

Question #1: You spoke about a sign. That's kind of cryptic, but I think you can probably recall it: when the seed of the woman was born, the Lion of Judah returns, and something about "a new star will appear," and there'll be people that are troubled. Do I get the gist of it?

Denver: Yes, you've got the gist of it.

Question #1 (continued): Can you expound on it?

Denver: Well, the answer is that I could expound. But let me give you some background about that.

For those of you who don't know what he's talking about, I have written up a description of a future event that's going to take place, that

I was inspired to write up.[122] But like what happens very often with things that are given to people by God, God tells you what to say and limits what you say about some things for purposes that He may understand a whole lot better than do we. You can read John's book of Revelation or Isaiah or Daniel or Ezekiel, and the debates about the content and the meaning of those more obscure passages are endless. And at the end of all the debate, what you wind up with is more confusion than understanding.

The way in which prophecies are handed to mankind by God is in a way that allows us (when the event takes place) to say, as Isaiah explained, "God knows the end from the beginning." Nothing's going to happen that surprises God, but the description that's given is not intended to tell us beforehand where to put our money in the stock market and when to sell, and when to get out of stocks and bonds and into real estate, or when to buy gold because it's all going to crap. The purpose is (once an event occurs) to ratify God's foreknowledge. It is to confirm to us that God knew what was going to happen.

Sometimes the way that God tells us that is by giving a specific date for an event. But if He gives you a specific date for an event, the description of the event will be such that you won't understand what the event is going to be until the date arrives. Alternatively, He can give you a reasonable description of the event but no date, and so, sometimes you wait generations—millennia—for prophecies. I mean, Isaiah lived at 725 B.C., and much of what Isaiah wrote about is happening now.

So, what I wrote was what I was told to write and confined to what was intended to be conveyed. And despite what some people may think, I try to be exact, obedient, and to take no step to the left, no step to the right, no step forward unless I receive instruction from God. The only

---

[122] "When the Seed of the Woman was born, a new star appeared in the heavens. In like manner, when the Lion of Judah returns, as with his first coming, there will be a new star seen. All the world will note its appearance and shall be troubled at its meaning. When it makes its appearance, you may know His return is soon upon the world. You may also know by that sign that He has given to me the words I have faithfully taught as His servant." Snuffer, Denver C., Jr. (2013, March 3). A Sign. www.denversnuffer.com.

reason I'm here giving this talk is because this was something God wanted to have take place.

So yes, I could tell you a lot more, but what I've written is what I was told to write, and therefore, when it happens, you'll say, "Oh yeah, God knew about that beforehand and gave a pretty good description now that I see what it involved."

Question #2: In the talk you gave in California, you referenced Matthew 24 and the signs of the last days—and that the signs have begun and that it'll all get wrapped up within one generation. Would you be able to shine more light on the vague description of "one generation"?

Denver: Ha! There've probably been as many Bible commentaries written on the definition of "generation" as…

One offered definition of generation is "while the teaching/religion/movement remains in an unaltered state." Almost invariably, however, the way a new revelation from Heaven works is that God will reveal Himself in a generation, and then when the prophet(s) of that time— the mortals living, the messengers—die, what survives cannot be kept intact. It simply cannot be kept intact. You need another Peter; you need another Paul; you need another Moses. You need another one with that standing, or it falls into immediate disrepair. So, the best definition of a generation is "while there are living oracles that are in communication with God."

But you don't "add on" to the work of a prophet. It goes downhill. From the death of Moses until the coming of John the Baptist, the only interruptions you get were when these singular men—Elijah, Isaiah, Ezekiel—came upon the scene, and their work was confined to them in that spot. You don't "improve upon" what God gives. When God gives something, it is living, and it is breathing. It is like a fire that has been lit, and it exists until the flame goes out. But when the visions of Heaven are gone because the recipient is no longer on the stage…

That's what happened with the death of Joseph Smith. Now, I use his name here, and I say that I accept him as an authentic prophet. You've probably got an image in your mind that's derived from those elders knocking on your door.[123] And that image I would hope to correct (if you take the book, and you read it). Joseph Smith was a very deep Christian thinker who confronted imprisonment because of betrayal by his own followers. He confronted the inability to convey the miraculous from himself to someone else, even though the someone else's were sincere believers. He did everything he could to try and bring them along, and they failed. Instead of saying, Woe is me, he backed up and attempted a project of educating them and bringing them along. And his writings are in the book, and an introduction is in the book. But time and time again, he was confronted by authentic Christian dilemmas just like our Savior was. I hope it's an interesting book. They are free if anyone wants to read it.

And we are out of time, so we're going to need to end. Thank you for coming. This is the second in three talks. There's a third one that will be given in Atlanta. That one, like this one, will be streamed live on the internet, so if you go to the website,[124] you'll be able to watch the Atlanta talk when it's given. All of them are being recorded, and all of them will be available to watch again afterwards.

Thank you for coming. In the name of Jesus Christ, Amen.

---

[123] Male LDS missionaries
[124] learnofchrist.org Christian Lecture #3, given in Atlanta, Georgia on November 16, 2017.

Third Address to All Christians

Atlanta-Fullerton Central Library
Atlanta, Georgia
November 16, 2017

Thank you. And thank you to everyone who has assisted in making the venue available, in organizing, recording, and ultimately broadcasting the talks. Everything that is done has been done voluntarily. No one is passing the hat or soliciting donations. Part of what we do, we do as a sacrifice to demonstrate our commitment. And everyone who has and does participate in this, sacrifices and provides their services as a matter of faith and commitment to what we believe in. And I can't thank enough those who have helped.

Religion should not divide us as it does. It's tragic that anyone's search to find truth and to connect with God should divide them from their fellow man. Christ said the greatest commandment was to love God but immediately added that the second greatest commandment was like unto it—and that commandment was to love our neighbor as ourself.[125]

Christ never taught us, "Love only those who love us in return." He taught:

> *Ye have heard that it hath been said, Thou shalt love thy neighbour, and hate thine enemy. But I say unto you, Love your enemies, bless them that curse you, do good to them that hate you, and pray for them which despitefully use you, and persecute you; That ye may be the children of your Father which is in heaven: for he maketh his sun to rise on the evil and on the good, and sendeth rain on the just and on the unjust. For if ye love them which love you, what reward have ye? do not even the publicans the same? And if ye salute your brethren only, what do ye more than others? do not even the publicans so? Be ye*

---

[125] See Matthew 22:36-39.

therefore perfect, even as your Father which is in heaven is perfect. (Matthew 5:43-48 KJV)

Let us make our search for truth one that brings us closer together rather than something to divide us apart. We share more than we disagree.

I want you to consider the meaning for us all in the account of Adam and Eve. We all have one set of original parents in common. All of the genetic potential for the entire human race comes from these two original parents. No man or woman possesses any genetic feature that did not first come from them. They set the limits on their descendants' height, they set the limit on how high their descendants could jump, how fast we could run, how intelligent we could become, how strong we could become. Every facet of us—their diverse descendants in the world at this moment—was determined by the genetic makeup of Adam and Eve. When we despise the differences we see in one another, we despise our first parents. Christ taught: *A new commandment I give unto you, That ye love one another; as I have loved you, that ye also love one another. By this shall all men know that ye are my disciples, if ye have love one to another* (John 13:34-35 KJV).

Menno Simons (who was one of the Reformation fathers after whom the Mennonites are named) said, "True evangelical faith cannot lie dormant, it clothes the naked, it feeds the hungry, it comforts the sorrowful, it shelters the destitute, it serves those that harm it, it binds up that which is wounded, it has become all things to all creatures."

Everything Christ taught is intended to change our inner self. He did not want me judging and condemning you. If you decide to abuse me, Christ teaches I should forgive you. If you offend me seventy times seven, Christ taught me to forgive.[126] If we believed in Christ enough to live as He taught, our families would heal, our communities would heal, our nations would heal, and the world would heal. Christ was an idealist, but He showed by His life that it is possible to live the ideal. As a Christian, I should commit to that ideal and, at every missed step,

---

126 See Matthew 18:21-22.

resolve to do better. Each of us controls only our own life, but your example is enough to change the lives of many others.

I hope to strengthen your belief in Jesus Christ by what is said here this evening and to encourage you to develop faith in Him. **Belief** does not require action. **Faith**, on the other hand, requires you to take action to live your belief. Far more people have belief in Christ than have faith in Him. Christ really is the Savior who offered Himself a sacrifice for sin.

Tonight we will examine what Jesus Christ did to save you and I from death and hell. To begin tonight, because this is the 500th anniversary of the Protestant Reformation, we look back on Christian history.

The Protestant Reformation was two things:

- First, it was a protest against the corruption of Roman Catholicism —hence the term "Protestant," because the protestors rejected the corrupt Roman hierarchy then in charge of western European Christianity.

- Second, it was an attempt to reform corrupted Christianity into something better—hence the term "Reformation," because the protestors hoped to recover and establish something marginally better than the institution headquartered in Rome. They hoped to reform Christianity into something better representing the actual commandments and teachings of Jesus Christ.

None of the Protestant fathers hoped to reestablish the original Christian church (or what is referred to as the "primitive church"), which once existed when Peter, James, John, Matthew, Luke, and other New Testament figures lived. When Emperor Constantine made Christianity the state religion of the Roman Empire, it did not improve Christianity; it compromised it. Christianity is best understood and practiced by the meek and the humble.

Christ came as a lowly servant, kneeling to wash the feet of others. He held no office or rank, commanded no fortune, and submitted to Jewish and Roman authorities. He was abused and rejected. His only tool was the truth. He was born in a stable and continually regarded by the leaders as unimportant. There was nothing about His position that commanded respect. When those who claimed to follow Him acquired the rank of "official Roman Empire state religion," Christianity could not have become more alienated from how Christ lived. Silk robes and gold headpieces worn by church leaders replaced the rough clothing and crown of thorns worn by Christ. This was a tragedy, not a triumph. Christianity was utterly broken. It has not been fixed, even by the Reformation.

Protestant reformer John Wesley candidly admitted the fallen condition of Christianity. He concluded that Christianity did not have the gifts of the Spirit because they were no longer really Christian at all. In Wesley's sermon, "The More Excellent Way," he explained:

> The cause of this [decline of spiritual gifts following Constantine] was not (as has been vulgarly supposed) "because there was no more occasion for them" because all the world was become Christians. This is a miserable mistake; not a twentieth part of it was then nominally Christian. The real cause was "the love of many," almost of all Christians, so called, was "waxed cold." The Christians had no more of the Spirit of Christ than the other Heathens. The Son of Man, when he came to examine his Church, could hardly "find faith upon earth." This was the real cause why the extraordinary gifts of the Holy Ghost were no longer to be found in the Christian Church—because the Christians were turned Heathens again, and had only a dead form left.

A New World Protestant leader, Roger Williams, admitted the same fallen state existed for Christianity but also envisioned the possibility for recovery of original Christianity. He conceived it would be possible for God to once again endow mankind with authority and knowledge that would allow us to have what had been lost. He wrote, "Christianity fell asleep in the bosom of Constantine, and the laps and bosoms of those Emperors who professed the name of Christ." This sober reflection led to his conviction that freedom of conscience was necessary to allow every soul to search for and accept all truth they could find. He declared, "There is no regularly constituted church of Christ on earth, nor any person qualified to administer any church ordinances; nor can there be until new apostles are sent by the Great Head of the Church for whose coming I am seeking."

I believe Christ has spent the last 500 years inspiring mankind to restore a more correct form of Christianity. He declared He would return again in glory to judge the world. But before His return, many prophecies remain to be fulfilled.

Almost the entire burden of prophecy focuses on two events: the First Coming of Christ and the Second Coming of Christ. And a great deal about the Second Coming of Christ will require that there be things that occur prior to His return in glory that will involve the Restoration and the presence of those who speak in His name with authority and have testimonies to be born. The world cannot be judged without an adequate prior warning being given. Even if the world is ignoring the message, it doesn't matter. God assumes the obligation of making clear His plans. He assumes the obligation of having the warning voice sound, and whether the world gives any heed or not, it doesn't matter. They've been warned, and they will be judged.

One of the prophecies came through Peter. He declared:

> *Repent ye therefore, and be converted, that your sins may be blotted out, when the times of refreshing shall come from the presence of the Lord; And he shall send Jesus Christ, which before was preached unto you: Whom the heaven must receive until the times of restitution of all things, which God hath spoken by the mouth of all his holy prophets since the world began.* (Acts 3:19-21 KJV)

The time of refreshing (or restoring) promised to come from the presence of the Lord has in fact begun. Jesus Christ has been sent again to prepare for His return. I believe that Joseph Smith was an authentic messenger called by Christ to help **us** become more Christian.

One message sent by Christ in 1829 explains more of what He (Christ) accomplished as the sacrificial Lamb who atoned for our sins. We know from Isaiah that *with his stripes we are healed* (Isaiah 53:5 KJV). God laid on Him the iniquity of us all. He bore our griefs, carried our sorrows, and the chastisement we earned was put upon Him.[127] Traditionally, Christians have understood that to have been

---

[127] See Isaiah 53:4-6.

accomplished in the Roman beating, scourging, and crucifixion of Christ. However, many men suffered similarly at the hands of Rome. Christ suffered to remove our sins and repair the fall of mankind. Isaiah's description suggests that this was cosmic and that Christ took the entire burden of mankind's sins upon Himself. Only Luke gives a glimpse into Christ's suffering in Gethsemane. Luke describes it in these words: *And being in an agony he prayed more earnestly: and his sweat was as it were great drops of blood falling down to the ground* (Luke 22:44 KJV).

In an 1829 revelation, Christ explained the price He paid for our salvation. His reflection on that suffering mentions **only** what happened to Him in Gethsemane, the place where Luke recorded He sweat great drops of blood. Let me read to you what Jesus Christ explained of that event in 1829.[128]

> *Therefore I command you to repent—repent, lest I smite you by the rod of my mouth, and by my wrath, and by my anger, and your sufferings be sore—how sore you know not, how exquisite you know not, yea, how hard to bear you know not.*
>
> *For behold, I, God, have suffered these things for all, that they might not suffer if they would repent; But if they would not repent they must suffer even as I; Which suffering caused myself, even God, the greatest of all, to tremble because of pain, and to bleed at every pore, and to suffer both body and spirit—and would that I might not drink the bitter cup, and shrink—Nevertheless, glory be to the Father, and I partook and finished my preparations unto the children of men.*
>
> *Wherefore, I command you again to repent, lest I humble you with my almighty power; and that you confess your sins, lest you suffer these punishments of which I have spoken.* (D&C 19:15-20)

Christ pleads with us in this revelation to repent of our sins so we do not experience anything like the dreadful price He paid for us. We

---

128 Revelation given through Joseph Smith at Manchester, New York, likely in the summer of 1829. In his history, the Prophet introduces it as "a commandment of God and not of man, to Martin Harris, given by him who is Eternal."

should let that message penetrate our hearts: God does not want us punished. God wants to relieve us from the bitterness of our sins.

In His kindness and mercy, Christ revealed yet more of His suffering in His atoning sacrifice in February of 2005 and December of 2007. Again, He provided us with a description of what happened in Gethsemane. This is the account:

> I knew a man in Christ about four years ago who, being overshadowed by the Spirit on the 26th of February, 2005, had the Lord appear to him again. And the Lord spoke to him face to face in plain humility, as one man speaks to another, calling him by name. As they spoke the Lord put forth His hand and touched the eyes of the man and said, "Look!" The man had opened before him a view of the Lord kneeling in prayer. It was in a dark place. The air was heavy and overcast with sorrow. The man beheld the Lord praying in Gethsemane on the night of His betrayal and before His crucifixion.
>
> All the Lord had previously done in His mortal ministry by healing the sick, raising the dead, giving sight to the blind, restoring hearing to the deaf, curing the leper and ministering relief to others as He taught was but a prelude to what the Lord was now to do on this dark, oppressive night.
>
> As the Lord knelt in prayer, His vicarious suffering began. He was overcome by pain and anguish. He felt within Him, not just the pains of sin, but also the illnesses men suffer as a result of the Fall and their foolish and evil choices. The suffering was long and the challenge difficult. The Lord suffered the afflictions. He was healed from the sickness. He overcame the pains, and patiently bore the infirmities until, finally, He returned to peace of mind and strength of body. It took an act of will and hope for Him to overcome the affliction which had been poured upon Him. He overcame the separation caused by these afflictions and reconciled with His Father. He was at peace with all mankind.
>
> He thought His sufferings were over, but to His astonishment another wave overcame Him. This one was much greater than the

first. The Lord, who had been kneeling, fell forward onto His hands at the impact of the pain that was part of the greater, second wave.

This second wave was so much greater than the first that it seemed to entirely overcome the Lord. The Lord was now stricken with physical injuries as well as spiritual affliction. As He suffered anew, His flesh was torn which He healed using the power of the charity within Him. The Lord had such life within Him, such power and virtue within Him, that although He suffered in His flesh, these injuries healed and His flesh restored. His suffering was both body and spirit, and there was anguish of thought, feeling and soul.

The Lord overcame this second wave of suffering, and again found peace of mind and strength of body; and His heart filled with love despite what He had suffered. Indeed, it was charity or love that allowed Him to overcome. He was at peace with His Father, and with all mankind, but it required another, still greater act of will and charity than the first for Him to do so.

Again, the Lord thought His suffering was over. He stayed on His hands and knees for a moment to collect Himself when another wave of torment burst upon Him. This wave struck Him with such force He fell forward upon His face. He was afflicted by this greater wave. He was then healed only to then be afflicted again as the waves of torment overflowed. Wave after wave poured out upon Him, with only moments between them. The Lord's suffering progressed from a lesser to a greater portion of affliction; for as one would be overcome by Him, the next, greater affliction would then be poured out. Each wave of suffering was only preparation for the next, greater wave. The pains of mortality, disease, injury and infirmity, together with the sufferings of sin, transgressions, guilt of mind, and unease of soul, the horrors of recognition of the evils men had inflicted upon others, were all poured out upon Him, with confusion and perplexity multiplied upon Him.

He longed for it to be over, and thought it would end long before it finally ended. With each wave He thought it would be the last but then another came upon Him, and then yet another. The one beholding this scene was pained by what he saw, and begged for the vision of the Lord's suffering to end. He could not bear to see his Lord suffering in this manner. The petition was denied and the vision did not end, for the Lord required him to witness it.

The man saw that the Lord pleaded again with the Father that "this cup may pass" from Him. But the Lord was determined to suffer the Father's will and not His own. Therefore, a final wave came upon Him with such violence as to cut Him at every pore. It seemed for a moment that He was torn apart, and that blood came out of every pore. The Lord writhed in pain upon the ground as this...final torment was poured upon Him.

All virtue was taken from Him. All the great life force in Him was stricken and afflicted. All the light turned to darkness. He was humbled, drained and left with nothing. It is not possible for a man to bear such pains and live, but with nothing more than will, hope in His Father, and charity toward all men, He emerged from the final wave of torment, knowing He had suffered all this for His Father and His brethren. By His hope and great charity, trusting in the Father, the Lord returned from this dark abyss and found grace again, His heart being filled with love toward the Father and all men.

These great burdens were born by the Lord not only on behalf of mankind, but also as a necessary prelude to His death upon a Roman cross. Had He not been so physically weakened by these sufferings and drained of power from within, the scourging and crucifixion He suffered at the hands of men could not have taken His life.

It was many hours after this vision closed before the one who witnessed this suffering could compose himself again. He wept because of the vision shown him, and he wondered at the Lord's great suffering for mankind.

The witness reflected for many days upon this scene of the Lord's great suffering. He read many times the account of the Lord's agony given to Joseph Smith, which reads, "Therefore I command you to repent—repent, lest I smite you by the rod of my mouth, and by my wrath, and by my anger, and your sufferings be sore— how sore you know not, how exquisite you know not, yea, how hard to bear you know not. For behold, I, God, have suffered these things for all, that they might not suffer if they would repent; But if they would not repent they must suffer even as I; Which suffering caused myself, even God, the greatest of all, to tremble because of pain, and to bleed at every pore, and to suffer both body and spirit —and would that I might not drink the bitter cup, and shrink— Nevertheless, glory be to the Father, and I partook and finished my preparations unto the children of men" (D&C 19:15-19). He pondered and asked: Why were there waves of torment? Why did they increase in difficulty? How were they organized as they seemed to fit a pattern?

After long inquiring into the things which he had seen, the Lord, who is patient and merciful and willing to instruct those who call upon Him, again appeared to the man on the 20th of December, 2007. He made known unto him that the waves of torment suffered by the Lord came in pairs which mirrored each other. The first of each wave poured upon the Lord those feelings, regrets, recriminations and pains felt by those who injured their fellow man. Then followed a second wave, which mirrored the first, but imposed the pains suffered by the victims of the acts committed by those in the first wave. Instead of the pains of those who inflict hurt or harm, it was now the anger, bitterness and resentments felt by those who suffered these wrongs.

From each wave of suffering, whether as the one afflicting or as the victim of those wrongs, the Lord would overcome the evil feelings associated with these wrongs, and find His heart again filled with peace. This was why, in the vision of the suffering of the Lord, it was in the second waves that there appeared oftentimes to be injuries to His body.

The greater difficulty in these paired waves of torment was always overcoming the suffering of the victim. With these waves the Lord learned to overcome the victims' resentments, to forgive, and to heal both body and spirit. This was more difficult than overcoming the struggles arising from the one who committed the evil. This is because the one doing evil knows he has done wrong and feels a natural regret when he sees himself aright. The victim, however, always feels it is their right to hold resentment, to judge their persecutor, and to withhold peace and love for their fellow men. The Lord was required to overcome both so that He could succor both.

In the pairing of the waves, the first torment was of the mind and spirit, and the second was torment of mind, spirit and body.

The Lord experienced all the horror and regret wicked men feel for their crimes when they finally see the truth. He experienced the suffering of their victims whose righteous anger and natural resentment and disappointment must also be shed, and forgiveness given, in order for them to find peace. He overcame them all. He descended below them all. He comprehends it all. And He knows how to bring peace to them all. He knows how to love others whether they are the one who has given offense or the one who is a victim of the offense.

In the final wave, the most brutal, most evil, most heinous sins men inflict upon one another were felt by Him as a victim of the worst men can do. He knew how it felt to wrongly suffer death. He knew what it was like to be a mother holding a child in her arms as they are both killed by those who delight in their suffering. He knew how it was for ambitious men to rid themselves of a rival by conspiracy and murder. He knew what it was to have virtue robbed from the innocent. He knew betrayal, treachery, and abuse in all its worst degrading horror. There was no cruelty, no offense, no evil that mankind has suffered or will suffer that was not put upon Him.

He knew what it is like for men to satisfy their ambition by clothing their hypocrisy in religious garb. He also felt what it was like to be the victim of religious oppression by those who pretend to practice virtue while oppressing others. He knew the hearts of those who would kill Him. Before confronting their condemnation of Him in the flesh, He suffered their torment of mind when they recognized He was the Lord, and then found peace for what they would do by rejecting Him. In this extremity there was madness itself as He mirrored the evil which would destroy Him, and learned how to come to peace with the Father after killing the Son of God, and to love all those involved without restraint and without pretense even before they did these terrible deeds. His suffering, therefore, encompassed all that has happened, all that did happen, and all that would happen in the future.

As a result of what the Lord suffered, there is no condition physical, spiritual or mental that He does not fully understand. He knows how to teach, comfort, succor and direct any who come to Him seeking forgiveness and peace. This is why the prophet wrote: "by his knowledge shall my righteous servant justify many; for he shall bear their iniquities" (Isaiah 53:11). And again, "Surely he hath borne our griefs, and carried our sorrows: yet we did esteem him stricken, smitten of God, and afflicted. But he was wounded for our transgressions, he was bruised for our iniquities: the chastisement of our peace was upon him; and with his stripes we are healed" (Id. v. 4-5). He obtained this knowledge by the things he suffered. He suffered that we might avoid sin by being obedient to His commandments. None of us need harm another, if we will follow Him. He knows fully the consequences of sin. He teaches His followers how to avoid sin.

The prophet Alma taught and understood our Lord's sufferings as he wrote, "And he shall go forth, suffering pains and afflictions and temptations of every kind; and this that the word might be fulfilled which saith he will take upon him the pains and the sicknesses of his people. And he will take upon him death, that he may loose the bands of death which bind his people; and he will take upon him their infirmities, that his bowels may be filled with mercy, according to the flesh, that he may know according to the flesh how to succor his people according to their infirmities" (Alma 7:11-12).

He can bring peace to any soul. He can help those who will come to Him love their fellow man. He alone is the Perfect Teacher because He alone has the knowledge each of us lack to return to being whole and at peace with the God and Father of us all after our transgression of His will. He is wise to what is required for each man's salvation.

As the Lord made these terrible things known to the man he cried out: "Hosanna to the Lamb of God! He has trodden the winepress alone! Glory, honor and mercy be upon the Chosen One forever and ever! I will submit unto anything you see fit to require of me! I will bend my knee in obedience to you! Let thy will, not mine be done! For worthy is the Lamb!" Then, thinking upon how trifling his difficulties and disappointments had been in comparison with the suffering he saw imposed upon his Lord, the man added: "Surely goodness and mercy have been mine all the days of my life!"

And the Lord responded: "And you shall dwell in the house of the Lord forever."

Then the man wept.[129]

From the forgoing accounts, Christ has finally made it clear to us that His death on the cross was not where He paid the price for our sins. Many have died in that same way and suffered that same dreadful agony. But Christ alone paid for mankind's sins because He alone was able to take on the terrible burden of our terrible failures. He conquered sin.

And so, what of the cross? He certainly needed to die, because without dying, He could not rise from the dead and conquer death.

In Matthew we have an account of something Christ declared as He hung on the cross: *Now from the sixth hour there was darkness over all the land unto the ninth hour. And about the ninth hour Jesus cried with a loud voice, saying, Eli, Eli, lama sabachthani? that is to say, My God, my God, why hast thou forsaken me?* (Matthew 27:45-46 KJV). This is misunderstood. Christ was not forsaken by God. He predicted in John, before His death, that the Father would never leave His side. Christ

---

[129] Snuffer, Denver C., Jr. *Come, Let Us Adore Him.* (Salt Lake City: Mill Creek Press, 2009), pp. 216-224

was reciting the opening lines of a hymn about Himself. The psalms were hymns. If I were to say, for example, "Silent night, holy night," in your mind, you could go to that hymn. If I were to say, "A mighty fortress is our God," your mind would go to that hymn. On the cross, Christ was taking the minds of those who were present to a hymn about Himself. Let me read some of that hymn:

My God, my God, why hast thou forsaken me? why art thou so far from helping me, and from the words of my roaring? O my God, I cry in the daytime, but thou hearest not; and in the night season, and am not silent. But thou art holy, O thou that inhabitest the praises of Israel. Our fathers trusted in thee: they trusted, and thou didst deliver them. They cried unto thee, and were delivered: they trusted in thee, and were not confounded. But I am a worm, and no man; a reproach of men, and despised of the people. All they that see me laugh me to scorn: they shoot out the lip, they shake the head, saying, He trusted on the Lord that he would deliver him: let him deliver him, seeing he delighted in him. But thou art he that took me out of the womb: thou didst make me hope when I was upon my mother's breasts. I was cast upon thee from the womb: thou art my God from my mother's belly. Be not far from me; for trouble is near; for there is none to help. Many bulls have compassed me....

They gaped upon me with their mouths, as a ravening and a roaring lion. I am poured out like water, and all my bones are out of joint: my heart is like wax; it is melted in the midst of my bowels. My strength is dried up like a potsherd; and my tongue cleaveth to my jaws; and thou hast brought me into the dust of death. For dogs have compassed me: the assembly of the wicked have inclosed me: they pierced my hands and my feet. I may tell all my bones: they look and stare upon me. They part my garments among them, and cast lots upon my vesture. But be not thou far from me, O Lord: O my strength, haste thee to help me....

I will declare thy name unto my brethren: in the midst of the congregation will I praise thee. Ye that fear the Lord, praise him; all ye the seed of Jacob, glorify him; and fear him, all ye the seed of Israel. For he hath not despised nor abhorred the affliction of the afflicted; neither hath he hid his face from him; but when he cried unto him, he heard. My praise shall be of thee in the great congregation....

All the ends of the world shall remember and turn unto the Lord: and all the kindreds of the nations shall worship before thee. For the kingdom is the Lord's: and he is the governor among the nations. All they that go down to the dust shall bow before him: and none can keep alive his own soul. A seed shall serve him; it shall be accounted to the Lord for a generation. They shall come, and shall declare his righteousness unto a people that shall be born, that he hath done this. (Psalms 22:1-31 KJV)

That was the hymn to which Christ pointed while on the cross. He started, *My God, my God, why hast thou forsaken me?* This was not a lamentation; this was a declaration that for this purpose, He came into the world, and for this purpose, He would die. Christ suffered for our sins in Gethsemane. Christ died on the cross while testifying He was the promised Messiah. Christ rose from the dead to break the bonds of death. Since He was entitled to live forever, His death was an infinite price to pay. Therefore, the demands of justice have all been met—and that, infinitely. We can benefit from that by accepting the ransom He has paid, repenting, and being baptized. Here is His doctrine:

Behold, verily, verily, I say unto you, I will declare unto you my doctrine. And this is my doctrine, and it is the doctrine which the Father hath given unto me; and I bear record of the Father, and the Father beareth record of me, and the Holy Ghost beareth record of the Father and me; and I bear record that the Father commandeth all men, everywhere, to repent and believe in me. And whoso believeth in me, and is baptized, the same shall be saved; and they are they who shall inherit the kingdom of God. And whoso believeth not in me, and is not baptized, shall be damned.

Verily, verily, I say unto you, that this is my doctrine, and I bear record of it from the Father; and whoso believeth in me believeth in the Father also; and unto him will the Father bear record of me, for he will visit him with fire and with the Holy Ghost. And thus will the Father bear record of me, and the Holy Ghost will bear record unto him of the Father and me; for the Father, and I, and the Holy Ghost are one. And again I say unto you, ye must repent, and become as a little child, and be baptized in my name, or ye can in nowise receive these things. And again I say unto you, ye must repent, and be baptized in my name, and become as a little child, or ye can in nowise inherit the kingdom of God.

Verily, verily, I say unto you, that this is my doctrine, and whoso buildeth upon this buildeth upon my rock, and the gates of hell shall not prevail against them. And whoso shall declare more or less than this, and establish it for my doctrine, the same cometh of evil, and is not built upon my rock; but he buildeth upon a sandy foundation, and the gates of hell stand open to receive such when the floods come and the winds beat upon them. (3 Nephi 11:31-40)

If you've not been baptized or if you would like to be re-baptized, there are people who have authority to do so who will do so without charge, without requesting or expecting a donation; indeed, they'd refuse it if you offered it. There is a baptism that has been arranged (for anyone who is interested) tomorrow, and you can find out details about that from people here after this ends.

Well, I got a number of questions sent in through the website that I'm going to take a few minutes to answer, and then we're going to invite anyone who is here that has a question to use the microphone (because this is being recorded, and the microphone can only pick it up if you use that in the recording), and we'll answer questions.

Question #1: One that was sent in was, "What drove Luther to create his own version of the Bible?"

Well, at the time that Luther did a translation of the Bible, the only version that was available was written in a language that most people did not commonly speak. He translated the Bible into the common tongue. (The first time the Bible got translated into English, for example, was only about 470 years ago. We take for granted that people can get access to a Bible that you can read and you can understand in your own language.) But one of the most important things that Martin Luther did—and one of the things that made the Reformation itself assume a durable form that would last past the generation of the Reform fathers—was translating the Bible into the common tongue so that people could read it in their own language, in language they would understand. That "let the genie out of the bottle," so to speak. You were no longer dependent upon someone else who could read a foreign tongue to read the text (that was written in a language you didn't understand) and tell you that they were speaking for God.

Now you could get access to the text yourself, and you could compare what you were seeing in the clergy with what was written in the biblical text. And the gap between what you saw in the biblical text and what you were seeing in the clergy was so enormous that immediately (upon access to the Bible), you began to have the same reaction that the Reformation fathers had to Catholicism. As the Bible has been made available in more and more of the vernacular tongue, what's happened is that Christianity has divided and redivided and redivided again because now anyone has access to the text.

As we stand here today, there is no official registry that we can go to that says how many different kinds of Christian churches there are. But it is estimated that there are at least 40,000 different Christian churches in existence today. You know, the apostle Paul wrote in one of his letters about the hope he had for seeing us all come into the unity of faith.[130] It seems like the more access that we have gained to biblical understanding, the more disagreements we've managed to have with one another—which is one of the reasons for the things I said at the very beginning of this talk.

We should not let our individual search for truth become a breeding ground for resentments, disagreements, and conflict between one another. If you have found some great truth that you can articulate and persuade me also to accept, then I should welcome you in doing that. And if I have some truth that I can present and persuade you to accept, then we're both benefited. But if you and I read these things and study these things and have our own religious experience, and if we accept Christ as a Redeemer, as a Savior, as the Son of God, and as what He said He was, then why can't we rejoice together in that fact? Because it is greater than any of the petty disagreements that divide us.

---

[130] See Ephesians 4:12-13.

Christianity needs to take a very sober assessment of itself and decide there is no room for venom in the Christian heart; there is no room for conflict. Celebrate what unites us. And as for the petty disagreements? Well, if you're from Jersey, you just "fo' get about it."

Question #2: "Did the Catholic Church ask Luther to retract all 95 Theses?"

No. Well, the purpose of the 95 Theses was to demonstrate the corruption of the sale of indulgences that was going on in order to finance St. Peter's Basilica in Rome. The papal signature on the indulgences was given to franchise holders, and then the franchise holders could go around and fill in the name on the indulgence (with the papal seal on it) and sell that to someone for money; and the guy who was selling it (the franchise holder) got to keep part of the money, and part of the money went back to Rome. It's like owning a McDonald's franchise. You get to keep part of the money, but you've still got to pay some for the franchise holder. They were financing the construction of St. Peter's Basilica by this process of selling.

There were a couple of the 95 Theses (if I can find those real quick) that I really like a lot—number 45 and number 87. I could summarize them, but I'd rather read them. Well, number 87, for example: Martin Luther was saying that anyone with common sense can think of reasons to doubt the practice of selling indulgences. For example, if the pope really can get people out of purgatory and end their suffering by a papal decree, why would he not just do that because it's a nice thing to do? Why do you have to pay him to do something that's good?

The entire burden of the 95 Theses does not question the primacy of the pope or the position of the pope. It says that the primacy and position need to be exercised under the constraint of what the Scriptures say. And if the pope violates the Scriptures, then the pope is wrong. He does not possess independent authority to do stuff. You don't get to be God. You have to submit to God, even if you're the pope. So, they didn't condemn them all, but the burden of it was offensive.

Question #3: In that first talk that I gave in Los Angeles, someone listening to that was concerned because I referred…

Jesus Christ's most extensive prophecy is in the 24th chapter of Matthew, where His disciples were asking Him about the future. And among other things, they wanted to know about the signs of the times when He's going to come. And Christ answers them, and well, you can read the 24th chapter. There's a lot of really tragic, ugly things that will go on before His coming, but it has a happy ending. He's coming, and when He comes, He's going to fix everything that's wrong with the world (primarily by destroying the wicked by the brightness of His glory—but if you're not wicked, that's still good news).

Question #4: So, this question comes in, and it says: "You addressed this in your lectures. Let's say, for argument's sake, I believed you. What can or should a university student do? I can't drop out, because I would immediately have to pay back student loans. Do I just keep attending school and trust that everything works out? Or let's say I'm in high school—would you recommend young people even go to college? Should young people who want to be lawyers just quash their dreams because everything is going to hell? That's my general problem with gloom and doom prophecy, it stagnates individual growth and development. People isolate themselves from the rest of the world, spend a bunch of money on guns and emergency supplies, and generally waste their lives living in fear. Is there a balanced approach to watching out for that dastardly thief in the night?"

I would say, "Finish high school." I would say, "Go to law school." And, I mean, one of the first things on the agenda that Christ will destroy (it's not the lawyers) is the bankers (…and the insurance companies; they're all evil). But your student loans won't need to be repaid because there will be nothing left of the institutions who hope to collect on them. You don't live your life in contemplation of the fearful return of the Lord. You live your life in a grateful celebration for everything God has done and given to us.

As I was flying here, we were taking off just as the first rays of the sun were creeping up in the east, and there was this brilliant scarlet ribbon on the horizon. And my wife pointed it out to me. (I was sitting in an aisle; the only thing I get to see is the cart they bring you treats with.) As I looked across at the sunrise, it was spectacular.

Where I live in Utah, we have this Wasatch Front. These are jagged granite cliffs that go upward. The top of one of the ski resorts is 11,000 feet. We live at about 4,000 feet. When the sun sets (as you are in the valley), you see the sun go down in the west. But in the east, on the mountains, you see the sunlight creep up and creep up and creep up the mountain until finally just the very top peaks remain with light. Because of the refraction of the atmosphere, as the light goes up the mountain in its nightly retreat, it tends to shift to blue and to purple. And it's particularly spectacular when there's snow up there because the hues of the sunlight refraction become very colorful up there.

Now, I happen to like impressionist art, and my favorite impressionist is Monet. We have a couple of Monets. I mean, they're forgeries; they were given to me as a fee; we didn't pay for them. But they are actual Monet paintings, right down to the brush strokes being reproduced, and they're beautiful.

Every night as the sun sets, God does something on the mountains that is never the same, always beautiful, and greater in beauty and splendor than anything Monet ever put on canvas.

We ought to love life, and we ought to love one another, and we ought to pursue our education. And we shouldn't bunker down with guns and ammo, fearfully waiting for a direful end to things. Of all people, Christians should have the most hope, the most optimism, the most vitality, and the greatest amount of joy in life. We ought to celebrate every day.

Question #5: Oh, here's a good one: "Having studied evolutionary biology in college, I came to appreciate the vast amounts of evidence for this scientific theory." (Well, pause there. Read *Darwin's Black Box*.) "Recent anthropological data (Gobekli Tepe) is pushing the origins of civilization far beyond 4000 B.C. It is an increasingly tenuous position to accept a strictly literal interpretation of Genesis in regards to creation and chronology, especially among the younger millennial generation I am a part of. Having also had a few mystical experiences that led me to accept Jesus as Lord, I feel somewhat torn. Whatever I do, it seems like I am rejecting truth. Whether I consider ignoring physical scientific evidence or effectively dismissing parts of the Bible, both are not satisfying solutions to me. Is there a way to make secular data fit into the Christians metaphysics?"

Yes, there is. I'm going to go ahead and answer this fellow, for what it's worth.

The problem with biblical literalism is not necessarily that what is in the Bible is untrue, but it may be that what is in the Bible is speaking using a vernacular that mankind is unacquainted with. For example, the work of the creation is referred to generally as "a day." There is no reason to believe that calling it a day—in the language that gets employed in Scripture—has reference to anything other than a discreet event. It would be more accurate to say that there were labors that were performed during the incremental progression of the creation—which took however long—and when the labor was completed, then that labor was called "a day." There is nothing to suggest that the labor of the first day was exactly the same amount of time as the labor of the second day, nor is there anything to suggest that the labor of the third day was equal in time to either the first or the second, and so on.

However many eons of time were required in order for God—through the process that we see in nature—to form the earth was the first day. However long it took—through seismic and volcanic and other activities—to cause the dry land to appear was labor that took however long it took.

The earth is moving in two ways. It is circling the sun on a tilt. Twice a year, that tilt aligns so that we have an equinox—which means that there's exactly twelve hours of sunlight and twelve hours of darkness on that one day, twice a year. And then there are solstices—when (in the north) the days are the longest because it's leaning towards the sun; and when it gets to the other side, it's leaning away, and at that moment, the nights are very long because (in the north) you're leaning away from the sun.

As it makes this movement in one direction, it's also wobbling at the poles. The earth is not perfectly stable in how its axis fits. It wobbles. It takes 25,900 years (roughly) for it to complete one wobble at the pole. In the ancient vernacular—because of that wobble—we have a pole star. It happens, at this moment, to be Polaris, but if you go back several thousand years, we have a different pole star. That pole star changes.

We also have, around the circumference, a group of constellations that everyone on Earth can see. It doesn't matter if you're in the south; it doesn't matter if you're in the north ("south" being below the equator, not Atlanta; or the "north"—not meaning Canada; it means everything, the northern hemisphere and the south). There are a group of constellations everyone can see. There are twelve of them. All twelve of them had a story behind them in the beginning. All twelve of them have symbols that represent Christ. (That's for another day.)

When the pole star changes—which happens about seven times every 25,900 years—that change anciently was called a "new Heaven." Likewise, there is a different constellation that appears at sunrise on the vernal equinox, and that constellation tells you what "age" you're in. Star fields overlap, and sometimes there are gaps.

Christ said, I will make you fishers of men,[131] and the constellation that age was identified with is **Pisces**: two fish. One fish caught in the net is endlessly circling the equator; but another fish—and it's much smaller—this other fish is headed to the north where you will find God.

That constellation is going to be replaced by the one who is coming—we call him **Aquarius**. We also call him the Waterman. He is "pouring out" a new age that will come. If you go back far enough, what he is pouring out is two streams: One stream is water, which gives life, and one stream is fire. He who is coming in the great day of the Lord is coming for the great (the water) and dreadful (the fire) day of the Lord[132]—to pour something out.

---

131 See Matthew 4:19.
132 See Joel 2:11.

Well, it just so happens that the star fields of these two overlap. If you date the return of the Lord by the star field of Aquarius at its earliest star, then the first sign of the "times of refreshing" would have been about in the 1840s, when Joseph Smith was saying that Christ appeared to him and gave him a message to preach. We have not yet fully exited the star field of Pisces.

Now, all of that is to make this comment: When there's a new pole star, that's called a "new Heaven." When there's a new constellation on the horizon at the vernal equinox, that's called a "new Earth." There will be a new Heaven, and there will be a new Earth when Christ returns. And all of these are given, as Christ said in Genesis 1:14, *for signs and for seasons*, and everything testifies of Him.

So, there's a lot of scientific proof, but there's a lot of material in the Bible that is simply misunderstood. This earth is pretty old, and how long it existed before it was considered sufficiently complete for man to occupy it is not to be measured in days; it's to be measured in epochs of time referred to generically as a day—meaning a period, meaning an agenda.

Question #6: "If Christ never had buildings, then what is His church, and how do you know if you're a part of it?"

Christ and the apostles and the earliest Christians met in homes. They talked on hillsides, and they met in places that were convenient, but they didn't build buildings. The prophecies predict that in the last days, there are going to be only two buildings that matter to God. One of them will be a temple rebuilt in Jerusalem, and the other will be a temple built in the tops of the mountains in a place called Zion. And these two places will be the center of activity.

Question #7: Now, this is an answer to a question, but I'm not gonna read the question because I didn't print it out. The Eastern Orthodox and Catholic Church split at approximately 1000 A.D. (it's about 1054). Martin Luther was generally positive towards the Eastern Orthodox Church. He and they both rejected celibate clergy, both rejected the pope's supremacy, both rejected purgatory, both rejected indulgences. Martin Luther claimed the Orthodox or Greek Church was proof of Catholic deviation. Luther did not personally attempt to build a bridge to orthodoxy, but some of his followers did do so.

———————

Now, I wanted to finish my comments by reading you a few quotes from some of the Protestant leaders. A husband and wife team (William and Catherine Booth) founded The Salvation Army, and I want to read you a comment of William Booth's. William Booth cautioned us about the trends he saw in both society and religion. Here's his quote:

> I consider that the chief dangers which confront the coming century will be religion without the Holy Ghost; Christianity without Christ; forgiveness without repentance; salvation without regeneration; politics without God; and Heaven without Hell.

C.S. Lewis may be one of the most influential Christian apologists that have appeared on the scene. Let me read you a few things from C.S. Lewis.

> Each day we are becoming a creature of splendid glory or one of unthinkable horror.[133]

> There are only two kinds of people: those who say to God, "Thy will be done," and those to whom God says, "All right, then, have it your way.[134]

C.S. Lewis was the one that said, "No man knows how bad he is 'til he has tried very hard to be good."[135]

And I really like this comment: "Of all the bad men, religious bad men are the worst."[136]

---

[133] C.S. Lewis, *Mere Christianity*
[134] C.S. Lewis, *The Great Divorce*
[135] C.S. Lewis, *Mere Christianity*
[136] C.S. Lewis, *Reflections on the Psalms*

He also made this proposition: "Christianity, if false, is of no importance and, if true, is of infinite importance. The one thing it cannot be is moderately important."[137]

Dwight Moody (after whom the Moody Bible Institute was named—although when he founded it, it had a different name) said,

> Christians should live in the world, but not be filled with it. A ship lives in the water; but if the water gets into the ship, she goes to the bottom. So Christians may live in the world; but if the world gets into them, they sink.

He made this observation: "Moses spent forty years thinking he was somebody; forty years learning he was nobody; and forty years discovering what God can do with a nobody."

He said, "Out of 100 men, one will read the Bible, the other 99 will read the Christian," hence your obligation. "The world does not understand theology or dogma, but it understands love and sympathy."

And then this, and I'll end with this. (And then if any of you have something you'd like me to comment on, I'd be glad to.)

There's a great difference between recognizing the signs of the times and knowing the detail of how prophecy will be fulfilled. An example of the difference is found in Matthew. Matthew 2:1-18 tells of wise men who studied the Scriptures, watched the signs in the heavens, recognized a star that testified of the birth of the Messiah or newborn King of the Jews, traveled a great distance (perhaps as long as two years) to worship Him, fulfilled prophecy by their presence in Jerusalem, and were visited by God in a dream. You know the story.

They came, and when they got to Jerusalem, they asked Herod, *Where is he that is born the King of the Jews?* (Matthew 2:2 KJV), which caused Herod to say, "Get in here and tell me about this," and his advisors said, *Bethlehem...not the least...out of [these] shall come a Governor*

---

[137] C.S. Lewis, *God In The Dock*

(ibid. v.6). So, he sends the wise men to Bethlehem and says, "Hey, when you find him, you return to me, and you tell me so that I can go (wink wink, nod nod) worship him, too." And of course, they were warned by God not to go back and tell Herod. And when Herod found out that he was not going to be advised to make this job easy, he sent soldiers to kill all the kids two years old and younger. In the meantime, Joseph and Mary were departed into Egypt.

Despite all the wise men were able to know, they did not know where to find the newborn King. They mistakenly went to Herod's people to inquire about Christ's birth. They did not know—and God did not reveal to them—that Christ would be born in Bethlehem. It's unlikely they would have willingly acted to fulfill the Jeremiah 31:15 prophecy of the slaughter of the children, yet Matthew credits their involvement with fulfilling this prophecy.

So ask yourself, can men unwittingly fulfill prophecy? Can anyone—even wise men who are well-studied in Scripture and prophecy and acquainted with the heavens and the stars and the signs up there—ever fully understand prophecy?

One of the lessons from the scriptural account is that all wise men whose diligence and faithfulness lead them to understand God's hand is at work may still not understand how or where God will act. There remain mysteries which God will accomplish but men cannot understand beforehand. If the wise men knew He had been born but could not identify where Christ's birth happened (despite all else they were able to do), then how can anyone know how God will accomplish His strange act in the last days? This is what the Lord has said:

> *What I have said unto you must needs be, that all men may be left without excuse; That wise men and rulers may hear and know that which they have never considered; That I may proceed to bring to pass my act, my strange act, and perform my work, my strange work, that men may discern between the righteous and the wicked, saith your God.* (D&C 101:93-95)

Prophecies are not given to know **details** beforehand; they're given so that they, **once fulfilled**, **PROVE** that God knew the end from the beginning. I'm here as a witness to tell you: God is working. There are signs in the heavens above, there are signs on the earth below that testify that He intends to come again. Don't interrupt your life because you want to buy guns and ammo and go live underground somewhere. There's a U2 song, "You've been living underground, eating from a can, Talking about things you can't understand."[138] Don't be like Reba McEntire and her husband in *Tremors* when they slayed the beast with the elephant gun and said, "You broke into the wrong damn rec-room."[139] Be like Christ, hopeful and helpful and positive. He went about doing good. That's who we're supposed to follow, and that's what we're supposed to do. That's how we're supposed to live. Be hopeful; be helpful.

The story of Adam and Eve that I mentioned at the beginning makes every single one of us descendants of a common set of parents. I keep thinking about these "23andMe" genetic ads that say, "Figure out who you are and where you reckon from." They've gathered genetic databases in order to try and segregate us into regions and into groups. But at the end of the day, they just don't go back far enough. Because if they went back far enough, everyone's genetic makeup would be half Adam and half Eve, and well, you wouldn't spend $49 to learn that. But if you want to spend $49 to learn that truth, then donate some money to the poor and the homeless instead of sending it in elsewhere.

Let me end by bearing testimony to you that I didn't come here because I thought it was a good idea; I came here because the Lord asked me to. This is the third location I've been in to accomplish what He's asked me to do after telling me the things that I ought to say and the subjects that ought to be covered.

I hope you realize that God is real, and that He is as concerned about you and your day and in your life as He was concerned about Peter or Paul or John or Mary or Elizabeth or Abraham or Sarah. Every one of you matter to Him. And if He were to speak to you out of Heaven today, He would call you by name, just as He has done with everyone to whom He's ever spoken. And if the Lord calls you by name, it's not

---

138 U2. "Mysterious Ways." Achtung Baby. 1991
139 *Tremors*. Dir. Ron Underwood. Perf. Kevin Bacon, Fred Ward, Finn Carter, Michael Gross, Reba McEntire. Universal Pictures, 1990.

going to be by your full legal name; it's not going to be by what's on your birth certificate. He will call you by that name your best friend knows you—because God is intimate with every one of us. He knows everything, including the desires of your heart. And even though we are all rough customers, the fact is, the only reason you're here is because your heart is inclined to follow Him. Your aspirations, your desires, and your hopes can be perfect—and your conduct can be reprehensible. God takes into account the perfection of your hope, and He evaluates you based upon your most noble aspirations. And He's cheering you on, trying to get you to move a little closer throughout your life to that ideal/that perfection that you would like to have. We get hungry, we get tired, we get ill, we get weak—and so, we excuse ourselves. But through it all, we can maintain the aspiration, the hope, the love of Christ. If you do that, He will take that into account as He deals with you.

In the name of Jesus Christ, Amen.

LIVE AUDIENCE QUESTION AND ANSWER SESSION

Question #1: The Scriptures talk one day about a day where we're all filled of the spirit, and some call it a day of Pentecost. Is there another day like that to come?

Denver: Yeah. Yes! (That was an easy question.) You're talking about the generality of mankind. The gifts of the spirit are intended to flourish in the hearts of those who seek the Lord. There are ways of having that develop in individual lives. But to have a community in which that happens... Consider for a moment all of the ills and illnesses, pathologies, and defects of any community that you live in.

Within Jerusalem at the time of Pentecost, there were a group of believers who had so fully dedicated themselves to the Lord that they had, at that point, all things in common. They were living as a society in a way in which they had consecrated themselves, not only to God but to one another, so that they were all equal with one another. There were two people (a husband and wife) who in that community had lied about what they had done. They had sold property, and they had kept back part. In essence, they were trying to live a law that one would live with Christ dwelling among them. But this married couple conspired, lied, and then broke any number of the ten commandments—bore false witness, they coveted, they stole—and when confronted, they were judged, and the wages of what they did resulted in both of them dying.[140] In essence, they committed to live on a level in which sin of that sort, that base of misconduct, is not permitted.

The general outpouring into a community is going to happen with a community of people who are willing to abide by those kinds of terms. You can accomplish it in an individual life, but we don't have a society that is sufficiently healed. We have the last days' society—identified generically by the name Babylon the Great Whore—which is the society in which you live. The Great Whore does not abide the conditions for that outpouring, but you (as a Christian soul) can and should; and therefore, if you do that, you're entitled to that outpouring in your life.

But make no mistake about it: If you sign up genuinely and sincerely to follow the Lord, what you're going to encounter is the hostility, the anger, even the rage of this world because this world is not interested in surrendering to Christ's control. That's why when He comes, He's going to judge the world. In the meantime, Christians—sincere Christians, devout ones who will obey Him—are going to encounter a necessary opposition. The challenge is to not let it overwhelm you. And I'd encourage every one of you in your faith to press on and to stay committed. Christ is real, and He paid a terrible price, and He did that so that you would not have to pay a price. He suffered *for* you. But He expects that we have not merely belief in Him, but faith in Him, and that we *act* consistent with our belief. Thank you.

Question #2: I also have a question for a friend. Do you believe Joseph Smith came reincarnated?

Denver: No, I don't believe that anyone comes back here to live a second mortal experience in this creation. I do think that when the Scriptures use the phrase *worlds without end*, that the work of God is

---

[140] See Acts 5:1-11.

infinite in scope and reach and that God's redemptive work is—in each individual case—adapted to the development of the individual, until they grow and are fashioned and are developed to the appropriate godly stature that we become like our Lord.

Christ went, and He preached to the spirits in prison—meaning that when He died and He went into the place where the dead are, He continued His ministry. Peter writes about that. Well, the continuation of a ministry among the dead suggests that when you die, there's still work to be done—at least preaching to be done. And if you read real carefully some of the content about the things that occurred before the world and the things that will occur at the end of the thousand years of peace when Lucifer/Satan is released, the very, very beginning of what went on before the world was created and the very, very end (when Satan is loosed from the pit after a thousand years of peace) look an awful lot alike. But that's a subject beyond the challenges and the problems of this mortal life and what we today confront and are faced with.

There's a lot of stuff in the far distance that isn't relevant for the challenges we face now. In fact, we were just looking at that phrase *worlds without end*, which is how it's rendered. The original language (if you take it literally) means, "As you look out at the horizon, it's something past your ability to see; it's beyond the end of the world, as *you* see it," meaning that what comes after we finish our sojourn here will be trouble for another day, because sufficient is the evil of this day for the purposes God has in mind for us and our challenges here.

And I know there are people who believe that you do come back, and I know there are people who think that they're Peter or David or Solomon or Isaiah—but I've met too many Peters to believe all of them, and there's a whole lot of Mary Magdalenes and Marthas. So, I don't put any stock in that.

Question #3: What advice would you give to other intellectuals (or even an analytical person) that would struggle with seeking for those answers or those truths that they desire to know, and they're struggling with finding those truths and not allowing those things to drive a wedge in the faith that they put in Christ?

Denver: Yeah, I believe that there is tension, if not outright hostility, between charity as a priority, on one hand, and knowledge as priority, on the other hand—and that as between the two, it is more important to acquire the capacity for charity or love of your fellow man than it is to gain understanding. It's like what Paul said—if I have all gifts and know all mysteries but have not charity, I am nothing.[141] Charity—or the love of your fellow man—is the greater challenge and the more relevant one; and when you've acquired that, you can add to it knowledge. But knowledge has the ability to render the possessor arrogant and haughty, whereas charity renders the possessor humble. If you want the greatest challenge in life, try loving your fellow man unconditionally and viewing them as God would view them—and then behaving according to that view. And out of that you will learn a great deal more about Christ than you can simply by studying. Walking in His path is a greater revelation of who He is than anything else that's provided.

Joseph Smith once remarked that, "If you could gaze into heaven for five minutes, you would know more about it than if you read every book that has ever been written on the subject."[142] Likewise, if you live charitably for five minutes in the presence of what you would normally condemn or what you would normally find repugnant, and if you can deal with that charitably, you will understand Christ better than if you spend a lifetime reading books written about Him.

Well, we need to let these fellows wrap up and close their stuff out. Thank you for coming. Thank you for the attention you've paid. And thank all of you who have helped, participated, and sacrificed in order to make this event and the others before this possible. Thank you all.

---

[141] See 1 Corinthians 13:1-3.
[142] *The Prophet Joseph Smith*, p. 324; cf. *History of the Church*, 6:50-51

FOURTH ADDRESS TO ALL CHRISTIANS

Recorded in Sandy, UT
September 7, 2018

The following five lectures were delivered subsequent to the first three talks included above, which were planned and delivered in California, Texas, and Georgia. They build upon the themes initially presented in those first three talks.

I think for an understanding of Christianity, you have to go back to the condition of Israel at the time of the birth of the Savior. Christ was introduced into an environment in which the whole of Judaism had been transformed by events that took place between ~600 B.C. and the time that the Lord was born.

Judaism divided at the time of Solomon's death into a Northern and a Southern Kingdom. The Northern Kingdom was taken away captive into Assyria, and they ultimately never returned (they're the lost ten tribes of Israel). And while there is some reference to them departing out of Assyria as an organized group being led by prophets, they did not return to the area of Palestine. They turned instead and went north (into the North countries), and we lost record of them. There are prophecies about their return, but history and their accounting for themselves is absent from the record.

It was some time later that the Southern Kingdom (which identified itself as either the "Southern Kingdom" or the "kingdom of Judah," or still later, they identified themselves as the Jews—but some of the anachronistic statements in the Bible identify them as Jews earlier than when they were self-identifying as that) also got taken captive, dispossessed, and moved into the foreign power of Babylon. It was while they were in Babylon that Judaism underwent a fairly significant revisioning.

Up until the time of the Babylonian captivity, they had (from the time of Moses until that moment) either a tabernacle in which they could practice their formalized religion or the temple that had been built by Solomon. In Babylon, they were dispossessed of their homeland, their sacred sites, their temple, and their functioning religion. And so, the first dispossession from their land—or their "first diaspora," their first separation from their holy land—in Babylon was a prelude and a practice to try and figure out how to make Judaism portable. In the Babylonian experience, you have a kind of portability to their faith that allowed it to survive dispossession of land, dispossession of sacred sites, dispossession of the temple, and a non-functioning Aaronic and Levitical Priesthood—it was literally non-functioning. When they returned again, they had to resort to genealogical study and Urim and Thummim in order to declare who could be a priest, because the priestly functions had lapsed into decay, disuse, and forgetfulness. And during that time, because of the Babylonian society, the religion took on a kind of Babylonian intellectualism that led in turn to Rabbinical Judaism in a way that Judaism had not existed before that moment.

When they returned, it was the time of Ezra and Nehemiah and the reconstruction of the temple. There is reason to believe (and I won't go into the details at this moment) that when they reconstructed the temple upon the return from Babylon that what they built was not a reflection of what had been there previously—that 70 years of captivity in Babylon was long enough that the people with the kind of continuity of knowledge/familiarity/understanding were gone, and so you get a reconstruction.

At the time that they were taken captive *into* Babylon, there was a lot of tension inside Judaism as reformers were trying to make the faith fit a model that was becoming popular among other competing religions and peoples; those reformers have been given the nickname of Deuteronomists by the scholars. The tension between the competing viewpoints had not been resolved at the time of the Babylonian captivity. They left with a fight going on and then had to reconstruct the religion in order to make it portable and fit into a new culture. When they returned, it appears that the people who reconstructed the temple and who re-established Judaism included people who had been persuaded by the Deuteronomists in the pre-exile. And so, the reconstruction of the religion that took place—including the books that were purportedly discovered (when the ruins of the temple were being rummaged through in order to reconstruct the temple site) by Ezra that were used to rebuild the Old Testament that had been lost— was rather more influenced by the Deuteronomists as the prevailing party in the argument than Judaism had been at the time of the Babylonian captivity. It's a whole bunch of historical events that together create a different look, feel, and flavor to Judaism even after its return.

In the prophecy that you have of Daniel interpreting and explaining Nebuchadnezzar dream, you have the head of gold, you have the shoulders of silver, you have the arms, and so on through the body, down to the feet of miry clay and iron—which is our day. Daniel declares that the head of gold is Babylon; it's the kingdom in which the Jews were being held captive at the moment of that prophecy. So, why the head of gold will persist all the way down to the time when there's clay and iron in the feet that will need also to be ground into dust by the "stone cut out of the mountain without hands" should perplex people—because Babylon fell, and Babylon's been gone and off the pages of history beginning sometime shortly after the Jews returned and rebuilt their temple in their holy land. So, when the Jews returned, they returned knowing that there was this head of gold that not only followed them, but would follow all religion; it would follow all society; it would and does follow all culture on into the last days.

Well, there's a series of kingdoms that came through between the time of the return to the holy land and the time in which Christ was born— because the Medes and Persians, the Greeks, and then the Romans were all part of that vision of Daniel, and all of them came through and swayed Israel, held influence, and brought culture, attitudes, viewpoints, and understanding. They brought government. They brought a variety of invasive ways of thinking that cumulatively had an effect on the landscape at the time of the birth of the Lord.

We have a statement in Luke that tells us when Christ was born: *And it came to pass in those days, that there went out a decree from Caesar Augustus, that all the world should be taxed. (And this taxing was first made when Cyrenius was governor of Syria)* (Luke 2:1-2 KJV). Cyrenius was a Roman puppet appointed by Rome, and Caesar Augustus was Octavius; he took the name of Caesar after he was the unquestioned head of the Roman empire, having defeated Mark Antony. So, you've got the dating in the record of the Savior and the birth of the Savior based upon what's going on in Rome. This is the legs of iron.

So, there is a stone to be cut out of the mountains that is going to grind to dust all of the components of the cultural, governmental, and economic influences that were foreseen by the king and interpreted by Daniel, going all the way back to Babylon. And Christ arrived in the middle of those pernicious, corrupting, social influences in the remnant of Israel/in Palestine with a reconstructed temple (this one built using Herod's family's money and influence) and under the Roman Empire's economic, social, governmental, and cultural influence. That was the society He came into in order to discharge His mission and ministry.

When you put the entry of Christ into the full sweep of both history and prophecy, you should not expect the Savior to establish the Kingdom of God on Earth that is intended, at some future point, to destroy all of those influences. He's going to leave all of those things intact. The Savior is going to come. He's going to minister. He's going to accomplish His mission. He's going to die. He's going to be resurrected. And the great image is going to continue happily on its way, developing down through the channels of history with all of those influences unimpeded, unimpaired, uninterrupted by the coming and going of the Savior.

Now, arguably, it was because of the presence of the Savior that some of those later anatomical developments occurred with the legs/the feet/the clay/the iron as the influence of Christ's ministry took over. And ultimately, the desire to separate church and state came about, the desire to have religious freedom came about, the desire to create a benign environment in which it's possible for people to worship according to the dictates of their own heart came about—because Christianity itself became a rather malignant force in the wake of the Savior coming and going.

But that gets ahead of where we are in the story. We're going to look at the time of the coming of Christ—because Christians tend to read Christianity as if it sprung into existence with Christ's birth, and it came fully formed, fully functioning, and fully capable of accomplishing the very thing that the culmination of the ages was intended to achieve. Christ didn't do that. It wasn't time yet for that to happen. In the "Lord's Prayer," He prays about a future kingdom: *Thy kingdom come. Thy will be done [on] earth, as it is in heaven* (Matthew 6:9-10 KJV) is a petition prayer begging the Father that the time will eventually come when that event will take place.

The stone cut out of the mountain without hands did not happen in Christ's time, and He knew it didn't happen. It didn't happen, but He prayed for that eventuality. And He said, "This is one of the things that when you pray (if I'm going to teach you how to pray) that you ought to be praying for. You ought to be asking that at some point this future kingdom will come about, so that God's will can be done on Earth like it is being done in Heaven." Because on Earth, we're down here in this cultural, social, legal, and religious environment that is heavily influenced by the head of gold and all of the cultures that succeeded one another in dominating the world.

Christ enters onto the scene inside a milieu that is corrupt; it is disconnected significantly from the pre-Babylonian religion of Israel. It holds very little content that reckons pre-Moses. It has hardly any connection to Abraham and the beliefs of Abraham, Isaac, and Jacob. And the "nation" includes only two of the twelve tribes—and for that, it includes only that remnant that returned from the Babylonian exile back to Palestine to reoccupy the land after they had been dis-possessed.

So, He's talking to a tiny remnant of what once was a great people, and it now primarily consists of the tribes of Judah and Benjamin (in the Southern Kingdom) who were willing to come back from Babylon. The ten tribes were scattered; much of those tribes were left behind. And in this Southern Kingdom, you probably had onesies and twosies of the other tribes (represented through marriage) that had stayed within the Southern Kingdom. But primarily, the blood of Israel is gone—and the religion that Abraham, Isaac, Jacob, and their family had was radically altered, revised, and poorly preserved. Abraham himself was trying to restore an even earlier version of the religion that went back to the first fathers.

When Christ came to minister and to serve and to sacrifice in Israel, He was dealing inside a very corrupt environment:

- He set up Peter, James, and John as three who were significantly isolated and elevated from the other members of the twelve (for such things as the Mount of Transfiguration—where they were taken up on the mount, and they saw Moses, they heard the Father, they experienced the events on the top of the Mount of Transfiguration).

- There were the twelve who were called to be a group that were ordained and sent out as messengers.

- And there were seventy who were called as missionaries to also go out.

If you go back historically and you say, "What is the 'type' that Christ is organizing as the way in which He's going to plant a seed for the religion that He's trying to get people to recognize? What is the model that Christ employed?" you would say:

- Peter, James, and John were an echo, an homage, and a remembrance of Abraham, Isaac, and Jacob.

- The quorum of the twelve that He organized and He sent out as messengers were a remembrance and an honor to the twelve sons of Jacob and the twelve tribes of Israel.

- And the seventy represented the seventy souls who went into Egypt at the time that the rest of the family joined Joseph and the brothers there.

What Christ was doing was reestablishing a kind of restoration of the family of Israel in a model that was pointing back to an earlier time before Babylon, an earlier time when there was a different religion on the earth, an earlier time—at the time between Abraham and the twelve sons of Jacob or Israel—when Judaism had not been influenced by Babylon, the Medes and Persians, the Greeks, and the Romans.

Much of the New Testament was actually written in Greek. If you don't think that the influence of Alexander the Great—in going through and conquering first in Persia, then second in Syria, and then next in Egypt (and they made Alexander a Pharaoh in Egypt)—wasn't persistent in the land at the time of Christ, then you're oblivious to the fact that the New Testament was written in Greek because Greek was a predominant language.

So, when Christ began His planting, He was actually a restorer of an earlier religion. Instead of this being something altogether revolutionary and new, Christ was a restorer. He was an antiquarian. He was bringing back something which once had been. He was trying to get people to understand.

See, the religion that Moses was trying to restore was originally significantly greater than the one that he wound up restoring—because the people were unwilling to accept the earlier versions. So those things were broken, destroyed, discarded, and a new innovation was established through Moses, the great lawgiver, who gave a law of lesser performances, observances, and rites in order to point forward to something else that would be coming—so that maybe when that something else came, it could explain to them what the law was intended to have them observe.

The paschal lamb (where the blood on the lintel of the doorpost saves you from the destroying angel) is a type of Christ because Christ's blood will save you from destruction. The rites involving the shedding of blood in the courtyard of either the tabernacle or later the temple were designed to be a propitiation, a form of paying the debt for sin. The wages of sin are death. Therefore, it's necessary that death be demonstrated through the sacrifice of animals in order to have your mind pointed forward to some great sacrifice whose effect will be saving you from sin. In the courtyard of either the tabernacle or the temple, when they sacrificed animals and they spilled their blood by cutting the neck and letting the blood flow out, blood got all over the ground—it got tracked; it got splashed; it got upon you. Prophets use this analogy of blood and sins, blood on your garments, and shaking the blood off of your garments as an analogy that's based upon the effect of performing the law of Moses—which itself is intended to point you to Christ.

Christ demonstrated, by His teachings and actions, that He fully understood *that* was what was happening and *that* was who He was and what His role was. Christ knelt to wash the feet of the disciples because one of the things that washing feet in that culture accomplished was cleansing the blood off the feet. It was tracked everywhere when you got near the courtyards of the temple and showed that they were accountable for sin. Christ was removing from them the guilt that the blood was intended to exhibit.

All of the sacrifices were intended to show that there was some great and final and last sacrifice that was intended to be offered. And Christ was that. The law of Moses pointed to a fellow; Jesus was that fellow. He came along to fulfill that.

Now, the people at the time predominantly rejected the idea that He was that great sacrifice. In fact, at the moment that the Savior was being tortured on the cross and in His last moments, He was mocked, ridiculed, and invited to come down off the cross and save Himself so that they would believe. But had Christ succumbed to the temptation to come down off the cross so they would believe, the effect of their belief would have been rendered null. It would have been made void because it was necessary for the shedding of that blood. He had to die in order for Him to complete the journey, the circuit, the atonement, the propitiation for sin, the actual sacrifice to which everything else pointed,. And therefore, Christ had to die. He had to remain on the cross, and He had to die. And the temptation to come down and do something demonstratively miraculous so that they could believe was an invitation to destroy the very object in which they were saying they wanted to have belief. He had to die, and He did.

But unlike all those who had entered the grave from the time of Adam until that moment, Jesus Christ did not have sin and error that kept Him in the grave. Death could have no hold on Him because the wages of *sin* is death, and Christ had not committed the kinds of things that can hold you in the grave. Anyone who can get through this experience without succumbing to the sins of this world is equally entitled to come forth out of the grave, because death can have no hold upon you. And so, the Savior came back out of the grave.

Once the Savior forfeited life in order to suffer death while in a state that did not require Him to die, His death became unjust. What was taken from Him was eternal; it was everlasting. If He should never have died because He led a life that did not justify death, then His death was, by definition, an infinite and an eternal loss, and His death compensated fully the law of justice that requires death. He died, literally, for all mankind. His death represents an eternal and an infinite sacrifice—which was the very point that the law of Moses was intended to point to because the people were unwilling to receive a restoration of the earlier religion.

Christ came and sacrificed and fulfilled the law of Moses. People didn't necessarily accept or believe that the mission of the Savior was designed to achieve and did achieve the things that He was sent to achieve. And so God, using those legs of iron, achieved the end of the law of Moses **externally** with the siege of Jerusalem and the destruction of the temple so that, as Christ said, Not one stone shall be left upon the other.[143] The observances of the law of Moses ended in about 70 A.D. when they destroyed the temple at Jerusalem, and the organized practice of the law of Moses inside a sanctuary or a temple set up for that purpose ended a second time. And that time it ended from that moment until today. It's gone. It has not been returned.

When Christ's missionaries—His messengers—went out to proselytize and bring people aboard the religion, people believed and taught Christianity (for the most part) as if it were the culmination of all things Jewish—the crowning jewel achievement of everything that was intended to be achieved in religion. Christianity was *it*. And yet, Jesus pointed forward to some future, still-greater event in which everything that had been around at the beginning would be fully restored; a time when there would be a refreshing or a restitution; a time when that

---

[143] See Matthew 24:2.

kingdom He prayed "would come so that God's will could be done on Earth like it's done in Heaven" would come to pass.

Christ spent some time prophesying about what the signs would be that would be immediately preceding His return. And while He talked about some more immediate prophecies about the destruction of Jerusalem and about the coming loss of the temple, the greater part of what He explained in that chapter of Matthew is about one single generation that would live at the time when He would return in glory. The prophets have pointed forward to that future event repeatedly. Prophets that existed in the Northern Kingdom spoke about it. Prophets (whose records we actually have preserved) in the Southern Kingdom also have spoken about it. And the prophecy that Daniel interpreted in the dream of Nebuchadnezzar points to it, in which something will happen—likened to a stone being cut out of a mountain—which will roll down and grow and fill the earth and grind into pieces this false religious/economic/cultural construct that still prevails on the earth today.

And so, Christ made an initial effort at restoring something that was far more ancient and that has yet to be fully achieved. Christians and Christianity fail to contextualize either Christ or His teachings when they look at Christianity as if it were an end in itself. It was a step in a process. And the ministry of the Savior was essential to the salvation of all mankind.

But God's work? God's work has not yet been fully revealed. And God's religion has never been fully restored.

Fifth Address to All Christians

Recorded in Sandy, UT
September 7, 2018

When we have the history of the Jews—with the loss of the Northern Kingdom and the ten tribes (the lost ten tribes of Israel) and then the captivity of the Southern Kingdom (or the Babylonian captivity of the Jews)—there's an intermediate event that occurs between the moment that you lose the Northern Kingdom and the moment that the Southern Kingdom gets taken captive. And that was an event in which another "planting" of Israel took place by the out-migration of a small group that were in the Southern Kingdom. They had been warned by God to flee before the destruction of Jerusalem by Babylon. That record or account is contained in the Book of Mormon.

The Book of Mormon details the history of people who left the land around Jerusalem and took with them some records in order to preserve their religion. They migrated across the Arabian Peninsula and settled into a place where they were commanded to build a ship. They built a ship and began to migrate. The route that they took appears, from the record, to go down the eastern edge of the continent of Africa, around the cape at the bottom of Africa where there was a terrific storm (coincidentally, a terrific storm at the very moment when things were getting out of hand inside the family, and there was a rebellion of sorts going on), and they returned to peaceful navigating after that. They appeared to come up the western edge of Africa and then across the English Channel, Iceland, Greenland, and the northern Canadian shore, and then down somewhere into the Americas where they settled. And this "planting" then practiced their religion in a new land in which they were **never** exposed to the head of gold. They were **never** exposed to the influence of the Medes and Persians, the Greeks, or the Romans.

They preserved their civilization for a period of about a thousand years. And over the course of that thousand years, they not only practiced the earlier, more ancient form of the religion that they had, they also qualified to have their own prophets come teach and preach. They had their own instructions, revelations, and connections with God. And ultimately, they were visited by Christ who came to minister to them as one of the scattered branches of the house of Israel.

We should be looking for the fulfillment of the prophecy about "a stone cut out of the mountain without hands" that will succeed in defeating the head of gold (Babylon) and all the other cultural influences that came about thereafter. And one of the chief candidates that every Christian should be curious about investigating is a record that is preserved in the Book of Mormon that is independent of and uninfluenced by the head of gold, the shoulders, the belly of brass, and the legs of iron. It is uninfluenced by any of that because it sprang into existence separate from those influences and was never taken captive, overrun, or imposed upon culturally, religiously, economically, or governmentally by any of them. They simply had no influence.

One of the big criticisms of the Book of Mormon by people who have taken the time to look at it is that there is too much Christology in the Book of Mormon for it to be an authentic 600 B.C. reflection of what the Jews believed. What you are accepting when you make that statement is the idea that the correct barometer/measuring stick to use should be the traditions that got handed down from those who **were** influenced by the head of gold—the Babylonians, the Medes, the Greeks, the Romans. You're saying that's your correct measuring stick, instead of saying: Let's flip that, and let's apply the measuring stick that has been handed to us from the source that purports to be free of those influences, and let's see if the Book of Mormon can't give us a more accurate gauge from which to measure all these things.

There was a Christian radio preacher who styled himself the "Bible Answer Man," Dr. Walter Martin. (I listen to a lot of radio preachers even when I disagree with them, because they entertain me. And one of those I'm entertained by today is Joel Olsteen. And there's a Catholic program on the Catholic channel on SiriusXM that gives some interesting stuff.) Dr. Walter Martin, the Bible Answer Man, used to use this slogan in almost every other broadcast: "It is the first principle of Biblical Hermeneutics that you interpret the old in light of the new" —meaning that when you encounter in the New Testament an interpretation of a prophecy that came in the Old Testament, you don't go to the Old Testament to decide whether or not that prophecy fit the events in the New Testament. You reverse that, and you say: What does the New Testament tell us that the Old Testament means? And the Old Testament means whatever it is that the New Testament says it means. You always arrive at your biblical interpretation by using the new to tell you what the old meant—which is another way of saying that prophecy is so obscure that it requires it to be fulfilled in order for you to understand what it was all about. When it is fulfilled, then the evidence of what was in the mind of God and the prophet when it first got composed is apparent, but it's not apparent until the events happen. This is why all of the people trying to date and foretell all of the events are always surprised—because they missed something. They're advising Herod when the wise men show up and say: "Now, where's the king that was born?"[144] And they're shocked there was a king that got born, and they have to search around and rummage before they say: *And thou Bethlehem, in the land of Juda, art not the least among the princes of Juda: for out of thee shall come a Governor, that shall rule my people Israel* (Matthew 2:6 KJV). And lo and behold, "Well, he must be in Bethlehem."

"If you find him, hey, you bring him to us so we can worship him,"[145] (wink, wink, nod, nod)—because they had the prophecies in front of them, but they didn't know what God was doing. And they wouldn't know it; they couldn't know it. It's just like today. God's doing things, but no one knows it because it requires its fulfillment before people can comprehend what happened.

Well, if we accept Dr. Walter Martin's biblical injunction that you interpret the old in light of the new, then if you're a faithful Christian and you accept that premise, what that requires that you do is that you interpret both—because the Book of Mormon did not come translated into English until 1830, so it is the latest in time. (Even though it is a composition that began 600 years before Christ and continued to record until 400 years after Christ, it did not come forth for **our** access until 1830.) Now clearly, the last 400 years were post-Christ, but the

---

[144] See Matthew 2:2.
[145] Ibid. vs. 8.

entirety of the text reckons in its public availability post-Christ by 18 centuries. So if we accept the edict to interpret the old in light of the new, then if you want to know what the New Testament was about—and in turn, the Old Testament, the ancient religion—then the first principle of interpretation is that you must go to the Book of Mormon to find out what that was all about.

One of the clearest examples—right in the Book of Mormon—that helps you see why Dr. Walter Martin's edict is useful is when Christ appeared as a resurrected being and showed the wounds in His hands and in His side and in His feet to the people who were gathered as a faithful body on the American continent, and He told them, *Ye are they of whom I said: Other sheep I have which are not of this fold; them also I must bring, and they shall hear my voice; and there should be one fold, and one shepherd.* (3 Nephi 15:21)

He explained that the disciples at Jerusalem didn't ask Him about that, and they didn't understand Him when He said it. They wrongly supposed that what He meant was that He would only come to speak to other sheep through the ministry of the people in Palestine as they spread the message outward.

Instead, what He meant was that **He** (Christ) would go **as a resurrected being** to scattered remnants of the House of Israel and that **He** would let them hear His voice and see Him, and He would minister to them. When He made that statement that is preserved for us in the New Testament, the people who were writing the Book of Mormon were included within the body of those that Christ intended to minister to. And then He extended it, and He said, "I have still other sheep, in addition to you, and I'm going to go visit with them also."[146]

So in just one example, if you want to understand the obscure statement/prophecy that Christ made that was preserved in the New Testament that He had other sheep to whom He was going to go minister, you go to the last in time/the later record (the Book of Mormon) to interpret the earlier. And the Book of Mormon supplies

---

[146] See 3 Nephi 16:1-3.

you that interpretation and explains: Yes, Christ meant that He would go and He would appear as a resurrected personage.

The record of Christ's appearance in His post-resurrected state in Palestine included appearing first to two women. Then He spent the better part of the day walking on the road to Emmaus with two disciples—Cleopas and an unidentified other who wrote the record (Luke). Then He appeared to the twelve. Still later, He would appear to the apostle Paul. And then there were more than 500 gathered together at the time that He ascended from the mount. And so, there were multiple sightings, multiple witnesses, and **multiple audiences** to whom He ministered as a post-resurrected being. In the Book of Mormon, He did exactly the same thing. He appeared as a resurrected personage, and He ministered.

The Book of Mormon helps contextualize Isaiah, Psalms, and Christ's Sermon on the Mount. It helps contextualize the prophecies about that time that is coming in which the head of gold is going to be ground to dust. It foretells the coming, ultimately, of the Kingdom of God on Earth. There are a lot of prophecies that are requiring fulfillment right now that must precede the return of the Lord in His glory.

In addition to everything else that you learn from the Book of Mormon, there are prophecies about a kingdom, an incipient planting, and a return of a religious body (small though it may be) that will build what's called a New Jerusalem—an antecedent to the establishment of Zion. The Old Testament prophecies about "Zion" and "Jerusalem" at the time of the Lord's return are not talking about one location but about two separate locations. When the Lord returns, the sun will never set on His kingdom: One of them will be on one side of the world, and the other will be on the other side of the world. He will establish in Jerusalem (that is, at old Jerusalem) a kingdom. And He will establish in the New Jerusalem (that is, in Zion) a second part of His kingdom. And out of Zion and out of Jerusalem will go the law and the teachings that will constitute the effort, the government, the society, and the culture that's going to finally free itself from the toxic influences and corrupt traditions that have been passed down from generation to generation, having been influenced all the way back to Babylon.

That's why the prophecies of John talk about the fall of Babylon the Great, because the head of gold is still with us. The Babylonian influence still remains with us in our banking, in our profit motive, in our culture, in our education, in our false ideas about what's important and what's not, and in our desire for power and wealth and influence. All of those things remain with us still today. And they corrupt everything. They corrupt business. They corrupt governments. They corrupt churches. They corrupt society. Everyone is vying with one another to gain influence, power, and in turn, wealth and the acclamation of this world. And it all goes back to Babylon, which is why John prophesies the fall—not of every one of these components of the great image that Nebuchadnezzar saw, but he goes right to the head, because as soon as you destroy the head, everything else is gonna unravel. And he prophesies about the destruction of Babylon, the head of gold that holds sway over all else.

So, if you're a sincere Christian and you want to tune in to the work that God began in 1830 to preliminarily prepare for a coming harvest, you have to consider the possibility that the Book of Mormon is an actual planting of something God wanted in order to permit that work of God to be fulfilled in the last days. The Book of Mormon came forth as a record of a fallen people in order to testify of the great work of Christ.

I mentioned that one of the criticisms of the Book of Mormon is the prevalent Christology found within it. People generally don't believe that Christ was so openly known, openly talked about, and openly expected in the pre-Babylonian captivity of the people in the Bible. But in the Book of Mormon, we learn that there were some prophets who came before Isaiah who left a testimony and a record that clearly influenced Isaiah and spoke openly about the coming of Christ. One of those prophets was named Zenos.

At one point, I went through the Book of Mormon, and I copied and pasted every quote of the prophet Zenos into a single Word document. And I'm going from memory, and my memory could be off, but it was in excess of 3000 words (and I think it was 3200 words) that are from the record of Zenos, as quoted in the Book of Mormon.

From the vernacular within the Book of Mormon, the references there about "the prophet" appear to identify **Zenos**. When *we* talk about "the prophet" of the Old Testament, *we* think about Isaiah; *they* thought of Zenos. Zenos and Isaiah talk about the same topic. Zenos went before, and Isaiah came after. Zenos was apparently a Northern Kingdom prophet, and Isaiah was a Southern Kingdom prophet. Isaiah's record about Christ is poetic and, like most poetry, tends to be obscure, beautifully-crafted language with difficult allegories to understand. Zenos, on the other hand, was pretty blunt and pretty straightforward. You could not miss the point of Zenos, whereas it's very possible to take the Isaiah text and construe it (because of its vague allegories) to mean just about anything.

Zenos could not be reformed to eliminate Christology. It was blatantly present in the Zenos text. Therefore, Zenos got dropped from the Old Testament. Isaiah, on the other hand, could be used to obscure the Christology. Although he points forward in magnificent ways to the coming of the Savior and His sacrifice, his "suffering servant" passages could be interpreted to not mean an individual Savior (Jesus Christ) but rather the people of God (or Israel) who went through so much persecution because they preserved a religion that testified of the true God. And therefore, the language of Isaiah was susceptible to interpretation that could construe it away from pointing to Jesus Christ. Zenos could not be so handled or interpreted; he clearly spoke about this coming Savior.

As a result, in the reconstitution of the Scriptures at the time of Ezra and Nehemiah, the references contained in Zenos were too plentiful to allow it into the canon, and it got obliterated from the Scriptures that were re-gathered. But the record of Zenos *was* included within what that "planting of people" in the Book of Mormon took with them. They didn't lose the prophecies of Zenos, and so it informed them about Christ in very specific ways. The presence of Christology in the Book of Mormon is the inevitable result of possessing Scriptures that speak candidly, openly, and frankly about the coming of this Messiah.

And so, when you pick up the Book of Mormon and read it, you are literally reading a text that has not been corrupted by these other influences. The abundant presence of a Christological theology in the

Book of Mormon is not evidence that the Book of Mormon is false; it is evidence that the **traditions** that surrounded the religion of the Jews (as it came to be understood when Christ came to Earth) were what were corrupted, what were incomplete, and what failed to preserve the original religion. That "original religion" was at the beginning with the first fathers, when **they** learned of death entering the world and of a promised Messiah who would save us from the fall of Adam, by reversing that as the "second Adam" (as the apostle Paul described Him) who would plant a restored family who was brought back to life through the power of the resurrection, so that *as in Adam all die, even so in Christ shall all be made alive* (1 Corinthians 15:22 KJV).

We also learn through the Book of Mormon that the first fathers were not so ignorant as we think them, but they had (from the beginning) knowledge of a coming Savior and a promise of redemption from the Fall. They had (from the beginning) the practice of baptism. They had (from the beginning) animal sacrifice to point to as a type and a shadow of the sacrifice that Jesus Christ would make to redeem them from death.

That Christology was not merely present at 600 B.C. (at the time of this planting the Book of Mormon refers to), but the Christology was present in the religion from Adam to Enoch, and from Enoch to Abraham, and from Abraham to Moses. And then because of the slave culture of Egypt and the corruption that they experienced there, Moses had to bring them along with the lesser law of carnal performances and ordinances in order to point their minds forward to the coming of a Savior who would offer an infinite and final and eternal sacrifice for the redemption of mankind.

If you want to begin to get your hands around what it is that God has **yet** to do in order to set the stage so that "His kingdom may come and His will be done on Earth as it is in Heaven" and you're a Christian, the place you ought to begin your search to find what God is really up to **now** is the Book of Mormon. And you ought to interpret the old in light of the new and accept the Book of Mormon as a guide in order to bring you along. The Book of Mormon poses a question that I'll paraphrase: "Wherefore murmur ye because ye receive more of the word of God?"[147]

It ought to be self-evident to anyone who claims themselves to be a Christian and to love the Lord that if a record comes about that purports to testify of Christ and of being written by people who believed in, obeyed, and followed Him, then that record bears not just **serious consideration** but **prayerful acceptance** if it is true.

I was raised by a Baptist mother and a Christian (but non-denominational) father. My father was a Mason, and Masonic lodges require that you be a believer in God, and my father believed in God. He just didn't necessarily extend that belief all the way to the exuberance of the Baptist faith. But my mother was ever hopeful of turning the whole clan into Baptists. We had our Baptist preacher over for Sunday dinner with some regularity, and I always liked the fried chicken. (For some reason, Baptist ministers and fried chicken dinner just go together like hand in glove; and if you're a Baptist and you're listening to this, you know this is authentic because you've been there and done that). So, when missionaries came and said, "Hey, here's the Book of Mormon. It's about Jesus, and it's gonna help you," my response to that news was less than enthusiastic. I mean, I'd had all of the indoctrination that comes from Dr. Walter Martin and all the other anti-Mormon critics. I'd read his book, *The Kingdom of the Cults*. I'd heard all the flaws and problems with this idea. The Book of Mormon grew on me very slowly.

I had actually determined there were reasons **other** than the Book of Mormon to affiliate with Mormonism, and I did so for years before I ultimately discovered the Book of Mormon to be something **terribly significant**. It took years of reading, of study, and of actually teaching the Book of Mormon before it began to penetrate into my understanding and my heart. Once the Book of Mormon began to be taken seriously by **me**, I discovered things in there that were beyond the capacity of a forger and a fraud to assemble (as the critics of Joseph Smith and Mormonism have claimed).

---

[147] See 2 Nephi 29:8.

Now, I am not a member of the Mormon church today (although they've recently asserted that their name isn't the "Mormon" church; it's The Church of Jesus Christ of Latter-day Saints). I was one time a member; I have been excommunicated because I prize historical truth above institutional loyalty—and the institution, as it turns out, is disloyal to "believing followers of the Restoration" if they're not sufficiently institutionally-loyal. At present, I don't hold any institution up as the ideal model or as an example of the work of Jesus Christ. I think Jesus Christ's work has to be done independent of institutional control at this point because every institution that's out there—just by reason of being institutional—becomes the subject of laws and taxes and rules and Babylon. Just because the institution exists, it's part of the great conglomerate that includes the head of gold/Babylon, the Medes and Persians, the Greeks, the Romans, on down to the present. I believe that Christ's work must stand independent of every other influence under heaven and owe its allegiance, owe its loyalty, and owe its faith to Christ and Christ alone, which makes me really ill-fitted in an institution that prizes loyalty to the clan above everything else.

Well, the more I began to take in the truths of the content in the Book of Mormon, the greater the gap grew between the lip-service paid to the Restoration by the Mormons/the LDS Church and the practice of the institution itself. In fact, if the Book of Mormon is used as a guide or measuring stick, it **condemns all** of the institutions of Christianity. It condemns everyone, except the few who are the humble followers of Christ, and points out that despite **that few** being *humble followers of Christ; nevertheless,* **they** *are led, that in many instances they do err because they are taught by the precepts of men* (2 Nephi 28:14, emphasis added).

If you want precepts that come from God, the best place to look, at this point, is the Book of Mormon text. The closer you look, the more you'll see. The more you see, the more you'll find that the religion of Jesus Christ is hardly practiced anywhere on this earth right now. If it's going to be practiced at all, it needs to be done by **you**, by someone who is eagerly searching for and trying to find words that come from Jesus Christ to use as your guide, as something to lead you back to Him, as the message intended for the last days, and as the means by which you can interpret the earlier New Testament and Old Testament to find out exactly what they mean. The key to unlocking **all** of what God has been, is presently, and will ultimately be involved with to fulfill all the prophecies is contained primarily in the text of the Book of Mormon. And so, if you want to escape before the ultimate destruction of that great image with the head of gold and be prepared for the coming of the Lord, if you're a sincere Christian, you don't need to go and join another denominational institution, but you better take seriously the Book of Mormon and study it and take its interpretations, its meaning, and its guidance seriously. It is the standard that has been planted in the last days as the ensign of truth to which all Christians, if they believe in Christ, need to rally in order to be part of His great latter-day work.

In the name of Jesus Christ, Amen.

SIXTH ADDRESS TO ALL CHRISTIANS

Recorded in Sandy, UT
September 8, 2018

In examining the mission of Christ, what was accomplished during His lifetime, and what was left unaccomplished during His lifetime (but intended by the Lord to be accomplished at some point before His Second Coming), even the record of the Lord's accomplishment is incomplete. It suggests that there is a great deal more that might have been learned or might have been recorded at the time of His ministry that was simply omitted from the record of the New Testament.

After His resurrection and His appearance to the women at the garden tomb, He appeared and spent the better part of the day walking with two disciples on the road from Jerusalem to Emmaus, about a seven-mile walk. He sidled up beside them, and He walked with them, and they talked throughout the day. It was evening when they arrived at their destination, and they asked Him to come in and to sup with them (to eat with them) because they had enjoyed the fellow's company. And He went in and blessed the food. Actually, He took bread, blessed it, and brake it, and gave it to them. And then their eyes were opened, and they realized it was Him. But their reaction to Him (after they recognized who He was) was a reflection on how they ought to have perhaps recognized Him earlier in the day—not because of seeing Him as He is and recognizing His person, but instead because of the message. Reflecting on what He had said, they asked one another, *Did not our heart burn within us, while He talked with us by the way, and while He opened to us the scriptures?* (Luke 24:32 KJV). And then they rose up from there and scurried back to Jerusalem to announce the news that He had appeared.

So, we know that the Lord spent the better part of a day walking with two disciples on the road to Emmaus and that the subject that He discussed with them was the Scriptures. And it was done in such a way that the Scriptures were opened to them, and the effect of that was to have their hearts burn within them from the conviction that what they were being taught was truth. There is not one word about what the Lord said or taught when the disciples' hearts were touched and they were brought to understand by having the Scriptures opened to them.

When something is missing from a record (a page or a hole in the record), that's called a "lacuna." One of the more obvious lacunas in the narrative is the failure to tell us anything about what Christ did to open the Scriptures to them in order to have these disciples/these people whom He deliberately chose/these believers become priority witnesses of His resurrection.

It's an interesting study to take a look at who the Lord appeared to and in what order He appeared. There seems to be a pattern in the appearances of the Lord and the priorities of the people to whom He appeared in order to have witnesses of His resurrection. But these are two of the earliest, and so, they have a high priority. And I believe that one of the two witnesses was, in fact, Luke (although he leaves his own name out). He identifies the companion who was with him as Cleopas, but he doesn't identify himself. But I think that it was Luke—the one who wrote the books of Luke and Acts, in which he explains:

- The history,
- The life,
- The death,
- The resurrection of Christ,
- The message,
- The importance of the message,
- The vindication of the promise of Him being a Messiah because of His resurrection, and then
- The immediate effect of the post-resurrection ministry of the apostles.

All of those things were written about, and they were written in some detail by Luke. And yet, that talk (that was so convincing that the hearts of both him and his companion, Cleopas, burned within them) is left as a glaring lacuna in the narrative by a fairly exhaustive biographer. Luke picked up upon some details of Christ's life that **only** appear in the Gospel of Luke. This incident on the road to Emmaus is one of those. But some of the more intimate details about the birth of

Christ are preserved by Luke. There are things that Luke was fully capable of preserving and conveying. If his heart was burning within him, **that** kind of a message is going to have some durability, some persistence—he was clearly **capable** of writing it, and yet it's gone from the record.

In the Book of Mormon, there was an early visionary encounter before they migrated very far from Jerusalem, in which Nephi was shown the whole sweep of history, and he began to record the account of what it was he saw. But he was interrupted and told: You can't write a record of what I'm going to show you hereafter because this record is going to be entrusted to another person who is going to write it. His name is John. And the Book of Mormon doesn't recite the account that John would record, but we all can identify it as the book of Revelation. And so Nephi was told: Don't write about this visionary material; someone else is going to do that.[148] Nephi was told he couldn't write it; a fuller account was going to be given by John. But Nephi was also told that this same kind of material had been shown to others.

Some time later, Nephi composed a second book. And by that time, 40 years had passed from the time of the visionary encounter near Jerusalem. He was now on another continent, in a new world, and a promised land had been given to them—and he'd had 40 years of reflection on what he saw and what he heard. And from that 40 years of reflection, he realized that he could bear testimony of what he saw (without infringing upon the right of John to write the fuller account) simply by quoting Isaiah, who wrote about much of the same material.

And so, Nephi adopted as his text, in large measure, the text that came from Isaiah as it appeared on the brass plates, which was slightly different than the version that we have in our Bibles that descends from the Masoretic Text. But he preserved, as his testimony, words that were composed by Isaiah in the form that he had them. And as his entire account was winding down (at the end of his second book[149]), he began to change from *quoting* the Isaiah text to *paraphrasing* the Isaiah text, in order to adapt it to a **very specific, prophetic foretelling** of the

---

[148] See 1 Nephi 14:20-25.
[149] See 2 Nephi 27.

coming forth of the Book of Mormon in the last days (in order to make the Isaiah text fit exactly what would be happening with the Book of Mormon coming forth). **Then** he gave his interpretive key from that point (explaining exactly why it was that he put those Isaiah materials in) in order to have people understand that it was his testimony of what he knew and what he was shown and to convert the language of Isaiah into the prophecy of Nephi to convey Nephi's message.

Well, we don't have any explanation from Luke as to why there is a lacuna in the record with the omission of Christ's post-resurrection exposition, His opening up of the Scriptures, and the explanation of what it was in the Scriptures that bore testimony of Him. We just have Luke leaving it out. But in the Book of Mormon, the record that we have of Christ's appearance to the Nephite descendants includes Christ opening up the Scriptures in order to show how they bear testimony of Him—not merely of Him coming as the sacrificial lamb but also of Him coming in the last days. Christ's missing material from the Book of Luke is back-filled by the Book of Mormon account of Christ's appearance and Christ's ministry and teachings to the Nephite people.

If anyone is a devoted follower of Christ and attentive to the scriptural record as the way in which they come to understand and know who Christ is and to gain a conviction of His status as the Redeemer of mankind, then anyone who is sincere about searching into and trying to find how and why and what the Savior was, is, and what He did should be eager to back-fill the lacuna that appears in the Gospel of Luke and find out what it was that the Lord was saying. And they'll be eager and willing to look at the Book of Mormon with that in mind.

I can tell you that the Book of Mormon has received perhaps the greatest amount of neglect since its coming forth in 1830 of any volume of Scripture. The one who translated the record, Joseph Smith, made almost no use of it in his public ministry. He was dealing with people who were largely converts from other denominations—including, initially, predominantly people who had been followers of Alexander Campbell; they were among the most devoted people to the Bible. New converts who came in BELIEVED the Bible and "accepted" the Book of Mormon—but they regarded the Book of Mormon largely as a sign that God was "up to something." When Joseph Smith taught (even as the one who translated the Book of Mormon), he largely focused upon the Bible and an exposition of the content of the Bible, because prospective converts and new converts to the idea relied upon and had a priority for the Bible above any other volume of Scripture. Adapting to the audience, Joseph Smith's teachings largely focused upon the content of the Bible.

You can see leaking through in the transcripts of the talks that are preserved of Joseph Smith that there was tension that ran all the way up to the highest level of the church, including with Sidney Rigdon (who was a counselor to Joseph Smith). Joseph gave a talk that has been called the King Follett Discourse. It was a funeral sermon about a recently deceased man named King (first name) Follett (last name). King Follett was a fellow who had been killed in an accident in a well, and he was recently deceased at the time that Joseph gave the King Follett Discourse. In the discourse, he talked about a variety of things that stretched on into the eternities and the post-death course that mankind will take. In the middle of that discourse, Joseph made an aside. (Sidney Rigdon was not in the audience at the time. He wasn't in the city of Nauvoo; he was elsewhere.) But Joseph made an aside, specifically calling Rigdon by name and saying to the absent Sidney Rigdon, "I suppose that the inquiry has to be supported by the Bible." And then he went on to use the Bible in order to demonstrate that the teaching he was advancing to the audience was biblical; it was based in the content of the Bible itself. So, Joseph Smith was saying, "Rigdon, I'll prove the truth of what I'm about to teach from the Bible. I suppose I have to support it by the Bible."

That tells you that one of the problems Joseph confronted was that people (including those very closest to him at the top of his organized church at the time) didn't want to hear anything that wasn't supported by the Bible, didn't want to hear him talking about the Book of Mormon, and didn't want to accept something based upon the new revelations.

At a still later time, there was a fellow who was one of the three witnesses to the Book of Mormon whose name was David Whitmer. He was excommunicated and disassociated himself with Joseph in

1838, and he later wrote (in the late 1870s or early 80s) a pamphlet that was called "An Address to All Believers in Christ." And in that, David Whitmer, one of the three witnesses to the Book of Mormon, complained that the revelations of Joseph Smith were given too much priority. I assume that the attitude that David Whitmer reflected 30 years after the death of Joseph Smith was an attitude that he held even while Joseph was alive and may be one of the reasons why he became disaffected. He didn't want to see the revelations of Joseph Smith expounded upon. He didn't want to hear material that was more recent (although David Whitmer *did* hold the Book of Mormon in some considerable regard, and he remained true to his witness as one of the three witnesses to the Book of Mormon).

After the death of Joseph Smith, among the people who are nicknamed "the Mormons" (The Church of Jesus Christ of Latter-day Saints being the largest one of those, the one that most Christians would be familiar with, the church that sends out the missionaries two-by-two in their white shirts and ties to knock on people's doors, the one that sponsors the Tabernacle Choir, the one that sponsors Brigham Young University, the largest single denomination: The Church of Jesus Christ of Latter-day Saints), no one gave any serious consideration to the Book of Mormon until the 1950s. It was then (in the 1950s) that the church president (at the time it was a man named David O. McKay) asked a professor at Brigham Young University (whose name was Hugh Nibley) to write a priesthood manual that could be used by the institutional church to teach a course in Priesthood Meeting for a year. When that interview took place (in the accounts that Hugh Nibley tells of it), he wanted to focus upon the Book of Mormon, and David O. McKay's reaction was surprise—because no one took that book seriously; and Hugh Nibley was saying, No—he believed in it. The seriousness with which the Book of Mormon was taken after the 1950s is largely the result of a now-deceased Brigham Young University professor, Hugh Nibley, and his **conviction** that the Book of Mormon was an authentic book.

I say that to a Christian audience because the Book of Mormon has largely been so neglected by the people who are nicknamed "Mormons," that if Christians were to take that book up and to examine it through the eyes of a devoted believer, I believe that they would find treasures within the Book of Mormon (an understanding, as a result of their Christian background) that the Mormons themselves have never been able to harvest, have never noticed, and do not have the eyes with which to even see its presence. The Book of Mormon remains a **Christian treasure** that has yet to yield its greatest results.

In 1950, there were leaders in the Mormon church who had never read the Book of Mormon, much less understood it. It was quite some time after that before the Book of Mormon became something in which there was some regular study among Latter-day Saints.

Because the Book of Mormon was published before there **was** an LDS Church and because the Book of Mormon stands as an independent witness, there is no reason why accepting the Book of Mormon requires you to be institutionally loyal to **anyone**. You can be a Baptist and believe in the Book of Mormon (and there is at least one minister out there who is doing that right now). There is no reason why Catholics and Presbyterians and other mainstream Christian denominations can't pick up the Book of Mormon and make use of it without pledging allegiance to any institution that claims ownership over the Book of Mormon.

In fact, the most accurate edition of the Book of Mormon currently in print is one that was prepared independent of any institution and is available for purchase.[150] It's one of two books that are combined in a single volume called The New Covenants: the first half of the book is the New Testament, and the second half of the book is the Book of Mormon. They were intended to go together as a witness by people who both—on one side of the world and on the other side of the world —witnessed the ministry of a resurrected Lord. He showed them the wound in His side and the prints of the nails in His hands and His feet, and He had people bear testimony that it was He who was sacrificed, that rose again from the grave, and who is the Savior prophesied of by Isaiah. (He used Malachi in the Book of Mormon— He used other texts to demonstrate and to teach His identity as the Son of God and the Redeemer of mankind.) And I believe if the

---

[150] Print-on-demand paperback and hardback Scriptures, as well as leather-bound sets are both available on www.scriptures.shop.

Presbyterians and the Baptists and the Catholics were to pick up the Book of Mormon and treat it seriously, it would yield truths to them which they could then preach independent of the LDS Church or the people who are nicknamed "Mormons," and they would find themselves growing closer to Christ as a consequence of having this material available to their study.

It's been too long that the Book of Mormon has been neglected. It's been too shoddily handled by the people to whom it was originally given. The copyright has expired. The book is now available to the public. The institution that got it originally has made precious little use of it. And if you find yourself not only disbelieving the LDS Church but accepting your institution's native hostility towards the LDS Church, you will find in the Book of Mormon a great deal of ammunition to use to condemn, to criticize, and to censure the LDS institution—because the Book of Mormon spares very little ink in criticizing, condemning, and judging harshly the people to whom the Book of Mormon would be delivered, including the LDS Church.

The use to which the Book of Mormon can be put by Christians is so relevant to the Christian belief system that if Christians will soften their hearts, consider it, and allow for the record that is latest in time to be used to help understand the records that are earlier in time (because God's latest word clarifies and governs the interpretation of His earlier word), Christians are going to reap a fabulous reward in doing so.

Many of the texts that we have in the New Testament are copies of copies of copies that we know have been altered in the process of transmission. Bart Ehrman (a one-time believer, now agnostic) parsed through the text of the New Testament, compared it to quotes from the ante-Nicene/pre-Nicene fathers and to internal evidence in the New Testament itself, and reached the conclusion that the New Testament text deserves a great deal of skepticism because the method and manner of its transmission has been demonstratively shown to be inaccurate and the record to be muddled.

In one place, the less-altered text of Hebrews preserves the words that are drawn right out of the seventh chapter of Proverbs: *This is my son; today I have begotten you* (Hebrews 5:5 KJV), a statement that was made prophetically about Christ. The book of Hebrews preserves it in that form. The Gospels, however, were altered, and the statement that was made at the time of the baptism of Christ when John the Baptist baptized the Lord was changed to: *This is my beloved son in whom I am well pleased* (Matthew 3:17 KJV) because of a controversy that erupted over the nature of Christ during the Christological debates of the third and fourth century. And it's one of the illustrations that Bart Ehrman points to in his book, *The Orthodox Corruption of Scripture.* That title tells you something about the transmission of the New Testament: *The Orthodox Corruption of Scripture.* Bart Ehrman isn't the only scholar, but his books are fairly easily available through Amazon (if you're interested in the topic).

Another scholar who has done essentially the same thing in picking apart the Old Testament and the integrity of the transmission of the Old Testament text is a Methodist scholar in England named Margaret Barker, whose works demonstrate that there was an earlier—an older—religion that got defeated at about the time that the Jews were taken captive into Babylon. And on the return from the exile, a new religion emerged that had been altered. Christians generally view information like that as threatening the very core of their religion because if their Bible is flawed and not inerrant, if their Bible has been poorly transmitted and is inaccurate, then the basis upon which they seek salvation is itself threatened.

The Book of Mormon, on the other hand, bears witness of the very same Lord in essentially the very same kinds of terms, identifying Him as having accomplished the work of the redemption by the sacrificing of His sinless life in order to defeat death and to restore mankind back to life. But unlike the transmission of the Bible record, the Book of Mormon record was preserved for generations by a singular transmission through a line of record holders. At the end of that line, a prophet named Mormon (hence, the name for the book) did a summary explanation, excerpting from all of the prior records a final and inspired, God-commanded, and prophetically-infused record-summary of the preceding nearly-millennium of history, giving us the truths that God wanted preserved. He turned that record over to his son, and his son finished it up and buried it.

When it came forth out of the ground, it was translated by the person who accomplished the translation through the means he called "the gift and power of God." The original language in which the Book of Mormon was first published in these last days was English, and part of the original first transcription has been preserved. It was put into a cornerstone, and water damaged it—and so we only have about 28% of that original. But the original was hand-copied before it was taken to the printer for the first printing. And all of that printer's manuscript still exists. Then later, the one who was responsible for the translation of the Book of Mormon had the opportunity to review it for another edition in 1837 and to review it and again publish it in 1840.

We do not have the transmission issues with the Book of Mormon that are existing with the current Bible. Christians hear this criticism about the Book of Mormon: that there's been 9,000 changes made to the text. Those 9,000 changes have been located and largely dealt with—every single one—in The New Covenants edition of the Book of Mormon that is currently now in print. (Most of those purported changes are punctuation changes. Many of them come from the fact that when it was first printed, it was printed like a book, but it later became versified and divided into chapters, and footnotes were added—and in the tally of changes, many of the changes are superficial changes to versification and chapter divisions and other such things. There were some errors made. There were some lines that were dropped out between the original manuscript and the printers manuscript that have been located and have been put back in.) But even with every one of the identified changes to the Book of Mormon, the fact is that it is demonstrably—on a whole other order of magnitude—more faithfully preserved and more reliably a text attesting to Jesus Christ than anything that we have transmitted in the Bible.

In short, if you are a Christian who feels some insecurities as a consequence of the criticism leveled at the Bible because of its clear transmission issues, it's very demonstrably-true problems of conveying the text from the original authors down to what we get printed, and the vagaries of how you convert some Greek lettering into other languages, the Book of Mormon has far greater integrity.

(At the time the New Testament was written, the form of Greek that was used didn't have lower case; it only had uppercase. It didn't have punctuation. And in almost every text, there's no separation from the end of one word and the beginning of another. Dividing it up into words and upper- and lower-casing the alphabet that was used was accomplished by monks many hundreds of years after the original text had been handed down.)

So, if you're insecure about the reliability of the content of the Bible, **none** of those insecurities should attach to the text of the Book of Mormon. The Book of Mormon is not only a testimony of Jesus Christ, but it is perhaps the most reliable testimony of Jesus Christ that exists in available print right now, today, in the English language.

If you're a Christian and you're sincere about your faith, I think you neglect the Book of Mormon at your peril. If God has sent you a message and a testimony about His Only Begotten Son in order to bring you closer to Him and to prepare you for the day of His coming to judge the world, and you decide that you're simply going to dismiss that message (that came from God), then what kind of a Christian are you really? Have you no faith? Do you think that God cares less about the generation of people who will be on the earth at the time of His returning to judge the world than He did about the people to whom He came and ministered when He came here to sacrifice His life to redeem mankind?

Now, it's true at His first coming that precious few took seriously the message and accepted Him. But God bears testimony whether you will listen to it or not. Wise men who were some distance from the place of the Lord's birth watched for and understood the signs testifying of Christ in the heavens above. Based upon the appearance of the sign and the journey and their arrival, it took them two years (according to the New Testament record) to get from where they were to where the Lord was. And Christ is called a "young lad" when they brought gold and frankincense and myrrh in order to worship the newborn king. And when they departed, they departed without advising Herod where they'd found the newborn king because they'd been warned in a dream —which means God was talking to them also—and they returned perhaps on a two-year journey somewhere else. The people who were on this continent (the American continent) watched for signs in the heavens, knew about His birth, knew about His death, and were anxiously testifying of Him before He came to visit with them.

The testimony of Christ to the world by God at His first coming was not local. Admittedly, the record begins with Zacharias bringing incense to burn before the veil of the temple to recite the prayer asking God for the redemption of Israel to take place. And an angel appeared, and the angel announced that, "Your prayer about the redemption of Israel is going to be answered, and your wife's going to have a son who is going to go before the face of the Redeemer of Israel,"[151] which seemed improbable to Zacharias because of the age of his wife. Nevertheless, it was vindicated. But that's not the beginning of the testimony concerning Christ by God throughout the world. And at least some company, two-year's journey away, heard the message and appeared to worship Him. How many others were there throughout the world? Has a Christian ever contemplated the fact that God's testimony to mankind was not tightly confined to a small group of people in Palestine, but it went out so far and so wide that one group responding to it took two-year's journey to get there? The Book of Mormon testifies that there were yet others—on the entire other side of the world, separated as they were by oceans—to whom Christ went to minister.

The purpose of the Book of Mormon, among other things, is to remind us living at the time when Christ's return is imminent **that His message is global**. If you think you can just brush off a message that was intended to help prepare Christians for His return, well, you're like those whose hearts were hard and refused to hear even when Christ walked among them. We ought to be rather like those who would undertake an arduous two-year journey just to come into the presence of the Redeemer of mankind.

If you refuse to take the Book of Mormon seriously as a Christian, you are no more Christian than the Jews who crucified the Lord, giving lip-service to a false and inadequate religion, rejecting the message of a Messiah who intends to save your soul because you prefer your false,

---

[151] See Luke 1:5-13.

inadequate, partial tradition to the truth of a living Redeemer. The Jews didn't reject Jesus because they had no religion. The Jews rejected Jesus because the religion they had did not adequately encompass the truth concerning Him. And so, they felt comfortable rejecting Him—just like Christians who feel themselves adequately informed (from a false and incomplete set of beliefs) about the work of Jesus Christ and are unwilling to accept the record that was intended to come forth to prepare the world for His return. You're no different if you reject the Book of Mormon.

And I testify of that in the name of Jesus Christ, Amen.

Seventh Address to All Christians

What is God Up to Today?
Recorded in Boise, ID
November 3, 2018

Christ made a comment about those that would be able to enter into the Kingdom of God, and He said that except you become as a little child, you shall not be able to enter into that Kingdom.[152] The idea of being "as a little child" is one worth considering; it's one worth puzzling over.

Hold that thought for a moment—because I want to talk about a related subject, and that's perfection. If I say the word "perfection," every one of us has something that comes to mind. In the course of your life, my guess is that every one of you have had moments that you could point to and say, "That moment was absolutely perfect. There's nothing about it that I would have changed."

Roads have a design that is, for safety reasons, capable of handling traffic at speeds that are called the "design speed," which means that a vehicle can operate up to that design speed on that road safely. But the speed limit is never the design speed, because they build in this margin of safety. So, they tell you to drive five or ten or fifteen miles below the design speed of the road so that there's a margin of safety built into it. If you're riding a motorcycle on a road—particularly a rural, winding road like Idaho State Highway 5 that goes from the Montana border to the Washington border—and you go the posted speed limit, the motorcycle does **not** cooperate with you. It doesn't like that speed. It's hard to handle. But if you speed up to where the motorcycle and the road and you are in syncopation with one another and you're riding at the design speed, everything is easier. In fact, it is almost thoughtless as you go—the rhythm of the road, the design of the road, and the pace the motorcycle is at.

---

152 See Matthew 18:3.

On Idaho SH-5, there are places where the banking (they call it "super elevation") of the road is 25 or 30 miles an hour above the posted speed limit. We were returning from the Black Hills of South Dakota, (coming through Northern Idaho on Idaho SH-5) going the design speed. It was a moment of absolute perfection when the joy of the experience, the feel of the humidity, the pace of the road, everything about that moment was perfect—until it was interrupted by an Idaho State patrolman who, fortunately, was pointed in the opposite direction as we went by at the design speed of the road. Well, he had a lot of recovery to do to reorient himself and to start from zero to get to where we were. And we happened into, fortunately, a little village and went a block off the road, found a gas station, and hopped off. There was a fellow there who owned a Moto Guzzi, which in northern Idaho is a pretty rare motorcycle to be driving. (It's a V-twin, but unlike a Harley Davidson, which is an inline V-twin with a front and a back, this one has V's that go out either side. It's still a V. It's not like a BMW; that's a Boxster, horizontally opposed.) And so, we acted like we'd been there all week. And the police came through, making their noise, and they went on their happy way, and he said, "They looking for you?" We said, "That's possible…"

There are moments where (because you can't be planning next week or regretting last month) you can't be doing anything other than that moment. If you're on the bike and you're going the design speed and your mind is elsewhere, you can kill yourself or badly injure yourself. You can do extraordinarily stupid, haphazard, dangerous things if you're not absolutely in the moment. Perfection is one of those things which occurs absolutely in the moment.

Think back over your lifetime at those moments where you would not change a thing. You were so content that there was nothing else that you could want or you would change about that moment.

- There's a character, a Samurai, that an American struggled to try and understand in the movie, *The Last Samurai* (although they did grow to have this friendship with one another). Katsumoto was always looking for the perfect cherry blossom. He would study the cherry tree as it blossomed in the spring outside his temple, always looking for the perfect cherry blossom and never finding it; there was always a problem with it. As he lay dying on the battlefield at the end of his life, in one of his last breaths he's looking up and seeing the cherry trees blooming in the distance, and he observes, "Perfect, they are **all** perfect." And it didn't matter what flaws they had. The fact was, they were all perfect.

- I can remember a time when I was young; the scene presents itself vividly in my mind. I can't tell you how old I was or what grade I was in, but I remember playing marbles out in the dirt with friends during recess—and recess was maybe 15 minutes, but it was timeless. All eternity could come and go in that moment of such profound contentment.

- I have dogs, and dogs are always content. We're told that dogs don't have any sense of time; they may live only 10 to 12 years, but as far as they're concerned, they've lived for all eternity, because there's a timelessness to the experience of being a dog. They're not in a hurry to get somewhere (unless of course you've got the leash, and you're gonna take them out, in which event they'll anticipate that moment). But there's a timelessness to the idea of perfection.

- I can recall an afternoon when I had come out of my house, and I was sitting on the front porch. And I was all alone. The temperature that day must have been exactly the same temperature as the temperature of my skin so that I could not tell where outside of me and inside of me began and ended by feeling the breeze. The temperature was exactly the same temperature as I felt. And it was so calm an afternoon, so calm a moment sitting there that I was taken in by the moment itself. A bird flew by, and I could feel the movement of the bird's wings through the vibration of the air because it was just that calm. As I sat there, I thought, "This **is** Heaven. This moment, this experience—**this is** Heaven." Because at that moment, it was perfect and something that I would not change.

- I was out walking, and I came upon this songbird that was just singing the happiest little tune you could ever imagine. I don't know what kind of bird it was, but it was, you know, sparrow-sized and small and very happy and singing its tune and doing all that

God endowed it to do. And I came upon it abruptly, and because of where it had situated itself and because of where I came upon it from, it was trapped. And it was singing loudly. And when I got there, it was so loud and so startling that I stopped and looked at it, and it immediately stopped singing. And it knew—it was like the bird realized—if I wanted to, I could capture it; if I wanted to, I could kill it; if I wanted to, I could exercise whatever control I wanted over the bird. And it looked frightened, less than an arm's length away. Foolish to let a human get that close to you in that vulnerable of a spot. And the stopping of the singing was so abrupt; it was like the last notes still hung in the air as this frightened little creature looked at me. And I thought, "Hey, I'm harmless, but it doesn't know that." So, I thought, "What's the best way to communicate to this trapped little animal that I'm harmless?" I turned, and I walked away, and I tried to whistle a little like what the bird had been whistling like. It was a miserable imitation—I mean, it was probably screeching to that poor thing, but I whistled as I walked away. And within a few steps, if there's anyway to describe it, I would say that the bird's tune resumed on a happier note than it had been before. That was a moment that was perfect.

I'm sure every one of you have had moments in your life that you can point to and recall and say: That moment, that incident—**that**—that was perfect. If we can conceive of perfection or if we can experience it even for just a moment, that means perfection exists. It's real. It's attainable. It can be had, even in this place and even with you and even with me. Perfection is possible.

In this creation, there are two opposing forces that cause everything there is to be and to exist. Those two opposing forces are not good and evil—although we tend to call them "good" and call them "evil." The two opposing forces are, in fact, love and fear. Everything that is generative or creative comes about as a consequence of love. If you think about all the problems that people have with one another and what would solve them, the one thing that could solve every problem is love, if we loved one another enough. And all of those vices—all of the suffering, the anger, the pride, the envy, the impatience, the greed—have their root in fear: "I fear I will not have enough, and therefore, I envy. I fear for my own inability, and therefore, I resent your ability."

Everything that produces negativity comes about as a consequence of fear.

In a letter to the Ephesians, the apostle Paul wrote: *That in the dispensation of the fulness of times He might gather together in one* **all things** *in Christ, both which are in heaven, and which are on earth: even in him* (Ephesians 1:10 KJV, emphasis added).

The entire history of Christianity is plagued with disunity. Christianity was born inside the crucible of disunity. When Christ sent twelve messengers out as missionaries to deliver the message, calling them apostles (which simply means someone with a message), He sent these twelve out, and they brought twelve different versions of what they learned from Jesus. And there was no attempt at having a unified message.

The earliest studies of the Christian faith focus not upon Christianity in aggregate but on the various forms that Christianity took as a consequence of which one of the apostles happened to be teaching their particular view. Then the apostle Paul came along and taught yet another view. And so, you had such strong disunity among Christians in the first generations that by the time you got into the third century, **Christians were killing Christians over Christianity** because they harbored that much resentment at the different views that were held.

I don't know if the word "fortunately" or if the word "unfortunately" should be applied, but fortuitously, as it turns out, when Constantine wanted to unite his Roman empire, one of the features of the unification of that empire that he recognized he needed to incorporate was religious unity. And so, he chose Christianity to become the new state religion of a unified, intercontinental Roman empire (only to learn, after he had made Christianity the official state religion, that it would not do the empire any good because Christians within his empire were killing other Christians within his empire **over Christianity**). And so, he convened a group of bishops at Nicaea and placed them under house arrest to force them into agreement. In hindsight, in order to portray it as something really good and inspired, their unified statement is now called the "First Great Ecumenical Council of Nicaea." It's just a fancy way of putting a positive spin on a very ugly moment in which the emperor didn't give a crap what they agreed on, he just wanted an agreement: "If I'm gonna make this infernal Christianity the Roman state religion, by damn, it better be a religion in which I can have peace!" It's practical; it's pragmatic. But it certainly doesn't guarantee you a form of Christianity that bears anything other than the hallmarks of compromise in order to solve the violence.

And so, we get the state religion of Rome, which evolves over time from being the Roman empire and the Catholic (meaning universal) Church to the **Holy** Roman Empire, which **is** Catholicism. And you had a period of relative Christian unity (with "unity" marked by the absence of killing one another, not necessarily the absence of a Christian spirit). Christianity itself became a political power broker in which there were really only a couple of professions that had any status that would allow you to enjoy a good life—one of them being the clergy. So, the clergy became political, and it became economically a source of power. And the Holy Roman Empire, in the form of the Catholic Church, exercised all of the abuses and excesses that you would expect from any kind of dictatorial government that has power over people.

People that have power tend not to be respectful of those that lack power. And if you can treat people as your servants, your slaves, and your serfs, then you treat them accordingly. And so, Christianity developed into a monolithic and very abusive control that was centered in the Roman clergy headquartered in Rome.

For a whole variety of reasons (including ambitious local kings who wanted to declare their own independence from the Roman hegemony and who wanted their own ability to waylay the money that was being aggregated through the church and getting exported—they wanted to keep that money locally and get their own hands on it), a moment came in 1517 when it was possible for Martin Luther to enact change. Luther was pricked in his conscience because he believed what Paul had written; he believed what Matthew, Mark, and Luke had recorded; he believed in the faith. And he saw that what was acting itself out on the stage of life bore no resemblance to the lofty perfection that is spoken of in the teachings of the New Testament. He'd simply had enough.

His life was spared because there was a political leader who saw some political advantage in providing protection to Martin Luther. So, Martin Luther was spared from what had happened to others who had rebelled against Rome; he wasn't burned at the stake. He was instead allowed to post his disagreement, and ultimately, he founded a new brand of Christianity, in which he believed religion should be more authentically Christian and less inauthentically autocratic and authoritarian.

But just like what happened in the New Testament with the twelve apostles, immediately upon the emergence of Lutheranism, we get in that same generation John Knox, John Calvin, and Ulrich Zwingli. (These men met, spoke with, and knew one another.) Not only did the fracturing of Roman hegemony cause Protestantism, but Protestantism immediately began to say, "We disagree with you about _____ (choose your topic)," and you had multiple Protestant denominations immediately springing into existence.

There had been coercive unity through Roman dictatorship and artificial unification of Christianity for a millennium and a half. But immediately with the first fissure showing up, you had fracture after fracture and disunity after disunity—because Christianity simply disagreed about so many things. It was **inconceivable** to them that Christianity did not require you to divide up into mutually-exclusive camps in which **your** brand of Christianity ought to be (at least **claimed** to be) superior to **their** brand of Christianity. And if Heaven is only for those who have the truest form of Christianity, then those people really need to go to Hell because they aren't quite Christian enough in the truest way, in the most meaningful way, or in the most correct way.

So, let's go back and read that verse again: *That in the dispensation of the fulness of times He might gather together **in one all things in Christ**, both which are in heaven, and which are on earth: even in him* (Ephesians 1:10 KJV, emphasis added).

All things. I don't know how many of you sitting here today and hearing those who have spoken about Buddhism or about the Native American tradition or about Messianic Judaism have thought, "That speaker has said something true, and I believe that." The dispensation of the fulness of times, which has to occur before the return of the Lord, has to gather together **in one all things**. If that thing to be gathered has been fractured and lost to Christianity but preserved in Hinduism, if that thing to be gathered is a truth lost to Christianity and broken away and preserved in Buddhism, or if that thing to be gathered into one appears **anywhere**, then in the dispensation of the fulness of times it all must be brought back and gathered into one.

If you take a piece of art—a sculpture—and you fracture it into bits and then gather the bits and reassemble them, you will not have the unity and the perfection of the original until every piece has been found, every piece has been gathered, and every piece has been put into its proper perspective. Only when they've all been gathered and they've all been put in their proper place will you have unity. The sculpture ought not look like Picasso and the Cubists. **It ought to look like what it was when originally formed**. When that happens—so that you can now see the beauty that's there—then you've completed the gathering.

But the prediction is that it will be gathered together **in one in Christ**. So it doesn't matter if you're a Hindu and you think Christ is outside (He is "other than") your tradition. Your tradition must be gathered home also into Christ because it fits there. And if you're Buddhist and you say, "Ours is not a religion but a philosophy, a way of thinking, and a way of disciplining the mind," that way of thinking and that way of disciplining the mind likewise must be gathered together in Christ for it to find its home. His purpose is the salvation and eternal life of every being, of every person. Until we gather all the parts, it is not possible to gather in one all things that belong with Christ. The search must be global; the search and the invitation must cross cultures, traditions, and religions.

You see, the philosophy that motivated Constantine in coercing Christian unity was the desire to see Christians not fight with one another. If you say fighting with one another is the evil end to be avoided, there are really only two ways to approach conquering that evil end. One of them is to do what Constantine and the popes have attempted and what some other centrally-controlled religious organizations likewise attempt today, and that is to use coercion and exclusion and punishment to discipline the adherents so that they fall in line. That is a compressive, coercive, and dictatorial way of trying to achieve the Christian unity that we seek after.

Another, more benign, way of attempting exactly the same thing is to say, "You are free in all your thinking and in all your beliefs. We require very little of you."

We believe in the Doctrine of Christ, which was read to us here today. It's very short:

- Belief in Christ,
- Belief in His Father,
- Acceptance of the Holy Ghost,
- Being baptized in faith, and then
- Allowing that Holy Spirit/Holy Ghost to animate you in your search for truth.

And if we begin with diversity, then we begin with appreciation for that diversity, because coming together in the dispensation of the fulness of times in the unity that Paul speaks of is not because someone beat you into submission. It's because someone had something to say that resonated as truth to you in such a compelling way that you found yourself persuaded, you found yourself enticed to accept it, you found yourself prizing it, and you welcomed it and embraced it. And if someone has not yet embraced it, you explain to them why it's delicious to you. And if they reject it for a season, that's okay, too.

Joseph Smith had a revelation that was actually dictated from beyond the veil and then recorded by a scribe and read back. And then, once the transcript was read back and it was correct, Joseph and Sidney Rigdon (who shared in the vision with him) said, "Yes, that's correct," and then it would move on. Part of that revelation is talking about people who, at the end of this experience in this world, find themselves disappointed by what they did not accomplish while they were here. They did not accomplish what they wanted because they received not the gospel, neither the testimony of Jesus, the prophets, and the everlasting covenants.

There was a talk about the Book of Mormon earlier today, and the whole text of the Book of Mormon comes down to experience after experience being retold by people who, during their lifetime, had this opening up of the heavens to them, and they came into contact with Jesus Christ (having the heavens opened to them and recognizing who He is and what His role was.) It's an experience they tell over and over again throughout the entirety of the Book of Mormon, because the people that wrote the accounts in the Book of Mormon had that experience.

The testimony of Jesus is not something that comes from **you**: "I have this, and let me tell it to you." The testimony of Jesus is something that **He gives to you as His confirmation to you** that you have part in His kingdom. To receive the testimony of Jesus is to receive from Him the promise that He will give you eternal life. The Book of Mormon is filled with accounts of people that had that experience, and it shows that it is, at one point, an expected and normal part of the Christian experience. It became very rare and unexpected and is, in fact, denounced by many denominations as something that doesn't happen, can't happen, ought not happen, and "if you've think you've come into contact with a divine being, then you've been misled" because, well, Jesus is busy. I mean, He can't be troubled with your lot. He's getting ready for the Second Coming. He's got a lot of wicked to burn. He's got stuff to do. And so, "Don't think that you're going to have an encounter with Jesus." However, my view is that Christian salvation is based upon the testimony of Jesus to you of your salvation.

I also think that it doesn't matter when you lived or what the circumstances were. If you are true and faithful to Him, **you will have that experience**. In the case of Stephen in the book of Acts, he was in the process of being stoned to death, and it was in the last moments of his life that the heavens opened up to him. He saw Christ, and he forgave the people who were in the act of killing him. He was filled with a devotion that came from having Christ Jesus confirm and testify to him of his salvation, and he parted this life rejoicing.

Joseph Smith had an older brother whose name was Alvin who died when Joseph was still a young man. In the last moments of his older brother Alvin's life, Alvin said that there were angels in the room and that the angels were talking to him and that he was conversing with them. Many years later, Joseph Smith had a vision of the Celestial Kingdom, and he saw his brother Alvin. And he wondered, "Why is it that Alvin got to be in the glorious afterlife when he died before the gospel had been fully restored?" And he was told that anyone who would have accepted the truth, the gospel, the testimony of Jesus, the prophets, and the everlasting covenants—**anyone who would have done that**—even if they die when it's unavailable, will be saved.

St. Francis believed in and practiced the Sermon on the Mount. St. Francis lived at a time when Catholic hegemony made Catholicism "IT"—the only religion, the only brand of Christianity. He went to the pope, and he said he wanted to found an order (the Franciscan Order), that they would take a vow of poverty, and that they would practice the Sermon on the Mount. And the pope told him, "Well, that's ridiculous. No one can do that. And if you can find people who will do this, come back, and ask me again. But this can't be." (If you gave St. Francis a coat in the winter because he was cold and without a coat, he'd accept the coat, and he'd wear it until he met the next person that needed it more than he, and then he would give it away. So, he was always needing coats and always giving away what little he had.) St. Francis found twelve men who would practice that order. And the pope gave him the Franciscan Order. In the last days of St. Francis' life, at a time when the only brand of Christianity was corrupt, St. Francis said that angels were coming and ministering to him.

I believe it to be an authentic part of every Christian's life. There's a revelation that talks about how there are those people who will not taste death because it shall be sweet unto them.[153] Why do they not taste death? Because death means bitterness. And if, in the authentic Christian's life, the final moments that they spend here are caught up with the testimony of Jesus, confirming that they have part with Him in His Kingdom (like Stephen, in the very act of being stoned to death), they part this life rejoicing. Because whatever they're going through, it doesn't matter—it's joyful to be reunited with that person who represents perfection itself.

---

[153] See D&C 42:46.

The highest aspirations and the highest ideals of Buddhism are present in the gospel of Christ. The highest ideals of Hinduism are present in the gospel of Christ. The problem is that in that disunity and fracturing, some of the bits of the sculpture left Christian awareness and departed into the East, and they are understood, practiced, and accepted by the Hindus, but they're outside of the typical Christian awareness. You will no longer understand the sayings of Jesus in the same way if you could put on Hindu eyes for a moment and read what is in the sayings and the teachings of Jesus Christ and His followers. You'll not understand the teachings of Christ as well until you've put on Buddhist eyes, and you've relooked at the gospel of Christ through that prism, because part of the picture will be missing. Christianity may be disciplined and have its story down, but it lacks the depth, the richness, the kindness, the texture, and the meditative power that you find in Buddhism and Hinduism. But as you heard from the people practicing those philosophies, religions, and viewpoints today, the fact is that they're fractured, too. Part of reunifying everything in Christ includes reunifying the Hindu and Buddhist worlds as well.

What is God up to today? He's up to the work and the challenge of reuniting all things in one in Christ—not by exclusion and subtraction and coercion but by openness and by addition and by tolerance.

Thank you.

Eighth Address to All Christians

Recorded in Montgomery, AL
May 18, 2019

I want to talk about religion—but I don't want this topic to be what it usually is, and that's a source of unease and friction and conflict and debate and discomfort. Religion is one of those things where we find it really easy to do two completely contradictory things: 1—love religion because we want to be close with God, and 2—take offense at our neighbor because their religious views differ somewhat from our own—when, in fact, the Author of the religion is telling us all to love one another. If we've got Christ in common, we ought to be able to de-emphasize our dissimilarities and emphasize our similarities to find peace in Him.

If you study the events that occurred in that immediate generation following the New Testament Gospels (you can see it in the book of Acts; you can see in in the letters of the New Testament), Christ commissioned twelve apostles, and He sent them out with a message to bear about Him. But Christianity, in the immediate aftermath of Christ's life, had various kinds of Christianity. We had a Matthean Christianity that was based upon the teachings of Matthew. We had a Pauline Christianity that was based upon the teachings of Paul. We had a Petrine Christianity, and it was based upon the teachings of Peter; it was the Petrine version of Christianity that ultimately got the broadest sweep and resulted in the formation of the Catholic Church. But Christianity did not start out centralized. It started out "diffused." It's almost as if what Christ wanted to do was to get the word out and let everyone have in common some very basic things, in which we could find peace and love and harmony with one another—but outside of that, to explore, perhaps, the depths of what the message could be and not to have it insular, rigid, and one-size-fits-all.

During that very earliest period, you had obviously-commissioned companions that had walked with Jesus and been witnesses of His teachings. He had brought them aboard; they had heard the Sermon on the Mount; they had witnessed miracles. John (in his Gospel) makes it clear that they weren't really "up-to-speed" with what Christ was doing and what He was about, because He would say things, and they wouldn't understand Him. In John's Gospel, everything was written in retrospect; it was written post-resurrection. When the apostles now knew that Christ was going to come, He was going to die, He was going to be resurrected, and then He was going to ascend into Heaven to be in a position of glory, they looked back retrospectively, and they said, "Ok, now I get it. Now I understand what He was talking about. Now those statements about the necessity that He suffer come full circle, and we get it." But walking with Him during this time period, they were really not tuned in to comprehending what the Savior was intending to do and ultimately would do.

Then after all that, we've got this guy who is a persecutor of the Christians and an opponent of Christianity, and on his way to Damascus, with a commission to try and bring Christians to justice, he gets interrupted in what he's doing: *Saul, Saul, why persecutest thou me? ...It is hard for thee to kick against the pricks* (Acts 9:4-5 KJV). The pricks were what you'd use to drive the donkey—if it kicked, it impaled itself, and it could be a fairly nasty wound; they didn't kick without suffering. And Christ is telling him, "That's what you're like. You're like a mule; you're so mule-headed about what you're doing, and you're actually doing something that is, ultimately, going to be to your harm." So Paul comes aboard—he's told to go to Ananias; he goes to Ananias. He gets baptized, and then scales fall from his eyes (he's been blinded for awhile). "Scales" is a great word (as an English translation) because it not only implies, potentially, the scales of the fish, like a contact lens that's opaque, and you can't see through it. But it also implies judgment—that Paul's judgment about things was wrong, and the scales needed to be put aright.

So, Paul comes aboard. But Paul is just as much what Paul was "before" as he was "after." And so, Paul and Peter never do quite get on the same page. And Paul writes that he *withstood [Peter] to [his] face, because he was to be blamed* (Galatians 2:11 KJV), which makes it clear that you can be a Pauline believer in Jesus Christ, a witness of His resurrection, and in communion with Him, AND you can be Peter, who walked with Him and was told that upon the foundation that he was part of that this church would be built—and you can authentically be Christian in both cases, and the two of you absolutely not agree on much of anything! So Christ set up, at the beginning, a Christianity in which there was a necessary diversity, a necessary broad-mindedness, a necessary tolerance.

The apostle Peter would write about coming into the union of faith. It's a theme that you see in James and in Paul—about growing into unity. So, why would we have a Christian establishment at the outset (in which we have this diversity of thought) with the expectation that you will **grow** into unity—and we're told, *Love one another; as I have loved you...love one another* (John 13:34 KJV)? So, why would it be set up that way if Christianity was simply supposed to be "mutually-opposing camps with differing points of view," in which your particular brand of Christianity will ex-communicate their brand of Christianity, and your brand of Christianity will denounce Catholicism (as "the great whore"), instead of everyone saying:

• What has the Lutheran group observed about Christianity that can help bring light, knowledge, and understanding to me?

• What has Catholicism preserved from their traditions that can help enlighten my understanding because it's a treasure that we have not preserved in our own right?

• And what is it within the Baptist movement that has developed a keen insight into some of the most penetrating beliefs that Christ taught?

Why do we separate into denominational differences and hold this hostility towards one another?

One of the things that I personally believe in is that you have to take the money out of religion in order for religion to ultimately be its greatest self. I believe that in order to have faith, you have to sacrifice for your faith. That means that no one can or should pay me for anything I do as a religious individual. I have to sacrifice to come here. I have to sacrifice to prove my belief in Christ. No one gets to pass a plate, collect money, and give it to me. I have an obligation, instead, to donate, to sacrifice, to serve.

We have a very small incipient group of people that believes that we do have an obligation to give tithes and offerings. But we collect tithes and offerings in very small groups, and once the money's collected, then within the group, the question is asked, "What are the needs? Who among us has a need?" And if there is a health need, if there's a food need, if there's a housing need—the money is used to benefit those that are in need among the household of faith. And no one gets to be paid. The reason why Catholic priests are hostile to Lutherans, and Lutherans are hostile to Methodists, and Methodists hostile to Baptists, and Baptists hostile to the Church of Christ is because the clergy of the respective denominations have a financial stake in making sure that their version of Christianity survives.

I went out to a Christian Evangelical conference in Nashville, Tennessee a couple weeks ago—again, on my own nickel. It was a national conference that lasted for days. I went out with some Evangelical folks and met some new Evangelical friends. And our last day there, as we were on our way to the airport, our driver was a retired Air Force Chaplain. He'd been enlisted; he left and used the GI bill to get through ministerial school, became a Chaplain, came back in as a Captain, served his twenty years, and retired. And after he was retired, he went to work as a Methodist church leader (I think he was a bishop; he was ordained to something), and he led a Methodist congregation in South Carolina until he retired again. And he was being paid retirement from both the Air Force and from the Methodist Church because their clergy have a financial setup in which they're not only compensated during their time of ministry, but they are then also compensated in the retirement. So, he's all on board with Methodism, and that's just the way things work in this world.

During the period of time between that very first generation of Christianity and 324 A.D. when Constantine determined that it was a mistake to have made Christianity the religion of Rome—because they were in disagreement, and his internal strife was not going to be solved by making Christianity…

He thought it was **one** religion. But the factions were so opposed to one another over teachings that they literally were killing each other. Christians were killing Christians. And so, the answer to the need of the Roman empire to have a "state religion that would unify" was not going to be served. And so, he "held" the First Great Ecumenical Council (as it is called by the "historical Christian movement"—which includes **all** Christian denominations). He summoned all the Bishops to Nicaea, he put them under arrest, and he told them they could not leave until they reached an agreement on some fundamentals of what the Christian faith was—so that once that was adopted, we had an orthodoxy. And they nearly got unanimity, but there were a handful that would not agree, and they were exiled from Rome. But they now had a state religion that was agreed upon.

If you look at what are called the ante-Nicene (or the "prior to" Nicaea) fathers, and you read the works of those ante-Nicene fathers, there are a lot of teachings that were still left over from that first generation that began to evaporate once they reached the 324 A.D. time period. It still required years of conflict—and many more years of death and killing—before Christianity settled down into a stable form that you could call "orthodox."

During the time period prior to 324, there were multiple kinds of Christianity. One of them got identified as "proto-orthodox." The reason the one form is regarded as proto-orthodox is because **it** would eventually win the battle. Once it won the battle, then you could go back in hindsight and you could say, "Well, that was the one that was the predecessor to what would become orthodox Christianity over time." That was the Petrine church (or the Petrine view), which emphasized priestly authority and the necessity of a priestly intervenor.

That view held sway until a split that occurred at about 1000 A.D. between the East and the West, between Constantinople and Rome, between two Bishops who were vying for primacy. And so, you have the Orthodox Christianity that spread into Eastern Europe and Russia, with the Greek Orthodox Church and Russian Orthodox Church being part of that. They preserved some teachings in Christianity that got dropped off the table in the Western church (or the Catholic Church)—doctrines that you don't hear much about.

Then you get down another 500 years to 1517 A.D. and the time of Martin Luther. He was a very devout believer. He was as sincere a religious man as ever lived in the Catholic faith. He believed, and he believed with all his heart—believed so much that he saw signs in his life of God intervening to do things. He saw miraculous events that showed him that God was walking with him. Martin Luther went to Rome and was horribly disappointed by what he saw as corruption and as profiteering and as something that could not possibly be true because these men were doing vile things. Prostitutes were at court with bishops; everything about what was going on was unseemly.

But Martin Luther believed. In fact, in the universe of Martin Luther's Christianity, salvation required a priest "to save." If you did not have a priest, you could not access salvation. And so, Martin Luther's dilemma was, "Is it even possible to be a Christian separate from the clergy that comes down from the time of Christ? Is that even possible?"

Reading in the New Testament in the book of Romans, he came across the passage that says it is by grace that you are saved; it is through the instrumentality of faith. And that faith is, in itself, the means for salvation. So Martin Luther conceived the idea that salvation just might be possible separated from the Catholic clergy if you relied upon the grace of Christ and the faith that you have in Him. And Martin Luther took the brave step of trusting what he had read, and he founded the Protestant movement based upon the concept that it is possible to be saved separate from a hierarchy that was grounded in Rome.

Well, as soon as you have Lutherans, you're inviting someone else to come along (like John Calvin) to say, "Wait a minute. You've got part of the idea, but you don't have it really in place." You have John Wesley. You have Ulrich Zwingli. You have a number of Protestant leaders, all of whom say, "Yeah, Martin Luther got one thing right, but he didn't get everything right." And immediately they began to divide up, and the Protestant movement morphed into dozens (and then hundreds, and now thousands) of different denominational divisions that were saying, "Yes, BUT... All those other churches got some things right, BUT there's still something that they've omitted that needs to be done!"

I was raised by a Baptist mother, and I was shown the Baptist religion from my youth. I never joined the Baptist Church. My next door neighbor, my best friend, was a Catholic altar boy. (Rick was a Catholic altar boy! And so was Wayne. You'd need to know those two guys before you understand how broad-minded Catholics are about their altar boys.) And so, on occasion I would go to Rick's church. Mary (his mother) was really devoted, and Rick was just a pedestrian that happened to be, on occasion, in the Catholic Church. I was always interested in religion. I always thought there was something to this— that Christianity has a core that is true. I believed that. Over the years, the more I have examined it...

I'm an attorney, and I do trial work. In the courtroom, witnesses of an event (if they're telling the truth) will agree in broad-brush and will disagree on details. If they agree on all the details, someone's lying, because that's not the way witnesses work. If you're standing on one side of the street and you see an accident, and you're standing on the other side of the street and you see the same accident, what is left on one is right on the other. They will disagree—if nothing else, from the vantage point from which they observed it. You also have the tendency to focus on "something," as opposed to "everything." And if everyone is focused on a different "something," the story that you will get from people—swearing to tell the truth, under oath—will be different versions. It is the same general theme/same large-picture outcome, but they will disagree many times on the details. "Oh, I didn't notice that" —because that's the way humans are. "I didn't notice that. I didn't hear that. You're sure he said...? He really said that? Because when he was speaking, he said **this**, and I know he said **this**. The reason I know he said **this** is because **that** struck me to the heart. And when he said that, I was thinking back about twenty things in my life, and so when I tuned back in... You're telling me that one of the things I missed is what you heard about **that**? I find that astonishing! I wish I'd heard it." My story and your story and the next person's story of the event (if they're authentic, in the courtroom) will always find details that are different (but with the same major theme).

Jesus Christ had a group of witnesses in a single generation—**in a single generation**! This isn't a work of fiction! You have four different Gospel accounts that came into being **in a single generation of time**, in which they all agree on the massive truth that this was the Son of God who came into the world to be the sacrificial lamb, He was rejected and died, and He was resurrected and ascended into Heaven. All four of them agree on that. And yet, only Matthew has the Sermon on the Mount. Some of them mention feeding five thousand; some of them mention feeding seven thousand; and some of them mention both. But not all of them mention everything. There are differences. It's what you would expect if you're dealing with an authentic account of a real person that lived a real life and left behind people who were so astonished by what they witnessed from this man that they wrote accounts. And whereas, BEFORE they were cowering, and they were running, and they were denying that they knew that man, AFTER they witnessed His resurrection, they went forth boldly and proclaimed who He was, performing miracles themselves based upon the name of Jesus Christ. **Something actually happened**. And that **something** was the life of Jesus Christ. So whereas BEFORE they ran and hid, after His resurrection and after they became acquainted with Him, they went willingly to their deaths as witnesses of Him.

I believed that there was something authentic about Christianity. I just wasn't quite sure about the brand of Christianity that my mom, a Baptist, was teaching me in my youth. I also—going down to the Catholic Church—was skeptical. (It was Pope John VI—he was the pope back then. He seemed like a decent enough chap. The first Catholic pope that impressed me, though, was Pope John Paul I. That guy was... He was a fan of Mark Twain's, ok? Pope John Paul I was the greatest pope that ever lived, as far as I'm concerned.)

I thought there was something missing from the Baptist faith. And I thought there was something theatrical and hollow, even inauthentic, about what I saw in Catholicism—not because the pageantry wasn't depicting something noble and great and wonderful, but because the players weren't always up to the job of carrying off the pageantry. There were times when it appeared to me that the last thing the priest in Mountain Home, Idaho was interested in was celebrating the service/the Mass. He did it anyway, but it was lifeless. His heart wasn't in it. It seemed hard to me for that to drive religious conviction—if the heart of the priest was not in the celebration of the Mass. The Baptists were always into the celebration of what they did because it's based upon a sort of charismatic movement in which enthusiasm is an expected part of it. But I remember the pious gestures, the things from the pageantry of Catholicism that depicted things, that depicted holiness... And I believe there is holiness. I honestly believe there to be holiness. But I think it is hard to imitate it instead of authentically be it. That's why a Mother Teresa stands out as a global figure, because she didn't imitate it. And Mother Teresa stands as evidence that there is such a thing as Catholic holiness.

Another one that stands out in history as authentic evidence of Catholicism having holiness is St. Francis. He believed and accepted the Sermon on the Mount. He **lived** the Sermon on the Mount. He went to Rome to get an order commissioned by the pope, and the pope laughed at him and said, "You can't get anyone to live the Sermon on the Mount." He said, "I would give you an order if you could come back here and bring with you twelve men who would be willing to live the Sermon on the Mount." St. Francis was the guy that—if you saw him in the cold in winter and you gave him a coat—he would wear that coat until he ran into someone that had a greater need than he; and then he would give away his coat to the person in need. When he decided that he was going to become a priest, his father (who was a wealthy man) went and intervened and said, "You can't do this! Everything about you, I paid for! You are utterly dependent upon me, and I refuse to let you go do this." St. Francis took off all his clothes, handed them to his father, and came to the clergy a poor and naked man—literally. He was a devout man. When he came back to the pope with twelve believers, the Franciscans were commissioned, and the Order of the Franciscans came into being.

The current pope is named after St. Francis. I think St. Francis was an authentic Christian. In the last two months of St. Francis' life, he reported that angels were visiting with him. There are a lot of people that dismiss that end-of-life spiritual experience (and telling tales of angels and visits and such things) as the frailties of a dying body. I don't think so, in the case of St. Francis. I think that he was ministered to by angels.

There's an expression—it's found in places some of you would find dubious—but there's an expression about how some people do not "taste death."[154] The statement that they do not taste death doesn't mean they don't die. It just means that their death is sweet because they die in companionship with those on the other side who bring them through that veil of death in a joyful experience. There are a handful of people who have reported that, as they were dying, angels came and ministered to them. I think all authentic Christians, in any age, belonging to any denomination—I don't care what the denomination is—I think all authentic Christians who depart this world find that death is sweet to them and that they are in the company of angels as they leave this world. And I don't think it matters that the "brand" that you swore allegiance to and you contributed your resources to support matters anywhere near as much as whether you believe in Christ, whether you accept the notions that He advances about the Sermon on the Mount, and whether you try to incorporate and live them in your life.

Jesus took the Law of Moses as the standard. What the Sermon on the Mount does is say, Here is the standard, but your conduct should not be merely **this**. *Thou shalt not kill* (Exodus 20:13 KJV) is not enough— you must avoid being angry with your brother; you must forgive those who offend you; you must pray for those who despitefully use you. Just refraining from murdering one another, with a reluctant heart, bearing malice at them—"Well, I didn't kill the guy, but I got even!"—that's not enough! That's not the standard that Christ is advancing. *Thou shalt not commit adultery* (Exodus 20:14 KJV) is not good enough. Don't look upon a woman to lust after her in your heart! Jesus is saying, "Here's the law. And you can do all of those things and be malevolent; you can be angry; you can be bitter; you can be contemptible; you can hold each other out as objects of ridicule. Its purpose is to make you something more lovely, more wonderful, more kindly, more Christian."

Christ says to be like Him. The Sermon on the Mount is an explanation of what it's like to be like Him. St. Francis made the effort of trying that, of doing that. I suspect that the first time St. Francis gave away a coat in the middle of winter to someone else, that it pained him. He probably felt the biting sting of the cold and thought, "How wise is this that I'm doing?" Because it's always hard to accept a higher

---

[154] See D&C 42:46.

standard and to implement it for the first time. But I suspect by the hundredth time he'd done it that he didn't feel the cold anymore; he felt the warmth in his heart of having relieved the suffering of another person—because the practice of Christian faith involves the development of Christian skill and the development of Christian charity in a way that changes you. You don't remain the same character that you were when you began the journey! You become someone absolutely and fundamentally different.

While I was in the Air Force and away from home, I was attending a University of New Hampshire night class. It was some kind of organizational behavior class. Having grown up in Idaho, I knew what Mormons were, and this professor (Cal Colby—he's from Brandeis University, but he was teaching a night class for the University of New Hampshire) just gratuitously started attacking Mormons. And my honest reaction was, "What the hell are you talking about Mormons in New Hampshire for? That's a local infestation somewhere out in the West, and there's none of that going on here." And in the middle of his diatribe, a guy raised his hand, and Colby called on him. And a fellow named Steve Klaproth defended Mormons (because he was Mormon). I made the mistake afterwards of saying to the fellow (I didn't know his name at the time, but I know him now—Steve), "Good job!" I always hate it when a person in a position of strength picks on someone in a position of weakness, and so I went to the guy who was weak and said, you know, "Good job!" He mistook this for interest in his religion. And I wound up (trying to be polite) being hounded, literally pamphleteered, missionaries coming… It was gosh awful.

Well, I left New Hampshire on what's called "Operation Bootstrap" where they send you to college. I went to Boise State University. The Air Force paid for me to go to school. I came back. When I came back, there was this campout; the campout was at the birthplace of Joseph Smith in Sharon, Vermont. And I went to the campout. There was a book that was in the Visitor's Center, and they gave me a copy of that book for free. Steve said, "You should read this." I read it, and at that moment, I was surprised. My reaction to Mormonism had been very, very negative, but the ideals that were expressed in this one statement were lofty and noble and Christian and charitable, and I wanted to know, "Where did this come from?" It was something that Joseph Smith had written, a revelation that Joseph Smith had received.

Well, I got baptized for the first time in my life on September the 10th of 1973 into the Mormon church. I was a Mormon until September the 10th of 2013—forty years to the day. And on the 40th anniversary of becoming a Mormon, I was excommunicated from the Mormon church.

So, I don't say this to sound like I'm bragging or exaggerating, but I don't know anyone alive today that knows as much about Mormon history as I do. Because while I was part of that church (and then afterwards, still), I've read every historical document that I can get my hands on; I've read everything that Joseph Smith said that got recorded, wrote, or transcribed when he had a scribe writing for him. My understanding of Mormon history is encyclopedic, really.

There's a thing that goes on in Salt Lake City called the Sunstone Symposium. It's run by people who are, basically, renegade Mormons —intellectuals. And it started out being friendly to the Mormon church, then grew into outright hostility and anger towards the Mormon church, and then it converted into a mixed bag. And some of it is pro; some of it is con. And I've spoken at the Sunstone Symposium.

One of the things I've presented was a paper about Brigham Young, in which Brigham Young's megalomaniacal presiding over Mormonism (during the late 1840s, into the early 1850s) and the excesses that went on during that time period—including murders that occurred on Brigham Young's watch—were laid out. Sunstone asked the Dean of Mormon History (the guy that is most respected), Thomas Alexander, to respond to my paper. And Thomas Alexander came and responded to my paper. I was talking about Brigham Young's literal regarding of himself as an actual king from the time they came into the valley in 1847 until the time he was deposed as the territorial governor by the Army of the United States in 1857. I was talking about that period of time. Thomas Alexander got up and said, "No, Brigham Young didn't believe those things because he said things in 1860 and in 1870..." and he read the quotes from 1860 and 1870. Well, as soon as he was deposed as governor, he *knew* he wasn't king. All 1860 and 1870 have to contribute is the fact that Brigham Young ultimately managed to grapple with reality because he had been deposed. But what he was saying in that early time period is exactly what he meant. So after Thomas Alexander got through with his rebuttal paper, I got up and, for five minutes, dismantled the Dean of Mormon History's view.

The Mormon church is a cult. It is not an authentic Christian organization. But I believe that you can find Christians who are Mormons. I believe that you can find Christians in every denomination that is out there. I believe that there is an authenticity to belief in Christ that transcends every denomination that's out there. I've written books about the history of Mormonism that expose many of the things that the Mormon church represents to be true that I show to be false, including their authority claims and their inconsistent following of what the founder of Mormonism stood for, believed in, and practiced himself.

Joseph Smith raised the largest standing army in the United States in 1844; it was under the command of Major General Joseph Smith in Nauvoo, Illinois. Literally, he could have taken on the United States Army and defeated them. And do you know what Joseph Smith did with a standing army larger than anyone else in the United States, larger than the federal government, larger than any of the state militias? Do you know what he did? He disarmed his soldiers, he turned the canons over to the state of Illinois, he surrendered to the governor of the state of Illinois, and three days later, he was murdered while he was in jail. He would rather personally die and give up his life than to have people on both sides of a fight die as a consequence of a religious dispute.

In 1837, Joseph Smith was in Missouri; and while he was in Missouri, hostilities broke out between Mormons and Missourians. Part of the problem with the hostilities was that leaders around Joseph Smith were spoiling for a fight—literally spoiling for a fight. A guy named Sidney Rigdon who was a counselor to Joseph Smith gave a speech in which he said, "If you people show anymore aggression towards us, we're gonna wage a war of extermination, and we will wipe all you Missourians out." It's called the Salt Speech; it was delivered on July the 4th of that year. It's an incendiary talk.

There was a Mormon named Sampson Avard who went about provoking hostilities with the Missourians. Sampson Avard was a Mormon, and he had a group that he called the Danites (based upon the tribe of Dan—the blessing that is given to Dan in the 49th chapter of Genesis talks about Dan being an asp in the way that bites the horses; it's a preamble of the violence that the tribe of Dan would render in the posterity of Dan—so Sampson Avard took the name "Danites" as his group). And they began to retaliate by burning houses, burning fields, and stealing cattle and hogs and bringing them back. Joseph Smith found out about it, and he demoted Sampson Avard. He was relieved of all responsibility in the army, and Joseph made him a cook. So the guy who was the militant leader is now a cook.

Hostilities ultimately did break out. It was inevitable that there be retaliations. Each side was saying that they were the victim, and the governor of Missouri said, "We're gonna wage a war of extermination," quoting what the Mormons had said in that July 4th talk. And so, Mormons were expelled from the state of Missouri. The militia was outside of a town called Far West, Missouri. Joseph Smith and his family, friends, and Mormons were inside Far West. They had a defensive position from which they literally could have caused so many casualties that the militia could never have overrun the town. The cost in blood would have been too high. Joseph Smith surrendered and told his people to surrender their arms, and he deflated the tension.

He was taken into custody by the state of Missouri; he was charged with treason against the State for fomenting rebellion. And they had a series of hearings trying to get witnesses to prove that Joseph Smith should be held for trial on the charge of treason. And no one could prove that Joseph Smith was involved with any of the hostilities until the guy who actually caused the hostilities, Sampson Avard, came to the courthouse to testify and to blame Joseph Smith for everything he (Sampson Avard) had done.

Joseph Smith was held over on the charge of treason, based upon the testimony of the guy who knew what cattle were stolen, what hogs were stolen, and what fields were burned because he was responsible for it. And he simply said that Joseph had engineered all of it. And so, based upon the testimony of traitors, Joseph Smith was held in prison for a period of six months, over a winter time-period, in an unheated dungeon that had bars but no glass on the windows. And they suffered for six months in a Missouri prison.

He was allowed to escape and get back to his people, all of whom had been driven out of Missouri. But while he was in prison—and while he had the opportunity to think about everything—Joseph Smith composed a letter from Liberty Jail that breathes with the spirit of Christian compassion, forgiveness, love, kindness, and refraining from abusing others. This is a man who got betrayed by his friends, and he turned around and showed compassion to them.

One of the books that I've written is called *A Man Without Doubt*. In it, I set up the historical context out of which Joseph Smith produced the three longest writings of his own in his life. They are a letter from Liberty Jail, the Lectures on Faith, and a statement of his own history (because the church historian had stolen all the manuscripts). Time and time again, the worst enemies of Joseph Smith were Mormons, the people who claimed to follow the religion that he was developing.

Joseph Smith, in my view, is authentically Christian in the same way that St. Francis is authentically Christian. The problem is—and it is an enormous problem—that everyone outside of the Mormon world looks at him as the property of the LDS Church. They look at him as if he was accurately represented by a group of people that, time and time again, he condemned and, time and time again, betrayed him. *A Man Without Doubt* is an attempt to let people see Joseph Smith as a Christian, divorced from the LDS Church or any of the splinter Mormon groups. It's an attempt to see him, potentially, as an authentic Christian, in the same way that I think Martin Luther and John Wesley and even John Calvin (although Calvin was so militant; he's kind of a drum-beater that scares me a little) were authentically Christian.

I think that everyone who sacrifices for the cause of Christ can help contribute to my understanding of what it means to follow Christ— because people who follow Christ bear the evidence of that discipleship in the way in which they walk, the things that they do, the things that they give up, in how they discipline their heart and their mind, and in how they treat one another. When you find someone whose life bears evidence that they are authentically Christian because of what they **do** and what they **say**…

Christ said it's not what goes into the mouth that proves you're unclean, but it's what comes out. What do you say? How do you display the grace of God in your life? I can tell you one way you **don't** display the grace of God, and that's by condemning them as being inauthentically Christian, merely because of their affiliation with one Christian group or another.

Christ looks upon the inner person. All of His parables suggest there's something very different about authenticity and inauthenticity. There are ten virgins—well, what are virgins a symbol of? If Christ is using the virgin as a symbol, He's talking about good people. These are good religious people; they have to be. And of that group, only five were allowed in.

There's a wedding feast, and at the wedding feast, He invites friends, and they don't come. Well, who are the friends of Christ that are invited to come to His wedding feast, and they don't come? They don't come because their hearts aren't right, their words aren't right, their mind isn't right, and they are not authentically what Christ is trying to have us be. But He invites, and they don't come—because they will not be His. And so He goes out on the highways and the byways to try and find anyone that will come. And "anyone that will come" suggests that, well, they could be a Samaritan. Think about the Parable of the Good Samaritan from the perspective of a Jewish audience: They were nothing but apostates! And yet, He uses the **apostate** as the illustration of authentic Christian discipleship. They invite in **strangers** off the highways and the byways—people that you don't expect to be invited because they're not at your church every week; they're going to some other place or, perhaps, no place at all. And yet, they're invited in, and they're allowed to remain so long as they have on the wedding garment. In other words, if they come having donned the mantle of authentic Christianity, they're welcomed.

We care and we fight about religious issues that are of no moment at all to Christ. And we do that because we're paying clergymen every week to rile us up so that we'll stay loyal to them and their congregation, and we'll contribute—and we will view one another with fear and non-acceptance.

If you took the money out of Christianity, most ministers would go into politics. They would not hang around. I'm not lying; they have done polls of Christian ministers to ask them if they believe Jesus Christ is the Son of God who was resurrected. The majority of Christian ministers do not have faith; what they have is a career. And they can't abandon their career. "If I leave your employ, what's gonna become of me? Because I'll be a poor man." And so, they stay employed, preaching what they don't believe. It's one of the reasons why I think Father Ordway (in Mountain Home, Idaho) made the gestures, and his countenance was devoid of the holiness and joy that should be expressed. I saw that in my friend Rick's mother, Mary. I saw in her that fire of belief, that devotion. I didn't see it in Father Ordway.

I would like people to consider the possibility that authentic Christians could come from anywhere, among any people—and that we can fellowship with one another. And that it is possible to fellowship with one another—even independent of an employee-hireling priest—in which we study together, worship together, rejoice in Christ together, and we try to figure out how to be more authentically Christian in what we do, what we say, how we treat one another, and how we view one another. And then to take the next step and to contribute our tithes and our offerings to a group of believers to help believers, to help each other—so that it's not just the support of the clergy, the buildings, and the programs, but it's helping the fatherless and helping the mother who has no one to help her. And to have Christianity not just theoretically modeled in feel-good sermons, but actively part of life and how we deal with and treat one another, in which we all say, "We've all sinned; we've all fallen short of the glory of God, but **let's not let that cause me to condemn you. Let's not let that stop me from trying** (in as authentic a way as I can) to be charitable and kindly to you, and you to me, and us to the people in need among us." If there were ever an authentic group of people who are Christian who were helping one another, the appeal of that would cause everyone who comes into their midst to have a change of heart. They'd want to be part of that; they'd want to live that kind of life, because there's no better life than the one that Christ taught us to model in the Sermon on the Mount.

I know a lot about Mormon history, and it's not at all what the Mormon persona is represented to be—either by the church itself or by its critics. In some ways, its history is much worse than the critics tell you. And in some ways, the very beginning of it was much different and much better than what the church represents.

I believe that Brigham Young introduced the practice of plural wives. I believe that Joseph Smith was an ardent opponent of that. I believe that Joseph Smith has been falsely portrayed because Brigham Young didn't think he could bring plural wives into the practice unless he laid it at the feet of Joseph Smith. And I think there's been a lot of history in Mormonism that tries to lay at the feet of Joseph Smith the responsibility for the things that traitors and treacherous and evil men did—and escape responsibility for it by saying: "Joseph taught it. But, he taught it in private... Oh, he lied to the public—he lied to the public about it, but in private he practiced it, and he taught it to us."

Joseph Smith was not that kind of man. You can read the letters between Joseph Smith and his wife, Emma. Emma was a stronger personality than Joseph. She was his trusted counselor and guide. Joseph deferred to her; he took advice from her; he took counsel from her. She was better educated than him. The false stories that have been told about Joseph Smith are equally false about Emma by diminishing her.

You should read *A Man Without Doubt*. You should go back and reconsider whether your opinion of Joseph is it all supportable by a true-telling of history—I don't think it is. And that is the reason why I'm an excommunicated Mormon, because I think the truth is valuable, and it's worth searching out. Even if a church tells you to think otherwise.

Baptism is Required: An Invitation

And now what are you waiting for?
Get up, be baptized and wash your sins away,
calling on His name.
Acts 22:16 NIV

Christ's simple command to "follow me" was given repeatedly.[155] Christ showed the way, and as part of that, He was baptized to *fulfill all righteousness* (Matthew 3:15 KJV). It was only after Christ was baptized that the Father declared *Thou art my Son, this day have I begotten thee.*[156] Christ also had His disciples baptize His followers.[157]

Christ spoke to Saul of Tarsus on the road to Damascus and converted him by that contact.[158] Following his conversion, Saul was healed of blindness, renamed Paul, and immediately baptized.[159]

Paul linked baptism to resurrection.[160] He declared that to be baptized is to *put on Christ* (Galatians 3:27 KJV). There is only *one faith,* and it is in the *one Lord* whom we worship, and it requires *one baptism* to be included in the body of believers.[161]

Peter explained that baptism saves us.[162] Christians who follow Christ will all be baptized. Baptism is required.

If you have not been baptized or would like to be baptized again, there are those who have authority to administer the ordinance who will travel to you. The ordinance is free, and the service is provided without

---

[155] See, for example, Matthew 8:22; 9:9; 16:24; Mark 2:14; 10:21; Luke 9:23; John 1:43; 12:26, among many others.
[156] See Hebrews 1:5
[157] See John 4:1.
[158] See Acts 9:1-6.
[159] Ibid., vs. 11-18.
[160] See Romans 6:3-4.
[161] See Ephesians 4:5.
[162] See 1 Peter 3:21.

any charge or expectation of any gift or donation. If you are interested, you can make a request at bornofwater.org.

Whether or not you are a member of another church and whether or not you intend to continue to serve in the denomination of your choice, we respect your choice of where, how, and with whom you choose to worship. However, we believe that baptism must be performed by someone having authority from Jesus Christ. Our Lord was baptized to show us by His example how to obey God. He then directed us to "Come, follow me." If Christ needed to be baptized to fulfill all righteousness, how much more do we have need to be likewise baptized?

Baptisms are performed by immersion in "living waters" outside of a church building using these words: *Having authority given me of Jesus Christ, I baptize you in the name of the Father, and of the Son, and of the Holy Ghost. Amen.*

This baptism does not make you—or require you to become—a member of any organized church or religion but is only a sign between you and God that you sincerely believe in Jesus Christ, wish to follow only Him, and keep His commandments.

ADDITIONAL RESOURCES

The new Restoration Edition of the Scriptures was canonized in 2017. All three volumes are available online for free at scriptures.info.

Denver Snuffer has authored numerous other books, including *A Man Without Doubt* (Amazon, 2016), which may be of interest to readers seeking to know more about Joseph Smith.

Readers can learn more about what God is doing to restore the gospel today at learnofchrist.org.

Baptism is available for free at bornofwater.org to everyone who asks, with no obligation to pay, or join, or attend any church, group, or organization.

The Covenant mentioned in this book is available to review at receivethecovenant.com.

About the Author

Biography of Denver C. Snuffer, Jr.

Raised as a Baptist, Mr. Snuffer was converted and baptized into The Church of Jesus Christ of Latter-day Saints (LDS or Mormon) in 1973 at the age of 19, while serving in the U.S. Armed Forces. He was an active member of the LDS Church for 40 years, serving in various lay member positions, including Elder's Quorum President, Sunday School President, Bishop's counselor, Ward Mission Leader, Stake High Councilor, and Graduate Institute Instructor.

Mr. Snuffer has authored more than 16 volumes on Mormonism that cover both Mormon history and doctrine (one of which is now translated into Spanish). Mr. Snuffer maintains a website where he publishes short essays and posts links to his books, talks, and longer essays. He taught for three years at Brigham Young University's summertime "Education Week" on the BYU campus in Provo, Utah. He has presented papers at the annual Sunstone Symposium in Salt Lake City, Utah for several years.

He was excommunicated in September 2013 from the LDS Church on the 40th anniversary of his original baptismal date. His excommunication was due to the publication of a book on LDS history, titled *Passing the Heavenly Gift*, which the church demanded be taken out of print as a condition for his continued membership in the organization.

Professionally, Mr. Snuffer received his law degree from the J. Reuben Clark Law School at Brigham Young University in 1980 and has practiced law for over 40 years. He was a Senior Editor for the Journal of Legal Studies while a law student, publishing an article on Types of Zones in the Summary of Utah Real Property Law. He was also the Assistant Editor of the Clark Memorandum. He was appointed to the Ad Hoc Organizing Committee for the U.S. Inns of Court, serving with law school dean Rex Lee, U.S. District Court Judge A. Sherman

Christensen, Ninth Circuit Court Judge J. Clifford Wallace, U.S. Supreme Court Chief Justice Warren Burger, classmate and former congressman Bill Orton, and classmate Michael Eldredge. The National American Inns of Court Foundation presented Mr. Snuffer with a certificate recognizing his service in founding the organization.

Mr. Snuffer is a founding partner of the law firm Nelson, Snuffer, Dahle & Poulsen PC. Mr. Snuffer has litigated cases before state, federal, administrative, and arbitration proceedings primarily as counsel for plaintiffs. He is admitted to practice in the U.S. Supreme Court, U.S. Court of Appeals for the Federal Circuit, U.S. Court of Federal Claims, Tenth Circuit Court of Appeals, U.S. District Court for Arizona, U.S. District Court for Utah, and the Utah Supreme Court.

He served the bar as an editor for the Utah Bar Journal for eleven years, was a member of the Continuing Legal Education Committee, chairman of an ethics panel for the Utah Bar Ethics Committee for six years, and assisted lawyers in need for several years as part of the Lawyers Helping Lawyers program of the Utah State Bar Association. He has taught Continuing Legal Education courses on Discovery, Negotiations, and Ethics. He also taught night classes on business management, law, and negotiations for the University of Phoenix for five years.

EDUCATION

Associate of Arts: Daniel Webster Junior College, Nashua, New Hampshire

Bachelors of Business Administration: McMurry University, Abilene, Texas

Juris Doctor: Brigham Young University, Provo, Utah (1980)

Lightning Source UK Ltd.
Milton Keynes UK
UKHW012316060122
396749UK00010B/455/J

9 781951 168827